▪ **DENNIS KING**

GET
THE FACTS
ON ANYONE
SECOND EDITION

MACMILLAN • USA

ACKNOWLEDGMENTS

For their help on this second edition, I am especially indebted to Geraldine Pauling, Kalev Pehme, and Dave Phillips; my agent, Nancy Love; and my editor at Arco Books, Barbara Gilson.

Second Edition

Macmillan General Reference
A Simon & Schuster Macmillan Company
1633 Broadway
New York, NY 10019-6785

An Arco Book

MACMILLAN is a registered trademark of Macmillan, Inc.
ARCO is a registered trademark of Prentice Hall, Inc.

Library of Congress Cataloging-in-Publication Data
King, Dennis.
    Get the facts on anyone / Dennis King. — 2nd ed.
      p. cm.
    Includes bibliographical references.
    ISBN 0-02-860026-6 : $14.95
      1. Public records—United States—States—Handbook, manuals, etc.
  2. Biography—Research—Methodology—Handbooks, manuals, etc.
  3. Investigations—Handbooks, manuals, etc. I. Title.
  JK2445.P82K55 1995
  353.0071'4—dc20   94-30034
                                          CIP

Manufactured in the United States of America

10 9 8 7 6 5 4 3

CONTENTS

4 ▪ Finding "Missing" People 42

7 • Collecting the Basic "Identifiers"   114

8 • Credit and Financial Information 127

INTRODUCTION

The purpose of this manual is to assist researchers in compiling accurate background or profile information on individuals, business entities, and nonprofit organizations. It can be used as a "where's what" guide for finding the answers to relatively simple questions, or as a manual for comprehensive (deep background) investigations.

The manual is organized in a cumulative manner, proceeding from nuts-and-bolts techniques (e.g., locating a person whose address is unknown) to the backgrounding of individuals and then to more complicated research tasks. You will find that methods mastered at one stage not only retain, but increase their usefulness at later stages.

County courthouse and state government records are a major focus of this book. It is not easy to generalize about these records because of the variations in filing systems, laws, and administrative policies affecting the public's right to know. Sometimes the descriptions are based on my own experience with New York City records. In other instances, I rely on what I believe to be the most common system. To avoid oversimplification, I make frequent use of "may," "might," "sometimes," and "often." I try to provide several alternative methods for gaining each type of information, leaving it to you to select the way that best fits your investigative requirements.

While attempting to meet the needs of researchers of all types, this book includes special tactics for journalists and public-interest researchers who lack the access to confidential government records enjoyed by law enforcement officers and who wish to avoid the kinds of trickery employed by collection agency skip tracers and private investigators. Although I describe a few typical ruses (they are, for better or worse, part of the real world of investigating), I also try to show that a researcher who exercises his or her ingenuity can usually find an alternate path to the same information or else an alternate body of equally useful information about the person or entity under investigation.

This is the second edition of a manual that I hope will go through many more editions. I urge readers to send their suggestions and criticisms to me care of the publisher.

1·

Basic Concepts

1.1 The Paper Trail

We live in a record-keeping society. Millions of Americans work in white-collar jobs involving creation, storage, and dissemination of data for government, business, or private institutions. The computerization of this function since the late 1960s has produced vast changes in research techniques in every field. The great turn-of-the-century pioneer of investigative journalism, Lincoln Steffens, would be awestruck by the resources that have replaced the ledger books and filing cabinets of his day.

Years ago the term "paper trail" was coined to refer to the vast wealth of records accumulated about an individual during his or her lifetime. Today the trail of paper has largely become a trail of computer bytes, yet the underlying concept is more valid than ever: It is almost impossible for anyone in our society to avoid leaving a trail of personal information in the files of government and private institutions. These documents provide a record of virtually every major event in a person's life: birth, baptism, high school and/or college graduation, military service, marriage, births of children, purchase of a home, deaths of parents, movement from one job to another, major illnesses, retirement, death. Also on record will be divorces, personal bankruptcy filings, criminal convictions, judgments obtained against subject in civil cases (with any liens or wage garnishments resulting therefrom), and even a list of subject's unpaid parking tickets.

By following the paper trail, you can study the influences prior to your subject's birth that helped to mold his or her life—the backgrounds of both parents, their marriage(s), the births of older siblings, the family's genealogical records going back generations. You can also follow your subject beyond the grave—by going to the probate court to find out what happened to his or her estate.

Records compiled by utility companies, banks, and credit card vendors will also be part of your subject's paper trail. Usually kept for limited periods only, these records will include lists of every phone number dialed from subject's home or office phone, every deposit made into (or every check drawn upon) his or her bank account, and every credit card transaction. Although such information is supposed to be confidential, private investigators with the right connections routinely gain access.

Subject's paper trail may include dozens of news articles about his or her activities. A budding investigator should therefore learn how to access these articles through newspaper and periodical databases, clippings "morgues," and the microfilm collection at the local public library.

Corporations and nonprofit organizations also leave a paper trail. Like an individual, a corporation has its "birth certificate" (certificate of incorporation), its "marriage certificate" (merger papers), and its major and minor crises (lawsuits, bankruptcy proceedings). It may even have a "death certificate" (certificate of dissolution). National and local business periodicals often report on such events as assiduously as the tabloid press reports on the escapades of movie stars.

1.2 The People Trail

The aim of following the paper trail is not simply to accumulate as many documents as possible. Although documents are important in their own right, they are also useful because they lead you to live sources: first, people with direct personal knowledge of your subject; and second, experts with background knowledge who can steer you to the direct sources and can also help you to interpret what you find.

In backgrounding an individual, you might seek out his or her former neighbors, co-workers, or business associates. In backgrounding a corporation, you might contact its customers, suppliers, stockholders, or former employees. In backgrounding either individuals or corporations, you would want to talk to their adversaries in any lawsuits. You would also want to talk to someone with a rosier viewpoint: the individual's best friend or the corporation's public relations consultant.

Success in any investigation depends on the skillful interweaving of the paper trail and the people trail. The paper trail leads to people with special knowledge who in turn steer you to new documentation, which then leads to people with even more (and hopefully deeper) knowledge. This spiral process, from documents to people and back again, gradually leads you to the heart of the investigation, possibly even to the proverbial smoking gun.

1.3 Parallel Backgrounding

If your subject is closely linked to a particular business or organization, the latter will have its own paper/people trail. By following it, you may obtain information about subject that is unavailable from his or her personal records. For instance, the personal records on Mr. X may contain no negative information, but the city housing authority's files on his contracting firm may contain documents suggesting that this supposed solid citizen is involved in rigging bids.

The same principle also works in reverse: If your main target is a business enterprise or nonprofit organization, you may gain startling insights by examining the personal backgrounds of its principals or officers. That seemingly innocuous annual report of your local community development corporation may appear in a different light once you learn that the city has padlocked two buildings owned by the executive director because of illegal gambling on the premises.

Parallel backgrounding also may involve looking into the affairs of one or more of Mr. Y's business associates, relatives, etc., to gain information about or insight into Mr. Y himself. (A classic example of this was the media's focus in the early 1970s on Richard Nixon's close friend Bebe Rebozo.) Or, to gain insight into Corporation Z's business tactics, you might take a look at its chief rival (especially if the latter's business methods are better documented than Z's in lawsuits and government enforcement proceedings).

We are speaking of four basic types of parallel backgrounding: Personal/Personal; Personal/Corporate; Corporate/Personal; Corporate/Corporate. If you are beginning a complicated investigation, you might draw up a chart with each of these headings. As you accumulate names and other information, jot down possible leads under each heading. You probably won't have time to follow up more than a few, but the chart will help you to decide priorities.

1.4 Indirect Backgrounding

Essentially, this method is parallel backgrounding on a grand scale. You may find that your subject is linked in complex ways to various economic or political interests. The only way to understand the significance of the relationships involved—and to identify which, if any, of the individuals or organizations warrant parallel backgrounding—is to analyze this larger environment. This approach can sometimes lure you into unproductive areas, but it can also pay big dividends. In one case, background research on the economy of a West African nation to which a New York businessman had often traveled helped to identify possible Libyan connections of that businessman. In another case, inquiries into the history of the Teamsters Union and of certain Midwest organized crime families led to a major breakthrough in understanding neofascist leader Lyndon LaRouche's links to the underworld.

This method, like direct backgrounding, involves both a paper trail (in this instance, books, newspaper and periodical articles, and various archival gleanings) and a people trail (chiefly, the "experts").

1.5 Operative Backgrounding

This is the level at which you put everything together. Operative backgrounding is the process of figuring out how things work in a particular area of money and power and then interpreting the facts in light of that understanding. To understand a city politician, you have to understand the world in which he or she moves—the relationships between the politicians and established wealth on the one hand, and between the politicians and organized crime on the other. You have to understand the mechanisms of legal and illegal graft through which transactions among these three forces are conducted. Likewise, to understand a local hoodlum you have to know how organized crime works—its division into so-called crime families, the characteristic businesses these families get into (and why), how they "launder" their illegal income, and how they deal with both the politicians and the police. The principle also applies to my own specialty, the study of cults and extremist groups. Here you enter a world where greed and the desire for power and status are covered up by high-minded ideologies (or theologies) that must be decoded to discover the underlying interests and the real meaning of the incessant factionalism (often just an inverted form of capitalist competition taking place in a frog pond with status rather than cash as the payoff).

As this book is not a political treatise, I have dealt with operational backgrounding only when necessary to explain specialized areas of research. But the best achievements in investigative journalism usually are a result of having an understanding of these matters—this is what guides the journalist almost uncannily to the right sources. You will not always learn much about this from academic social scientists, who frequently either prettify things or ideologize them and thus miss the main point. For a more pragmatic view (including a healthy cynicism about human nature), seek out veteran political and crime reporters. Better yet, cultivate insiders in the worlds of business and politics. It is not easy to get CEOs to open up, but you can always find someone on a lower echelon—or a retired or fired executive or an independent consultant—who knows as much if not more about the way things work and is willing to talk frankly.

2 ∙

Some Basic Research Tools and Resources

2.1 Getting Started

Your Office Reference Shelf
The following is a list of the directories, manuals, etc., that are most useful to have at hand in your office:

- **Telephone directories.** You should have *The National Directory of Addresses and Telephone Numbers*, which contains 125,000 of the most essential business, nonprofit, and government listings in all 50 states and can save you enormously on directory assistance charges; and the two-volume *AT&T Toll-Free National 800 Directory* (240,000 listings), which if used assiduously can also provide big savings on your long-distance phone bill. You should also have the current local white-page and yellow-page directories (the latter both business-to-business and consumer) for your entire metro area. When a new edition of your local white pages is delivered, don't throw out the old one—back edition telephone directories are often very useful in tracing people who are not listed in the current edition (see Chapter Four).

- **State and local government directories.** Most states and large cities publish annual volumes that give the addresses and phone numbers—and sometimes the functions—of all state or local government agencies and legislative committees. These volumes also provide the names and phone numbers of legislators, legislative committee staffers, and key administrative officials. Most important, they contain lists of all professional and commercial licenses required by the state or city government and the agency responsible for each license.

▪ **Directories and guides to the federal government.** The *United States Government Manual*, published by the Government Printing Office, outlines the organizational structure, functions, and key personnel of each federal department or agency. The *Congressional Directory* describes the various congressional resources, including committee and subcommittee research staffs. You should also have the *Washington Information Directory*, which is indexed by subject and government department or agency (and also includes nongovernment Washington sources), and *Lesko's Info-Power II* (formerly *Information U.S.A.*), which describes how to squeeze free information out of both federal and state bureaucrats. By juggling these four books, you can usually figure out which bureaucrat or congressional aide is most likely to have access to the information you need, and which department or agency is most likely to have public records (or records accessible under the Freedom of Information Act) relevant to your research.

▪ **Guidebooks to public records.** If you intend to do much investigating outside your own city or state, invest in *The Guide to Background Investigations* (the best one-volume compilation regarding state and local records) or in the print volumes or CD-ROM version (see below) of The Public Record Research Library (individual volumes are listed in the bibliography). Through these reference works you can learn not only where to write for particular records but also which offices will provide information over the phone (crucial for any reporter on deadline!). Another important work is privacy activist Robert Ellis Smith's *Compilation of State and Federal Privacy Laws*, which describes more than 650 state and federal laws affecting privacy. By telling you what's not available (and what shouldn't be, but is), this book will help you plan your public records' search strategy.

Note that in some localities in-depth "where's what" directories to municipal, county, and/or state records have been compiled (either in published or unpublished form) by college journalism departments, daily newspapers, or public-interest groups. Check with the librarian of your local daily newspaper—or with any nearby college journalism department—to see if there is a manual for your city or state. If a local newspaper has produced a private manual for its staff reporters, request a courtesy copy. A list of several of these guidebooks is contained in the bibliography. Since the same kinds of public records are kept in every locality, albeit in different formats and under varying restrictions, a manual for one locality will be useful in another.

▪ **Investigative how-to manuals.** Dozens are listed in the bibliography. The most essential is *The Reporter's Handbook* (third edition), the official manual of Investigative Reporters and Editors (IRE), a nationwide professional organization with headquarters at the University of Missouri School of Journalism.

- **Offbeat how-to manuals.** You can learn all about the use of false ID, illegal electronic surveillance, computer hacking, money laundering, and similar arcane skills from scores of pamphlets offered by mail-order publishers. Many of these manuals are written by and for criminals and rarely differentiate between what is legal and what can land you behind bars. Yet they contain much valuable information for an investigator. The most comprehensive mail-order catalog is offered by Loompanics Unlimited (see bibliography).

Library Reference Works

The current editions of most major reference works will be too expensive for you to purchase. Instead, you will have to consult them via your public library's telephone reference service (see section 3.1), a personal visit to the library, or (if the particular work is available online) a database vendor. The most essential single reference book for an investigator or journalist is *Directories in Print*, which describes almost 16,000 national, state, and local directories in 26 subject categories. The richness of information in this "directory of directories" is extraordinary. If you consult it at the beginning of your investigation, you can work out an efficient plan of which other reference works to consult and in which order.

Note that many libraries will throw out the old edition of a reference book or offer it for sale at a nominal price as soon as the new edition hits the shelf. If you become friendly with your local reference librarian (as every researcher should), you can learn when a book you need (say, the *Martindale-Hubbell Law Directory* or the *Gale Directory of Publications and Broadcast Media*) is about to be discarded. As out-of-date as these older directories might seem, they can often save you the bother of a trip to the library or the expense of an online search.

CD-ROM and Diskette Products

Although most CD-ROM and diskette research databases are best consulted at the public library, certain products are so useful on a daily basis and/or so modestly priced that a freelance journalist, citizen investigator, or individual private investigator will want them in his or her office library. The most essential is PhoneDisc PowerFinder, a nationwide telephone white pages/crisscross directory with 81 million residential and 9.4 million business listings (see section 4.2). Those who routinely track hard-to-find people might also want to purchase the Street Atlas USA (see section 4.11) and the Social Security Death Benefits Index (section 4.2). Essential for politically oriented journalists is NameBase, an index on diskette of personal, corporate, and organizational names from over 400 books and thousands of articles of investigative journalism (see section 6.5).

Periodicals

For tips on the latest investigative techniques, subscribe to *The IRE Journal*, a bimonthly magazine published by Investigative Reporters and Editors. Without fail, you should order a full set of the back issues since 1978 (available at a very reasonable price) and the latest cumulative index (covers 1978 to 1994). Other useful periodicals are listed in the bibliography.

Investigative Conference Proceedings

IRE holds annual national conferences, as well as regional and specialized conferences, with extraordinarily detailed panels on investigative techniques. Cassette tapes of every panel at every national conference and most regional conferences since 1980 are available from Sound Images Inc., P.O. Box 460519, Aurora, Colorado, 80046. An index to these panels was published in the Winter 1989 *IRE Journal*; Sound Images has a listing of all panels since then. Note that private investigators' and information industry associations hold similar conferences and conventions; to see if panel presentations from these events are likewise available on cassette or in published form, contact the relevant associations listed in the *Encyclopedia of Associations*.

Catalogs from Reference Book Publishers and Major Database Vendors

Get on the mailing lists of these companies for catalogs, supplements, and press releases that can keep you up to date on what's available in these rapidly changing fields. For a list of the most important publishers and vendors, see the bibliography.

2.2 City Directories

Ever since the nineteenth century, specialized publishers have produced household-by-household and store-by-store marketing directories, commonly known as city directories. These books are used by telephone or door-to-door sales teams, direct mail firms, fundraising experts, pollsters, newspaper subscription departments, and essentially anyone who needs marketing information that will identify potential customers and/or supplement the demographic information found in U.S. Census reports. Such directories are also used by private investigators, skip tracers, police detectives, and newspaper reporters to locate individuals and compile background information on them. By using back as well as current editions of such directories, along with back and current phone books, you can gather a remarkable amount of information about someone in a short time.

The city directory is compiled via door-to-door or telephone surveys. It may tell how many people live in a household, how long they have resided there, where the head of the household works (or at least what his or her occupation is), the name of each household resident, and the general income level of the neighborhood. By tracing a person's name through back issues of a city directory, you can get a bare-bones picture of his or her family through the years.

Usually revised each year, the city directories include alphabetical, street, and numerical listings. The street listings will help you find subject's present and/or former neighbors and also will give you a sense of the neighborhood environment.

Most large cities are no longer covered by city directories as urban mobility and the socioeconomic disintegration of inner-city life have rendered them impractical. However, city directories are often still published for the suburban communities surrounding the core cities. In addition, many medium-sized and smaller nonsuburban cities are covered, as well as many small towns and rural areas (the latter by rural route directories).

The current and back editions of a city directory may be found at the local public library or chamber of commerce. Among city directory publishers, the biggest name is R.L. Polk & Company (about 1,300 directories in the United States and Canada).

In cities no longer covered by a city directory, the public library will have copies up through the final edition. A researcher can thus trace a longtime city resident's life up to that point. Furthermore, many persons listed in now-defunct city directories in the 1940s and 1950s later moved to suburban communities that are still covered. You can thus sometimes compile an uninterrupted record of successive residences, household members, and neighbors. (Even if you lose the city directory trail, you can pick it up with back-edition crisscross and telephone directories; see section 2.3 below and section 4.3.)

2.3 Crisscross Directories

A crisscross directory is based not on survey information but on a rearranging of the telephone white pages. Whereas the white pages lists phone numbers alphabetically by customer's name, the crisscross directory lists them in numerical order and by street address (it is thus often called a "reverse directory"). When you have a number but no name, you can look in the numerical listings and get both name and address. When you have an address but no name, you can look in the street listings and get both name and phone number. Sometimes the street listings and the numerical listings will be in one volume, and sometimes they are separate. A volume including street listings is sometimes called a "street directory" or "household directory."

Crisscross directories cover the large cities abandoned by the city directories. Although providing less information than the latter, crisscross directories should never be underestimated as a source of information (especially if you use back as well as current editions). For instance, the latest editions of Cole's directories for the five boroughs of New York City will tell you how many years your subject has been listed at his or her current address, whether subject's new listing is altogether new to the directory or only new for the given address, the identities of two or more people with different last names who are sharing a phone number listed separately under each name, the identities of two or more people with different last names who have separate phone lines at the same street address, the names and phone numbers of subject's neighbors, and the approximate income level ("wealth rating") of the block.

Cole is one of the largest publishers of crisscross directories. It leases rather than sells them. Nonsubscribers can obtain access to its vast directory library by calling (900) 288–3020.

Like city directories, crisscross directories are usually available at the local public library or chamber of commerce.

Electronic Crisscross

The chief drawbacks of the print versions of crisscross directories, in addition to their price, are that each directory covers only a single city, and the directories for other cities are rarely available in your local public library. For years, information brokers have offered national crisscross searches online, but now you can use PhoneDisc (see section 2.1), SelectPhone, and other CD-ROM products to perform your own nationwide crisscross searches at leisure either at the public library or, if you choose to purchase the disk, in your office.

2.4 The Law Library

Whether you're investigating an individual, a corporation, a nonprofit organization, a trade union, or an electoral campaign committee, they are all subject to specific legal statutes, government regulations, judicial decisions, and administrative rulings. Hence, a law library (or the legal databases, LEXIS and WESTLAW) can provide important information about your subject. For instance, you can look up the laws and regulations relating to Mr. A's activities as a street peddler, Dr. B's as a podiatrist, and Ms. C's as a stockbroker.

To guide your search for such information, there are four essential sets of books: the city code, the state code (for instance, *McKinney's Consolidated Laws of New York Annotated*), the *United States Code Annotated*, and the *Code of Federal Regulations*. The designation "annotated" means that a set provides, along with the text of each section of the law, a summary of the most important decisions interpreting it. Each annotated volume, unless it is from the latest annual edition, will include a "pocket part," an annual update inserted in a pocket at the rear of the volume. The pocket part gives all new developments since the date of publication of the volume on the shelf and should *always* be consulted. Note that the *Code of Federal Regulations* does not have pocket parts; you must consult the *Federal Register* for the latest developments.

The various codes are indexed according to topics/key words in an easy-to-search manner. With the index (often itself a multivolume work) as your guide, your use of the federal, state, and local codes is limited only by your ingenuity and your knowledge of subject's activities. Mr. X is a café owner? Look at the municipal laws relating to eating establishments, including the health, fire, and sidewalk codes; also look at the city and state laws pertaining to registration of small businesses. Ms. B is a freelance writer? Look at the state and federal tax codes and regulations pertaining to self-employed individuals who file itemized deductions.

If a person is engaged in a licensed occupation, the state code may guide you to a surprising array of official records (see sections 10.11 and 10.12).

On the federal level, you might want to skip the *United States Code Annotated* and go straight to the *Code of Federal Regulations*, which includes a volume called the *CFR Index and Finding Aids*. Let's say you are investigating Mr. W., a right-wing arms dealer suspected of supplying machine guns to the Ku Klux Klan. Look under "Arms and munitions" and note the relevant subtopics, cited by "title" and "part." Turn to Title 27, Part 178 ("Commerce in Firearms and Ammunition") and Part 179 ("Machine Guns, Destructive Devices, and Certain Other Firearms"). Here you will find a description of the various filing requirements with which Mr. W. must comply. Your next step: Check with the Bureau of Alcohol, Tobacco, and Firearms to find out which of the government forms filed by Mr. W. are available under the Freedom of Information Act.

2.5 Freedom of Information Laws

For generations, bureaucrats routinely denied the public access to most records of the federal government's executive arm. Congress initiated a new "open government" approach in 1966 by passing the Freedom of Information Act (FOIA). This law, amended in 1976 and 1986, applies to all departments and agencies of the executive branch, including the armed forces and the Central Intelligence Agency (CIA); but it excludes Congress, the federal court system, and the president's immediate staff. Essentially, the law says that the bureaucrats and brass must provide copies, to anyone who requests them (even a mobster in prison), of any government document except those covered by nine exemptions. Exempt documents (or exempt portions of documents) include classified national security information; trade secrets and other confidential business information; information that, if released, would violate personal privacy; information about ongoing law-enforcement investigations; information that might jeopardize a law-enforcement informant; and certain internal bureaucratic memoranda.

The exemptions may seem to provide loopholes for the bureaucrats to weasel out of giving you just about anything. In fact, a vast amount of material is readily available to anyone who bothers to request it. America's corporations and their foreign competitors use the FOIA assiduously to gather government documents that will give them a business edge. Journalists use the FOIA in preparing scoops that blast the very agency releasing the information (if there hasn't been more of this, it's because most journalists are too lazy to master this tool). Public-interest foundations use the FOIA to gather large libraries of national security documents that illuminate every conspiracy and intrigue of the Cold War years. Former radicals have used it to gather their own files from the FBI, and then have turned around and successfully sued the FBI. I myself have used it to gain information from the FBI, the CIA, the Department of Energy, and the State Department. In each case I found that the particular department or agency's FOIA staff complied with the spirit as well as the letter of the law, even though the material released was potentially embarrassing to the government. My experiences may not have been typical—many journalists have complained of bureaucratic stonewalling. Nevertheless, a 1985 congressional study found that over 90 percent of FOIA requests were being complied with adequately.

These figures should improve even more during the next few years. In October 1993, the Clinton administration liberalized the rules for release of government information, thus reversing a 1981 Reagan administration ruling that FOIA requests could be routinely denied whenever there was "a substantial legal basis" for doing so, even if none of the interests protected by the exemptions would be harmed by the information's release. According to the new rule, agencies must grant requests, even if an exemption is technically arguable, unless it is "reasonably foreseeable that disclosure would be harmful" to national security, the privacy of individuals, and other interests covered by the exemptions.

How can you use the FOIA to background a local businessman or mobster? Because of the Privacy Act, you can't expect a government department or agency simply to send you everything they have on someone. (Nor should you ask for information that is clearly personal, since the FOIA unit may contact the person and tell him or her about your request.) However, documents pertaining to businesses, nonprofit organizations, government contracts, and so forth with which subject is associated will be available. You thus can do parallel and indirect backgrounding (see sections 1.3 and 1.4) on a broad scale, gaining much information about subject in the process.

Let's say you need information about Arthur, a community development corporation director in Chicago who has wangled tens of millions of dollars from the federal government to finance development projects for the black community but has only a collection of almost bankrupt enterprises to show for it. Under the FOIA, you can obtain the relevant files of the succession of federal agencies that gave him the money. These files will include much of the correspondence and many of the intra-agency memos that led up to each grant. (If the FOIA officer is really conscientious, you may even receive a copy of the letter from a U.S. senator in Arthur's state supporting

Arthur's request for yet more money.) You also can get the audits and the records of any resulting investigations. You can see who in the agency pushed for the investigations and who, higher up, apparently quashed them.

Furthermore, you can look at the records from the Department of Housing and Urban Development (HUD) on a housing project financed by Arthur's organization. You can look at the files of the Federal Deposit Insurance Corporation (FDIC) on the community savings bank controlled by Arthur—files that may include devastating criticism of the bank management selected by Arthur and his cronies. You can get the FBI's file on Arthur's late bodyguard (a former Black Panther) who died in the mysterious crash of a plane owned by Arthur, as well as the Federal Aviation Administration (FAA) report on that crash, license information on the pilot who died along with the bodyguard, and perhaps even Drug Enforcement Administration (DEA) files regarding the mysterious airstrip from which they had taken off. And as you collect all these documents you will automatically be gaining the names of potential sources—those people in government, formerly in government, or outside government who opposed giving money to Arthur or who tried to blow the whistle on him.

The main problem with the FOIA is the time it takes to get an answer. Although the government is supposed to reply to any request within 10 days, that reply is simply an acknowledgment that the request has been received and that it will be processed in its turn. During the Reagan years the staffs of FOIA units were deliberately cut back, creating backlogs at some departments (especially the FBI). However, departments with a low volume of requests and little need to redact documents for national security reasons will usually meet requests with reasonable promptness.

The FOIA is best used in investigations that are not run on a tight deadline. But even if you have as much time as you like to gather the story, you should make your FOIA requests as soon as possible—the documents you receive may open up an entirely new avenue of inquiry.

Before making an FOIA request, always make sure that it is really necessary. I once asked the Federal Election Commission (FEC) for information, under the FOIA, that was already on the public record as a matter of law and thus routinely available for the asking. The press officer called me to suggest gently that I withdraw my request so he could send me the information immediately. Not all government agencies will volunteer such advice.

You should also check to make sure that FOIA documents you've requested have not already been released. Each department or agency covered by the FOIA keeps an index of released (or "preprocessed") documents. If what you want or part of what you want is on the index, you can order copies directly from the agency's library without delay. Also, many released documents may be available directly from journalists, authors, or scholars who have previously obtained them; others may be accessible in the files of the nonprofit National Security Archives in Washington, D.C., or via the

Declassified Documents Reference System at your local research library. And even if none of the information you seek has been released pursuant to the FOIA, the very same information (or information just as good for your purposes) may be available in a government audit report or a published congressional hearing.

Even if none of the above applies to your information needs, there are still steps you can take to avoid a formal FOIA request. First, you can make an informal request to the agency in question, giving the bureaucrats a chance to look good by releasing the information immediately and thus demonstrating that *their* agency has nothing to hide. (If they display resistance at first, you have something to "threaten" them with: the paperwork they'll be stuck with if you're forced to go ahead with your FOIA request.)

A variation on this is to contact the press office of the agency and ask for the documents in the same manner as if you were making a routine request for a copy of a press release. Press officers often see themselves as expediters rather than by-the-book prevaricators. In some instances, if you tell them you are on a tight deadline, they will get you the information directly. (This works best if you have a very simple request, such as for a single document you already know exists.)

You might also ask your congressperson or U.S. senator to obtain the information for you. He or she can go through the particular department or agency's congressional liaison office and often get the records you need within days. If your senator or congressperson won't help you (or is newly elected and lacking in clout), try a member of Congress who has a special interest in the issue you are researching.

If none of the above options work, you will have to file your FOIA request and go through the red tape. The following suggestions, however, will help you get the maximum information with the minimum wait:

- Do your homework. Each agency is required under the Privacy Act to publish an annual description of its records systems and the categories of individuals on whom records are kept. These notices can be found in the *Federal Register* (which is computer searchable via DIALOG; see section 2.6), or you can obtain a copy from the given agency's FOIA unit. The biennial *Privacy Act Issuances* is a compilation of these notices from every agency covered by the act. Much of the same information is contained in the *Code of Federal Regulations*. Also useful in figuring out what's in an agency's files is the Office of Management and Budget's monthly agency-by-agency inventory of every red-tape form and procedure by which information is gathered from the public. Printouts of the inventory for a given agency can be obtained from that agency. To learn about defunct forms and procedures, request back copies of the inventory.

- Phrase your request clearly and be as specific as possible. If your request is vague or overly broad, the bureaucrats may use this as an excuse to deny it altogether. For detailed information on how to prepare a request, see *How to Use the Federal FOI Act*, a pamphlet published by the Reporters Committee for Freedom of the Press. Also see *A Citizen's Guide on Using the Freedom of Information Act and the Privacy Act of 1974 to Request Government Records*, a somewhat longer booklet available from the House Committee on Government Operations.

- Specify that you want all electronic records (bureaucratic e-mail, etc.) as well as all paper documents pertinent to your request. And insist that any such records be provided to you on diskette as well as in the form of printouts (see section 3.3).

- Touch base with the FOIA officer, or records analyst, assigned to handle your request. A discussion with this person will give you a better idea of what's available and will provide him or her with a clearer understanding of what you are looking for. The result may be a narrowing or rephrasing of your request in the interest of faster results. In general, if you indicate a willingness to be helpful (*without* making yourself a pest) the FOIA officer will be inclined to go the extra mile for you.

- When you make a request for especially sensitive information, have another researcher ask for the same information in a different form. If the requests are processed by two different FOIA officers, one may release things that the other withholds, and vice versa.

- Try more than one agency. Copies of memos from Agency X will often end up in the files of Agency Y as well. Agency X might regard the memos as too embarrassing to release; Agency Y may release them without hesitation.

- File your request with an agency's field offices and regional offices as well as with its Washington headquarters; in some agencies, these units make their own determinations about FOIA requests.

- Think creatively. James Bamford, author of *The Puzzle Palace*, wanted to know the number of employees at the top-secret National Security Agency (NSA), the electronic surveillance and code-breaking agency. The NSA stonewalled him on this and on everything else. He eventually obtained the number of employees by making an FOIA request to the U.S. National Credit Union Administration for its records on the Tower Federal Credit Union, which is located at the NSA. He also used a loophole in the FOIA to obtain copies of the NSA's internal newsletter.

- If an agency gives you part of what you want, but withholds more, file an immediate appeal and also let the bureaucrats know you'll take the matter to court if necessary. Get your congressperson to write a letter on your behalf. Alert the chairpersons of the House and Senate FOIA oversight committees (in the Senate, this is the Subcommittee on Technology and the Law; in the House, it's the Subcommittee on Government Information, Justice, and Agriculture). Almost always, the bureaucrats will release a few more items to avoid a hassle.

- Seek help from experts. Journalists can contact the Reporters Committee for Freedom of the Press in Roslyn, Virginia. Nonjournalists should get in touch with the Freedom of Information Clearinghouse in Washington, D.C.

Many states also have Freedom of Information statutes, known as "sunshine laws." Usually these laws (which apply to city and county governments as well as to the state) have fewer teeth than the federal FOIA, but if you keep pushing, threaten to sue, and gather the support of one or more state legislators or city council members, you can generally get at least part of what you need. If your state or city has an ombudsman's office, enlist its help. Note that state and city agencies often keep duplicate files: When reporters in Springfield, Massachusetts, were stonewalled by the Springfield License Commission regarding certain mob-connected liquor licenses, they turned to the state Alcoholic Beverage Control Commission for the duplicates. In general, the tricks for using the federal FOIA will apply to state sunshine laws with only minor variations.

2.6 Computers and Databases

Overview

Thousands of commercial and government databases can now be accessed by any home computer user who has a modem. The range and depth of information available online is awesome. Sitting at your computer, you can search everything from Department of Motor Vehicles auto registration data through synopses of Ph.D. dissertations. You can retrieve the full text of over 3,600 magazines and newspapers, in some cases going back 10 years or more, and find every mention of a person's name. You can call up on your computer screen the Securities and Exchange Commission (SEC) filings of every publicly held U.S. corporation.

Generally, an end user of databases does not purchase access directly from the database producer. Instead, the producer licenses one or more vendors to market the database. The vendors will offer a large number of databases from different producers within a single database system. Each database is downloaded into this system, which includes the vendor's value-added software, so that all databases on the system can be searched in a uniform and "user-friendly" manner.

One of the leading vendors is Dialog Information Services, Inc. Its DIALOG Information Retrieval Service offers over 450 academic, business, and newspaper/periodical databases with a heavy focus on abstracts and indexes.

Another large vendor is Mead Data Central, which offers LEXIS/NEXIS, a vast collection of legal, business, and full-text newspaper/periodical databases.

Database vendors generally charge a start-up fee and/or annual or monthly subscription or minimum-usage fees. These fees are not a major burden if you are subscribing to only, say, DIALOG ($295 initiation fee with $75 annually thereafter). The fees can get out of hand, however, if you sign up with several of the major database vendors (not to mention the vendors of specialized investigative databases) all at once. Most database searchers end up using a gateway service to access multiple database systems. Essentially a gateway is a vendor of vendors—it gets you into the various database systems via a single subscription fee. Other advantages: you use a single set of search routines, pay only a single monthly bill to the gateway, and minimize costs by using the gateway's software. CompuServe is among the most popular gateway services, offering access in whole or in part to major vendors such as DIALOG, WILSONLINE, NewsNet, and DataTimes.

Keeping Your Costs Down

With or without a gateway service, commercial database searches can be quite expensive, especially if you're not expert at getting in and out of the system as fast as possible. An unskilled searcher using LEXIS/NEXIS can inadvertently get stuck with a bill for hundreds of dollars for a single search if he or she types in the wrong commands. Even a veteran searcher can run up a bill of $200 per hour of connect time on a complicated search (as opposed to no money—but days of tedium—in fumbling through reference books and microfilm at the public library). Here are some ways to contain costs:

- Go online during evenings or weekends on special-rate plans such as Knowledge Index, a collection of over 100 DIALOG databases including many full-text newspaper archives. Knowledge Index, available only on CompuServe (*not* on DIALOG), can be used from 6 P.M. to 5 A.M., Monday to Thursday, and continuously from 6 P.M. Friday to 5 A.M. Monday.

- Take advantage of free online access at terminals in your public library (these terminals are often crowded—you may have to make an appointment in advance).

- Sign up for an evening course at a local college and then use DIALOG or LEXIS/NEXIS at the college library.

- Search for data on the Internet rather than via commercial vendors whenever possible. Many databases on the Internet are free (although you will have to pay a gateway for your Internet access if you're conducting the search from your home or office computer rather than at a library). The Internet cannot provide you with the full range of business and news information available via the major commercial vendors, but it will give you access to the Securities and Exchange Commission's EDGAR system, which includes the electronic filings of thousands of publicly held companies, and it will also get you into hundreds of research library catalogs (including LOCIS, the online catalog of the Library of Congress). In addition, you can use the Internet to locate and communicate with a vast range of experts on every conceivable subject via bulletin board systems, e-mail lists, and so forth. Many of these experts will be willing to send you information via e-mail that is more detailed and up to date than what you would find in a search of DIALOG databases on the same subject. (See the appendix.)

▪ Before going online, check in the *Gale Directory of Databases* (see below) to see if the given database is also available on CD-ROM. If so, check with your public library and other local libraries to find out which of them have it. CD-ROM products available at public libraries include regional or nationwide telephone white pages and crisscross directories (including powerful products that are far more accurate than PhoneDisc), compilations of biographical who's whos, periodical indexes/abstracts covering hundreds of scholarly journals or general-interest magazines, and full-text newspaper archives. CD-ROM will not give you the daily updates that some online databases claim to offer (most CD-ROM products offer quarterly updates only), but you can search the disks at your leisure, and at no cost, in your public library's reference section.

Nonprofit Help with Your Database Searching

If you are faced with a complicated search that is beyond your level of skill and involves getting into database systems such as LEXIS/NEXIS that are inaccessible via your gateway, you can get help from a public library or university library search service operated by professional librarians. Many of these offer online searches of DIALOG, LEXIS/NEXIS, etc., to the general public at below commercial rates or even for free. To find such help, Gale's *Online Database Search Service Directory*, although out of print, is still a useful guide. It indexes search facilities by online vendors accessed, subject areas searched, and geographic area. If you need a particular database searched, you can pick up the phone and call library search services anywhere in the United States for help.

Freelance journalists requiring help on a database search can contact Investigative Reporters and Editors (IRE), which will arrange for a University of Missouri librarian to perform your search for a modest fee.

Database Directories

Various guidebooks will help you take maximum advantage of the massive number of databases available from the various levels of government, from universities and other nonprofit sources, and from commercial database vendors:

- The *Gale Directory of Databases* is a semi-annual reference work that is also available on CD-ROM (and online with daily updates via ORBIT). It describes almost 9,000 online, CD-ROM, magnetic tape, and diskette products.

- Information USA's *Federal Data Base Finder* describes 4,000 free and fee-based federal government databases and specifies the mode in which they are available to the public, such as magnetic tape purchase or lease, online access direct from the government, online access via commercial vendor, or searches performed by the source agency itself. (Note that the above book is somewhat dated. If it describes a magnetic tape database you should always inquire from the source agency if that database is now or soon will be on CD-ROM.)

- Gale's *Information Industry Directory* profiles over 5,300 database producers, vendors, and gateway services. Study this directory and then get on the mailing lists of any companies whose products you think you might someday need.

- *The Internet Directory* (see bibliography) describes over 1,500 e-mail lists, over 2,700 news groups, over 1,000 online catalogs, over 250 electronic journals, and many other resources available on the Internet.

Investigative Databases and Information Brokers
Certain types of databases are of special interest to investigators. These include:

- residential marketing databases—compiled from telephone directories, U.S. Postal Service change-of-address files, magazine subscription and direct-mail lists, and many other sources. The largest, such as Metromail, cover upward of 100 million households.

- credit-reporting agency databases—for instance, TRW's Updated Credit Profile database, which contains information on 170 million people. Credit-reporting agencies are barred from giving out credit information on individuals except according to strict privacy guidelines, but this does not apply to noncredit "header" information on credit reports (address, date of birth, Social Security number, spouse's name, mother's maiden name, etc.).

- local, state, and federal government public records databases. Those most widely used by investigators include court indexes at the state trial court level, federal district court indexes and dockets, asset/lien records (especially Uniform Commercial Code [UCC] filings), county property records, and Department of Motor Vehicles (DMV) records.

The key to entering this new Sam Spade cyberspace is the nationwide network of information brokers. A list of several of these firms is provided in the bibliography; a comprehensive list can be found in *The Sourcebook of Public Record Providers*. These are vendors who lease or purchase data from the above sources for value-added resale and/or who serve as gateways into a wide variety of investigative databases.

Some information brokers provide data only to high-volume users who pay hefty monthly minimum fees; others also offer their services to nonsubscribers on a per-request basis. If you need only an occasional search, you can call a company that accepts such requests. It will conduct a search of its own databases and also of the larger investigative database net, and send you the results by fax or e-mail. The cost for a single search will be quite reasonable; but if you need frequent searches of motor vehicle records and other public records, find an information broker who charges a modest user deposit but no monthly minimum charges—and then learn to do your own searching via this broker's gateway.

If you are going to purchase data (or access to data) from information brokers on a regular basis, you should exercise the same caution as any consumer. *The Sourcebook of Public Record Providers* suggests that you ask where the information comes from (i.e., how reliable are the source databases), how often the provider updates its own database from the source database, how often the source database itself is updated, how long it takes for information to get into the source database (e.g., certain county records systems may have a backlog so that information is not entered into the computer until months after the filing), how well indexed a database is (i.e., how narrowly you can define your search), how the data was originally inputted (e.g., by scanning or by an operator typing it in) and with what margin of error, how many databases a provider has access to, how much experience the provider has in searching the particular databases you are interested in, whether the provider can help you interpret data that is retrieved in a coded or abbreviated form, and under what circumstances if any the broker is required to inform the subject of your inquiry that information has been requested about him or her.

To supplement what you get from the information brokers, you might consider developing your own collection of low-cost investigative databases. Such a collection could include commercial CD-ROMs available at a modest price (e.g., Street Atlas USA); inexpensive federal government databases (e.g., the National Geographic Names Database and the various Federal Election Commission databases—see the *Federal Database Finder*); and state and local public record databases, which in some localities are available directly from the source agency at cost. Some of the government databases will be on magnetic tape; for advice on converting them for use on your computer, contact the National Institute for Computer-Assisted Reporting (NICAR) at the University of Missouri. If you intend to work with government databases often, subscribe to *Uplink*, the NICAR newsletter.

Limitations of Database Searching

Databases are no substitute for leg work. Both veteran journalists and private investigators will tell you that online searches rarely provide more than a small fraction of the information needed in preparing an investigative news series or a background report. In addition, the information in public-record and credit-reporting agency databases (and thus in any databases that are based in part on these sources) invariably has a rather large percentage of errors. (Millions of Americans have been denied credit over the years because their name got confused in the databases with that of someone else who failed to pay a debt.) If you are writing for publication, any negative information gathered from public record databases should be backed up by a certified copy of the actual document. Even then, never assume the information is true without contacting the person about whom the record was purportedly compiled to make sure you have the right person and to get his or her side of the story.

3.

Some Basic Techniques and Procedures

3.1 Getting Facts Fast

Many times in the course of an investigation, you will need a fact immediately. You may need, for example, the home address of a corporate executive, the law school background and year of graduation of a local attorney, the name and address of a trade association, or a list of a major corporation's subsidiaries.

One way to get these facts is by online databases, but if you use them to answer every minor question your costs will soar. Fortunately, there is another way to check out vexing details without leaving your office. The central public library in many cities operates a telephone reference service staffed by professional librarians who have at their fingertips hundreds of basic reference works.

This service is free and takes only a few minutes—but keep your requests simple. If the librarian doesn't have on hand the book with the answer, he or she can at least tell you its title and refer you to the reference service at another library that does have it.

Library reference services can best help you if you know exactly what you want. This is why you should have a copy of *Directories in Print*. Find there the book you want searched before you call the reference service.

I have found that the public library reference services vary in quality. In some cities, the line may be perpetually busy or the number of directories at hand relatively small. In other cities, the service is excellent. If you can't get through to your local reference number, simply call a library in another city (the *National Directory of Addresses and Telephone Numbers* gives the central numbers for hundreds of public libraries). While researching an article on the Teamsters Union a few years ago that had to be finished fast, I used the telephone reference services of fifteen libraries around the country during a single week.

The Library of Congress's telephone reference number is (202)707–5522. Call it only if local public libraries can't help you.

3.2 Telephone Information "Pyramiding"

Public library reference librarians generally will allot only a few minutes to any given caller. If you have a question that is too complicated for them, the federal, state, and local governments maintain a vast cohort of public information officers, press secretaries, and legislative committee staffers who routinely answer questions from the public or who refer callers to the appropriate government expert. To find out who to call, look in the guidebooks described in section 2.1 (*Lesko's Info-Power II* is especially strong on government sources of free information). If you're stumped, call the legislative office (*not* the community office) of your elected representative at the relevant level of government for advice. Your regional Federal Information Center may also help you identify sources of information at federal offices, either within the region or in Washington. Once you reach the best expert in a given agency, he or she may steer you to an official in another agency or someone in the private sector for additional information.

You can also seek information on your own from a wide variety of private nonprofit organizations, ranging from trade associations through think tanks. Get a telephone reference librarian to look up likely prospects for you in the subject listings of the *Encyclopedia of Associations*.

Other good sources include newsletter editors (your local telephone reference librarian can find the right newsletter by looking in *Newsletters in Print*, which is divided into 33 subject categories) and corporate public relations or communications directors (the names and telephone numbers of these people at any large corporation can be found easily in any of several business directories). I received much help from both newsletter editors and corporate PR types in researching this book.

With the vast range of sources described above it is possible to find an answer over the phone quickly and efficiently, even to quite arcane questions. You are passed on from general to specific experts, or from experts in one aspect of your question to experts in another aspect. I call this "information pyramiding." Once you get the hang of it, it rarely takes you more than three or four calls to zero in on the person who has the definitive answer to your question.

3.3 Collecting and Filing Your Documentation

You can master every technique for gaining background information, but it won't do you much good if everything gets lost in a huge pile of unsorted documents on your desk. This doesn't matter much if you're doing a relatively simple investigation, but if you are preparing a major piece of investigative journalism or compiling a deep background report that involves parallel backgrounding you will be accumulating documents and also notes from telephone inquiries and interviews at a rapid pace. It is essential that you devote a period of time at the end of each day to filing and crossfiling this material. If you let this go for more than a couple of days it will get out of hand. Not only will you not be able to locate things, you will find it very difficult to plan out your future research efficiently. You may discover an important lead one day, set it aside thinking you'll follow it up next week, and then completely forget it.

There are as many filing systems as there are journalists. Here's my system: First, always have on hand several dozen filing folders at the beginning of your investigation. Use legal-length folders because if you use letter-size ones you'll have to fold documents before inserting them, which makes the file harder to search. When you label a folder use a pencil so you can erase and use the folder again. As the documents accumulate during your research into a local businessman's past, make a folder for each aspect or important event or stage of his life (e.g., college years, first job, 1987 lawsuit, divorce proceedings, 1989 federal prosecution—you might want to construct a chronology). Also make a folder for each of subject's associates, business entities, and so forth, as well as folders on appropriate background topics. Before you file a document, highlight the important parts with a yellow marker. You will find that many documents or interview notes relate to more than one topic; in such cases, make multiple photocopies of the document or of its most important portions and place each in the relevant folder with highlighting specific to that folder. If you don't have a photocopier in your office, you can place the document (with a red "X" on the front page) in the file to which it has greatest relevance and then insert in the other file(s) a yellow-pad sheet bearing the reminder "See—1987 lawsuit file." You will find that some documents are relevant to many or almost every folder; in such cases, make an "Urgent—Multiple Use" file, and keep such documents there (as well as placing them in the relevant folders if possible) to be consulted constantly. (Note that when you get down to writing it is always preferable to have a copy of a document or article in *every folder to which it is relevant*, even if the copying and filing seem tedious beforehand.) When a folder begins to fill up, divide it into primary-relevance and secondary-relevance folders.

A rule of thumb: If you're not spending at least 10 percent of your time doing such filing during a complicated investigation, there's something wrong.

My filing system flows from my approach to the gathering of documents: Photocopy everything of possible relevance in a court file, newspaper clippings file, library reference volume, and so forth. This is especially important in the early stages of an investigation: You won't know what's most important until you fit it into the larger picture.

When you find a damning public document—for instance, a deed of sale showing that a local politician bought a parcel of land two weeks before a zoning change raised the land's value dramatically—always get a certified copy from the county or city clerk's office immediately. Such documents have a habit of disappearing from the public files within a few days of your call to the politician to question him or her about it.

Now, one of this manual's most important pieces of advice (for which you will thank me many times over): *Whenever* you go to the courthouse or the public library, carry at least $10 in crisp one-dollar bills (for the photocopying machines, if they take dollar bills, and for the change machines if they don't). You should also carry rolls of coins: Courthouses and libraries don't always have change machines, and if they do, the machines are frequently broken or out of change. In general, rolls of dimes are preferable to quarters since some coin-operated photocopiers don't take quarters but almost all take dimes. If you forget this advice, you may have to traipse from office to office within the courthouse to find someone with change. And don't rely on the bank around the corner: many branches nowadays will provide rolls of coins only to depositors, and most branches close two hours earlier than the courthouse file room.

Computerized Files

If you have a choice of obtaining a document in (or converting it into) electronic form as well as obtaining and filing a paper copy, do both. A computerized document can be instantly retrieved, edited, sent to other computers by e-mail, copied instantaneously (no more trips to the local photocopy shop!), and merged in whole or in part with any of your other documents. Most important, you can search computerized files via powerful search software (see below) to find exactly what you need when you need it.

While conducting your research, always be alert to how you can maximize the use of your computer. When you highlight certain lines or paragraphs in a print document with a yellow marker, you should also key in the highlighted material (or an abstract of such material). If you made handwritten notes on a certain interview, you should key them in immediately (see section 3.5), adding further information from memory and also interpretive remarks. And if you taped the interview, you should transcribe the most important segments, again creating easily searchable files.

You may have a collection of clippings on a particular person or topic from your local newspaper that you have not yet manually indexed. If the back files of this newspaper are available online (say, from DIALOG), you might as well spend a few extra dollars to download the articles, thus creating your own electronic clippings library. Perhaps you have a copy of *Who's Who in America* on your desk? You can go online; search this and other biographical dictionaries for all entries on subject and on his or her present and past professional colleagues, business partners, college classmates, etc.; and then download these entries for instant searching of all personal, corporate, and government names therein whenever you like.

If you approach an attorney for access to the depositions or trial testimony in a civil court case (see sections 9.6 and 9.7), ask for a copy of the diskette the court reporter provided to the attorney (or a diskette of the computer file the attorney's office created by scanning the court reporter's paper transcript); you can then search the text to find the most minute interconnections of names and facts.

Often the richest source for your electronic files will be online information regarding subject's business entities. You can download, for instance, the latest SEC filings from every corporation with which subject has been associated as an officer, director, or insider owner. (This is much more feasible for a home PC user now that the general public has been given free access to SEC filings via the Internet.) You can also obtain vast quantities of data on these businesses (if you can afford the connect time) via DIALOG or CompuServe's IQuest.

A wealth of federal government data beyond the SEC filings is available for free via the Internet, while much federal, state, and local government data is available at a modest price, often simply at cost, on diskette, magnetic tape, or CD-ROM (note that the cost of copying a diskette may be pennies compared to tens of dollars for photocopies of the print version of the same document). In many states, certain heavily used public-record databases are sold only to designated vendors or else are offered to the general public at a price reflecting their commercial value rather than simply the cost of copying. But many other electronic records are available in these states and from the federal government *without* price gouging; for instance, that 400-page report from the state organized crime commission in which certain associates of your subject are featured may be available on diskette for just a few dollars if you *insist* on obtaining it in that form.

Some electronic records will be available easily through a call to the given agency's public affairs office; others might require an FOIA request. (Note that the federal executive branch is currently under court order to keep all its e-mail and other electronic records pursuant to the FOIA.) But when dealing with government entities on any level—federal, state, or local—always request your information on diskette or CD-ROM; never be content with a computer printout or other paper document.

Of course, much of your documentation on Mr. C, the infamous political fixer whose depredations on society began long before the era of electronic archives, will be available only on paper. But here you have the option of adding them to your computer files by using a scanner and Optical Character Recognition (OCR) software that converts the scanned text into searchable and editable electronic text. For years, scanning has been a feasible means of storing surveillance photos, photos of missing children, and so forth (using graphics software) and of creating electronic versions of court reporters' transcripts and other legal documents with OCR software. Recent advances in OCR have now made it possible to scan in the texts of books and magazine articles, newspaper clippings, faxes, and other materials—even with a handheld scanner—to create a workable OCR document.

The latest software will stitch things together neatly and give you (if you're working with clean copy) a 95 percent or better accuracy rate. Top-of-the-line software programs such as Omnipage Pro and Wordscan Plus can even read originals of poor quality and correct the OCR translation errors via spelling checkers. A new generation of OCR software promises to preserve the exact format of the scanned page, including the typefaces, thus giving you something very close to a photographic image.

In addition, you have the option of keeping the paper document (or even creating full images of key pages) to check against your OCR version when it comes time to verify your quotations and other facts with your fact-checking department and your editor.

Although scanning technology is improving rapidly, you should have an original that is as clean as possible. If you are a journalist or author who is going to be specializing in a particular topic for the next year or so, but you want to wait for the scanning technology to improve a bit more, preserve your manual files in a scanner-friendly form. First, make clean high-quality photocopies of all newspaper clippings (the backside of newsprint often shows through, confusing the scanner) and of any other documents you anticipate working with very often. Place the visually inferior versions (whether the photocopies or the originals) in working files, and the scanner-friendly versions in pre-scan files. You can then highlight, scrawl marginal notes on, fold, crease, smear, and spill coffee on the working copies to your heart's content.

Once you have created electronic documents via downloading of online data, scanning, and so forth, you must be able to search the hundreds of files on your hard disk efficiently. Among the most popular search software programs used by journalists and writers is ZyLAB's ZyINDEX. This program will index the entire contents of your hard disk, a process that takes several hours. Thereafter it can look through all your files in only a few seconds and retrieve information according to highly sophisticated search options. A still more powerful program is Windows Personal Librarian (from Personal Library Software), which can take you into the realm of hypertext (the programming of just about any desired links among words, images, or segments of text throughout your files).

For more information on search software, see Hy Bender's *Essential Software for Writers.*

3.4 Eliciting Information from Sources

Skip tracers and private investigators use various ruses to trick people into providing information. For instance, they may call up a friend of a skipped debtor and say they represent the estate of a relative who has left the skip some money. The friend, wanting to be helpful to his or her pal, often will reveal the new address or phone number.

Many times ruses aren't intended to elicit closely held information but simply to make a person feel comfortable about discussing something he or she has no strong reason *not* to discuss. The ruse allays his or her suspicions of a stranger asking questions about a third party. It also gets around his or her antipathy toward bill collectors.

Apart from ethical concerns, the use of a ruse makes it more difficult to go back to the same source later. The person you manipulated into revealing an unlisted telephone number may turn out later to be the key to far more important information, but the trick you used the first time may have destroyed the possibility of any trust.

Journalists can avoid ruses under most circumstances, because they have a built-in reason for their snooping—they are working on a news story, and their questions are part of that story. Most people understand this and respond politely and without suspicion. If they know the journalist is on a deadline, they'll often drop a pressing task to answer his or her questions on the spot.

Another advantage journalists have is that their craft emphasizes tracking down opponents and enemies of their subject. Whereas a skip tracer might pump a friend of subject for information using a ruse, the journalist will naturally gravitate to subject's enemy and get the same information (and more) in an above-board fashion.

Whether you are a journalist or a skip tracer, your success in eliciting information depends on your mind-set. Remember always that the average person has a natural desire to be helpful if he or she is not too harried at the moment or feeling ill. Approach each contact as if you were lost on a country road and seeking directions to the nearest town. As the conversation develops, let the contact know that you are trying to do a job on a deadline with your editor pressuring you (anyone who works for a boss can identify with this). Behave as if there's no question in your mind that the contact will help you. The more you believe this, the more it will come true unless you sabotage things by being rude, unctuous, overly aggressive, or otherwise disagreeable. If you haven't learned basic human communication skills, there are many good books and seminars on the subject.

If you need a source's help on anything more than a simple question or two, you should strive to make your investigation personally meaningful to him or her. This means stimulating the source's sympathy, curiosity, or self-interest, and appealing (when appropriate) to his or her moral or political convictions. For instance, if you are working on an exciting or colorful story, try to get the person interested in what you've found out. If you are working on a story about a crooked politician, appeal to the person's indignation and desire to do right. If you are working for a defense attorney, appeal to the potential witness's natural sympathy for a little guy caught in the toils of the legal system.

A corollary of the above is to never *assume* a source will be hostile. Once, in investigating an anti-semitic group, I came across a sales brochure of a related investment scam. In it was included a picture of a light-haired, crew-cut board member with a German name. I put him at the *bottom* of my list of potential sources to call. When I finally did contact him, however, he turned out to be a liberal Protestant college professor, not a far rightist or neo-Nazi. And he was eager to talk. The group, he said, had used his name and picture without his permission after he had turned down their request for investment cash. He had been trying for months to get law enforcement to investigate them.

If a contact refuses to talk and/or slams the phone down, try him or her again in a few days with a slightly different pitch. They may just have been in a bad mood, or you may have used the wrong approach the first time (e.g., calling them at work rather than at home, or vice versa). I've had people scream and curse at me on the phone one day and be perfect lambs when I called back 24 hours later. Also, when working on long-range projects, I've had sources adamantly refuse to talk at the outset but be eager to talk six months or a year later. If you can't wait six months to talk to Mr. X, try talking to a friend or acquaintance of his—not only to find out what the friend or acquaintance knows but also to elicit his or her help in getting Mr. X to open up. (In investigating a cult this might mean approaching a longtime defector to help line up an interview with a recent and still very nervous defector.) Also try approaching your Mr. X at a place outside his normal routine (e.g., at an out-of-town convention rather than at his office). If he is a yuppie investment banker, put on your jogging shoes and approach him during his evening run in the park (if you are a male reporter, do *not* attempt this with a female source). An additional tactic (if, say, you're trying to collect information to establish the innocence of a criminal defendant) is a heartfelt letter to your potential source appealing to his or her best instincts.

If a contact consents to talk but then gives only very limited and vaguely worded information (but you know that he or she knows much more than he or she is saying), don't give up. Thank them politely and ask if you can call them again when and if your research generates further questions. Most people will say yes, if for no other reason than just to get you off the phone or out of their office. But it lays a basis for calling them back without seeming too pushy. I have found that cautious bureaucrats or frightened cult defectors sometimes will open up marvelously during a second or third conversation if you don't push too hard.

If you are investigating the sinister Mr. Z, one of your most important sources will of course be Mr. Z himself. You must get his side of the story at some point, but when to do so is a complicated question. On the one hand, interviewing him early in the investigation may save you a lot of unnecessary digging: First, you may find he is not quite the villain you thought he was. Second, you may find him willing to provide important information in order to placate you, justify himself, or shift the blame onto one of his associates. Third, he may not perceive his own behavior the way you do; what is sinister to you may seem admirable to him and not at all to be covered up. For instance, I once spent weeks digging into a Teamster official's relationship to a far-right organization before calling him. I might as well have called him the first day and saved myself all that digging: He was proud of the connection and discussed it freely, regarding it as proof of his patriotism.

Of course, tipping off your subject too soon may trigger action that closes off important avenues of information. In investigating an elected public official, I suggest that you contact him or her early in the investigation with relatively noncontroversial but necessary background questions, then come back later with your zingers. In general, the less controversial or potentially damaging your investigation of a person is likely to be, the earlier you should approach him or her.

There is also the question of how to treat your subject (or a hostile source who is defending your subject) after interviewing him or her. Some practitioners of killer journalism (who are using their journalism to act out their neuroses) will indulge in gratuitous sarcastic remarks and value judgments about these interviewees in their ensuing article or column. Or they will gossip about an interviewee in scornful language to third parties (who sometimes will inform the interviewee and/or the interviewee's friends about this display of animus).

Such behavior is self-defeating as well as immature. It makes it very difficult for you to call the subject(s) of the article afterward for his/her/their reactions (such reactions can often set the stage for a follow-up article far more revealing than the first article). It ignores the fact that today's hostile source (e.g., George the closet-gay New Right fundraiser) may become tomorrow's friendly source (George the Act-Up demonstrator who has denounced his former colleagues as bigots). It guarantees that when the hostile source decides to stop being a sacrificial lamb for his or her superiors (as did Watergate's John Dean), you will be the *last* journalist he or she might choose as a conduit.

Rule of thumb: No gratuitous insults in your articles—stick to the facts. No attacks on aspects of subject's life that are not pertinent to the issue at hand (e.g., no references to Councilwoman Smith's son's drug arrests in an article on her campaign finances *unless* her son worked on her campaign or the information is otherwise directly relevant). And no gossiping about subject to third parties. In other words, drive the moneychangers out of the temple, but don't forget the Golden Rule.

A touch of Golden Rule–style tolerance is frequently essential in dealing with problems posed by putatively eccentric or disreputable sources. It would be nice if investigative journalism involved only interviews with priests, rabbis, and an occasional professor of business ethics at a local college. Unfortunately, in many investigations the only people with inside knowledge are those regarded as either weird or sleazy—you have to take what you can get. In investigating far-right politics I have had to deal with many such people. Although some journalists have been burned by such relationships, my experience with borderline sources is that they often provide information as reliable as—and certainly a lot more interesting than—the information provided by impeccably respectable people (who, by the way, have their own tricks for covering up the facts).

The basic rule in dealing with so-called eccentric sources is to afford them the same respect as anyone else and never violate their trust on grounds that they somehow don't deserve the same straight dealing as ordinary folks. This does not mean becoming their doormat. You may find that they have a narcissistic tendency to call you collect from Alaska at 2 A.M. with their latest brainstorm. An experienced journalist-therapist, however, knows how to put an end to these excesses with a bit of Pavlovian conditioning (if they call after midnight, hang up and then be noticeably cool to them at the outset of the next conversation).

Special problems of a different nature will arise when you encounter a government "whistle blower" or other source with vast inside information regarding a major story. You should always ask, at the outset of your dealings with such a source, for all the documentation—every scrap of paper, no matter how seemingly trivial—he or she has collected or can collect. Ask your source to bring as much of this documentation as possible to your first meeting (and also to bring the in-house phone directory of his or her company or agency so you can begin your search for additional sources). But be aware that even with a thick folder of documents a single conversation may only scratch the surface of what the source knows. Indeed, even a half dozen conversations and entire boxes of documents may fail to uncover a key piece of information that the source has but that he or she doesn't know is important and that you don't know enough to ask about. As you follow up leads from the earlier conversations and the documents—and thus get a clearer picture—you will often have to mull things over with your original sources again and again. All the more reason to be absolutely honest in your dealings with them: Maintain confidences and be careful not to misrepresent or misquote what they tell you. If you disagree with their interpretation of something, let them know forthrightly—don't spring it as a surprise in one of your articles.

I also suggest that you read the complete draft of your article (or of each article in your series) to your chief whistle-blowing sources; not only will it increase their sense of commitment, but also they will probably spot subtle errors of emphasis if not outright errors of fact. Most reporters don't do this as they feel it might undermine their "control" of the story. In my opinion, however, reading the draft to a key source is as natural—indeed, as obligatory—as submitting it to your fact-checking assistant or your editor.

3.5 Interviewing

An interview, as opposed to a brief telephone conversation with a contact, involves formal questioning at a prearranged time and often according to mutually agreed upon ground rules. The first thing to remember about interviewing is: Do your homework. If your subject is an expert in a given field and you come to the interview totally ignorant, he or she will be annoyed and thus will be less inclined to cooperate. (Your display of knowledge, however, should be restricted during the interview to the posing of intelligent questions; you are there to ask such questions and listen to the answers, not spout off. If you and the source want to *exchange* ideas, do so after the interview is over.)

Being prepared also means drawing up a list of questions and arranging them in some order of priority. You should ask yourself what the person might know *beyond* the obvious. Time and again while interviewing people, I've failed to probe far enough, failed to get to the key question—and it was usually because I called them hastily without preparing beforehand. (If, after you hang up, you realize you've missed a key question, call the source back immediately; this may actually start a longer and far more illuminating conversation.)

Whether you interview someone on the telephone or in person, you should consider carefully the best time and place for the interview. They might feel constrained talking in their offices, but if you talk to them at their homes they might feel equally constrained by the presence of a spouse who doesn't want them sticking their neck out (or who regards you as some kind of sexual rival). Thus, in some instances, the interview might best be conducted over lunch or at a tavern after work.

In both telephone and in-person interviews, you have a choice of taping the conversation, taking notes, or both. Taping someone on the phone without their knowledge is illegal in several states (and since you can't use the illegal tape in court or to convince your editor, why do it?). However, if you ask a person's permission to tape them over the phone, you may screw up the interview. If they consent to be taped, they often will be extremely cautious in what they say (remember, they are talking to a stranger they cannot see). If they don't consent to be taped, they'll think you have the machine on anyway and thus will talk much less freely than if you'd never raised the idea. These problems will probably not arise in a phone interview with an expert providing noncontroversial background information, but even then make sure he or she feels comfortable about being taped.

When you interview someone in person, there is more leeway for using a tape recorder. If you have established a rapport with them and don't intend to ask anything that might seriously compromise them (and if the conversation is *on* the record), I would say the tape recorder is appropriate—just don't place it in their direct line of vision while they are talking. Otherwise, simply take notes. And even *with* the tape recorder on, you should take notes: It will save you later from having to listen to and transcribe material of little or no importance. Also, taking notes ensures against such common mishaps as the recorder not working properly or background noise ruining parts of the recording.

Both cassettes and notes should be marked for identification immediately: Put on the cassette label the name of the person interviewed and the date and place of the interview (this and other identifying information should also be at the beginning of the tape itself, the first words you speak after turning it on). On the first page of handwritten notes or at the beginning of notes taken by computer, put the name, date, time, and either the place at which the interview was conducted or the telephone number that you dialed to reach subject (plus the number from which you called). In taking notes by hand, write on one side of the page only (for later ease in photocopying); also number each page (1 of 3, 2 of 3, etc.) and print "END OF INTERVIEW" right beneath the last line of notes on the last page. While the interview is still fresh in your mind type up and add to the notes on your computer (or make additions to the notes you typed during the interview). This should be done after brief telephone conversations (if they elicited significant information) as well as after formal interviews.

Unless you are using shorthand, the notes you end up with will be a mixture of the following elements: (1) subject's exact words (the exact quote) as written down in your notebook on the spot; (2) subject's remarks as paraphrased or summarized on the spot; and (3) subject's remarks as paraphrased or summarized later from memory. The cardinal rule is never to confuse (1) with either (2) or (3). Direct quotes from your interviewee, whether entire sentences or isolated phrases, should always be clearly set off in your notes either by underlining or by quotation marks. Also, additions made while going over the notes should always be placed in brackets.

After you have keyed in and added to your interview notes on the computer, do *not* destroy the handwritten originals (you will need them in dealing with your editor and your newspaper's libel attorneys before publication, and possibly in a libel defense thereafter).

A fourth element in note taking is your own interpretive remarks. Although a few of these will doubtless be in your original notes, you should in general write these down separately afterward, along with observations about subject's personal appearance, his or her office furniture, and so forth. As you will want to speculate freely to yourself in these jottings, you should keep them in a separate notebook or in a separate computer file; you don't want Mr. J to find, during his subsequent libel suit, phrases such as "uptight bureaucratic creep" or "egg on his tie—disgusting!" scrawled in the margin of your subpoenaed notes.

Before any interview you should get the correct spelling of the person's name and also any generational designation. In interviewing public officials or corporate officers, be sure you get their correct title *and* the correct name of the agency or company. There is nothing more annoying than to read an article in a weekly free-distribution newspaper (or a private investigator's report) in which the chairman of the city planning commission is referred to as the "director" of the "department" of planning. In dealing with a high-level official, get this information from his or her private secretary or an aide rather than bothering him or her with it during the interview.

If you interview someone in his or her office, observe carefully your surroundings: a diploma on the wall or pictures of family members on the desk may provide important leads. Also note the names of the interviewee's private secretary, the receptionist, etc. These people may hate their boss and become important sources later on.

Some journalists say you should observe carefully the interviewee's facial expressions and body language. I suppose it's better to observe these things than to keep your eyes closed, but I wouldn't make too much of it. The nerdish accountant who keeps clearing his throat when questioned about the sloppy bookkeeping in the city agency for which he works may not be manifesting job-related guilt at all. It may just be that he feels intimidated by members of the press or that he simply has a post-nasal drip. If lie detectors are notoriously unreliable, why should pop-psychology theories on blinking and leg-crossing be any better?

Journalists and their sources can choose among a variety of arrangements regarding how the information from a given interview will be used. Ideally the entire interview should be "on the record" (i.e., you can quote the person by name on anything he or she says). If he or she declines this, however, you can put forward various alternatives. First, suggest that some of the interview be on the record and some not (often, to make your story, you will need only a single quote on the record). If your source still refuses to be named, ask if you can quote him or her on a "not for attribution" basis, for example, as "a former top aide of Senator Foghorn" (no name given, but many people will be able to guess). Only if this doesn't work will you offer to do the interview as "background" (you attribute it only to vague "official sources" or "well-informed sources") or reluctantly agree to do it "off the record" (you use the information only if you can verify it from other sources or from documents and never refer even in the vaguest of terms to the existence of your original source).

A somewhat arcane arrangement within the Washington Beltway is that the reporter will attribute a statement to a certain official but will paraphrase rather than directly quote the statement. The source can then say the remarks were misrepresented if he or she gets any heat from the interview. Obviously this and most of the arrangements above will make sense only with media-savvy government officials and prosecutors. With ordinary people, just stick to "on the record" and "background."

In preparing for any interview, the question arises: Should you be the first to raise the question of attribution? In dealing with most government officials (except whistle blowers) or most politicians, I would say: Let sleeping dogs lie, and just assume everything is on the record. If the official is stupid enough not to set ground rules, he or she must pay the price. But in dealing with ordinary people, it's not so simple. Often they will tell you something openly, and then say halfway through the conversation or at the end, "Don't quote me on this." If you quote them anyway, they'll feel aggrieved and won't cooperate in the future. It is thus usually best to establish ground rules for the interview if you anticipate further dealings with the interviewee. However, I have had people agree to go on the record and then change their mind and call me at home afterward, begging me not to use their names. If this happens, you have to weigh carefully (1) whether you are willing to risk alienating them and cutting yourself off from further information they might provide, and (2) whether using their names will really create a hardship for them (they may just be having an irrational panic attack). Be aware that journalists who lack a caring attitude toward their sources not only lose them, but they also experience difficulty later in gaining the trust of friends or associates of the original source who may possess far more important information.

An important distinction to keep in mind in your interviewing is that between an anonymous source and a confidential source. The former is a source whose identity you will not reveal in your article or in conversations with third parties but whose identity you might disclose in a libel suit or under other special circumstances. A confidential source is one whom you have agreed to keep secret at all costs, even if you are jailed for contempt of court as a result. This should be agreed on at the outset if the source is giving you sensitive information. Obviously, you would prefer the source to be anonymous rather than confidential (and on the record rather than anonymous). I have had sources who began as strictly confidential agree to go public later on, as we got to know each other better.

Finally, there is an art to interviewing—of how to do it so as to extract the maximum information. Any reporter who wants to avoid blunders should read carefully the articles by Eric Nalder and Bruce Selcraig in the November–December 1992 issue of *The IRE Journal*. Also see the books on interviewing listed in the bibliography.

3.6 Getting a Signed Statement

If you are working for an attorney, or if you are a journalist working on especially sensitive material, you will want to get signed declarations from some of the sources you interview. Some interviewers may do this with a laptop computer and portable printer, but the method described here involves the good old yellow pad with ruled lines and a pen (never a pencil). Write at the top of the first page "Declaration of John R. Doe." Begin the text, "I, John R. Doe, was interviewed on [date] between [starting time] and [ending time] at [place of interview] by [name of interviewer] who is a reporter for [name of publication]" (or: ". . . who is an investigator for [name of attorney]"). Then write down the source's occupation, place of employment, and home address, followed by each relevant fact of which the source has direct personal knowledge; do not include any mere speculation, no matter how juicy. Read each sentence to the source before you write it down, so he or she can affirm its accuracy. Keep the statement as brief as possible, locking the source into an affirmation of the absolutely crucial facts only. If you need more than one page, number them "1 of 3," "2 of 3," etc. When finished, ask the source to read over the entire declaration carefully. If the source wishes to make changes at this point, he or she should initial each change.

When all changes have been made, the source should sign each page and then write in his or her own hand at the bottom of the last page that he or she has read the above X pages and X lines (count the lines on the last page) and know the contents to be true. Finally, have the source sign this affirmation on the spot or take him or her to a notary, who will verify his or her identity, witness the signing, and stamp the signature page with a notary seal. If you do much interviewing for attorneys, you should become a notary yourself. However, if you're a journalist who happens to be a notary, do *not* notarize the statement yourself: It won't be as credible as a statement notarized by a third party if you're subsequently sued for libel.

In most instances, a simple declaration (signed but not notarized) is sufficient. The notarized statement, or affidavit, is chiefly useful when the source is telling you explosive and potential libelous things. It's a way of putting sources to the test—if they are lying or wildly exaggerating, they will most likely back off from giving an affidavit. Even when you fully trust the information, an affidavit may be useful because it takes the source's commitment to a higher level—he or she becomes less likely to back out later. In addition, an affidavit is sometimes useful when a source refuses to allow you to quote him or her by name in your article; having the statement to show to your newspaper's editor and attorneys will help to convince them the information is reliable in spite of the source's insistence on anonymity.

Note: When you get a signed statement, also get the name, address, and telephone number of at least one person who will know how to contact your source if the latter moves.

3.7 "Advertising" for Information

When a person is searching for a missing relative and the trail runs dry, he or she may try placing classified ads in selected publications, asking those with information to come forward. Families searching for an abducted child may pass out flyers that include the child's picture and a reward offer, or they may go to the media. The police often circulate wanted posters and seek the aid of the TV program "America's Most Wanted." Well, journalists can do this also: Jessica Mitford, in preparing an exposé of the Famous Writers School (a correspondence school), placed a classified ad in *Saturday Review* (a magazine whose readers she felt were likely to have fallen victim to the school's scam) asking former students to contact her.

Journalists (or private investigators who are part-time journalists or have a journalist friend to feed a story to) can do a subtler but often more effective type of "advertising." It's called going with what you've got. You take the partial, imperfect story you've uncovered and publish it as a means of attracting sources who can tell you the rest of the story.

I first learned about this tactic while working for the Manhattan weekly *Our Town* in the late 1970s. Assigned to a story on local newsstand distribution companies and "swag" (stolen newspapers and magazines), I was able to write a story describing how the scam worked but with no hard facts on who was behind it. *Our Town* published the story, and within hours we were getting calls from anonymous persons in daily newspaper circulation departments—and also newsstand operators—offering us information about the role of a corrupt local union. A similar thing happened several months later when we did an article on right-winger Lyndon LaRouche: Within days, calls were coming in from defectors from LaRouche's organization who had a wealth of information, some of which was about LaRouche's hidden control of one of Manhattan's largest computer software companies. We published a piece on this, eliciting, again, a spate of calls, this time from former clients and employees of the firm in question. One morning I came into the office and found on my desk a complete computer printout of the firm's general ledger, apparently dropped off by a disgruntled programmer.

This technique worked in the above cases because the published articles were so easily available to people with the information we needed. The "swag" scam was centered in Manhattan, the LaRouche organization had its headquarters in Manhattan, and LaRouche's computer company did much of its business in Manhattan. People with knowledge of these topics could pick up *Our Town* for free in midtown banks and other busy locations, and all three articles were on the front page. The lesson is: Use your news articles as the journalistic equivalent of a wanted poster to find the sources you need. If your article appears in a paper that reaches the right audience (and that audience, depending on the topic, could just as well be a specialized newsletter with only a few hundred subscribers), the results may surprise you.

If you specialize in a particular journalistic topic—or have developed a reputation for going after villainy across the spectrum—you can advertise on a much broader scale: Go on radio and TV talk shows, solicit speaking engagements, hold a press conference on your latest findings, do newspaper and magazine interviews, and get other reporters around the country to quote you as an expert. Over the long run, this can pay big dividends. Much of the information for my 1989 book on LaRouche came from sources who first heard me on talk shows, or who saw my name in an article by another journalist, or who came up to the podium after one of my speeches.

Another approach is to cultivate people in organizations concerned with your topic who will then refer potential sources to you. In the mid-1980s, I had over a dozen Jewish, civil rights, labor, and anti-cult organizations passing on my name to victims of the LaRouche group; this also produced major leads. In addition, if you let other journalists around the country know that you are focusing on a given topic, they will call you when they are working on a relevant piece, and, in return for your help, will share their findings with you and introduce you to their sources.

I believe in getting other journalists involved to the maximum extent. If the story is a big one, there's always room for several people to work on different aspects. What one turns up will help the others. The tracking of LaRouche in the early 1980s, for instance, was the work of a network of journalists across the country. Whenever an article about LaRouche by freelancer Russ Bellant appeared in a Detroit paper, it would attract to him local ex-LaRouchians who would never have known to contact me in New York or Chip Berlet in Chicago or Joel Bellman in Los Angeles (and vice versa). Unfortunately, reporters on major dailies are often too paranoid or competitive to practice this cooperative approach.

One of the best forms of advertising is simply to have a listed home phone number in the telephone directory. This may produce some annoying messages on your answering machine (and certainly you might want to have your address unlisted), but to have an unlisted home phone number is, for an investigative journalist (especially a freelancer without a fixed office), the cardinal sin in my opinion.

If you are linked to the Internet, you can advertise in another way: by putting messages on electronic bulletin boards or sending messages to all members of a given e-mail list requesting information on the topic of your investigation. An appeal for tips regarding a local political scandal might go to certain bulletin boards on your local Freenet; a request for help on an article relating to a particular religious cult might go through the Campus-Wide Information System (CWIS) of each college at which the cult recruits. The latter request could also be sent to anti-cult e-mail lists and to academic news groups or conference groups that focus on the sociology of alternative religions. To draw attention to your request and stimulate curiosity, you might send along with your message the text of a previous article you wrote on the cult in question.

If you're not yet on the Internet, get someone who is to handle this task for you. For more advice about using the Internet, see sections 2.6 and 14.1.

3.8 Caller ID

This controversial service, which involves the use of a small display screen to show the telephone number from which an incoming call originated, was available in only a few areas when the last edition of this book was being prepared. Today, caller ID is available in all or part of over half the states, and plans are afoot to bring it even to rural phone subscribers. Its biggest early drawback—the fact that it would show the number for incoming calls originating only *within* the subscriber's calling area or state—has now been overcome: The Federal Communications Commission (FCC) has ruled that all telephone companies must (as of April 1995) transmit a caller's number to out-of-state calling areas for caller ID display.

To answer the concerns of privacy critics, all states with caller ID now provide per-call blocking by which a caller can prevent his or her number from appearing on the caller ID subscriber's display screen by entering a three- or four-digit code before dialing (the letter "P" or the word "private" will then appear on the caller ID subscriber's screen along with the date, time, and daily numerical order of the call). Some states also allow or require per-line, or all-call, blocking—a free service whereby the caller's number is automatically withheld unless the caller unblocks his or her line by entering a special code before making a call.

How is caller ID useful for you, the reporter? A hard-hitting investigative series often produces threatening or harassing phone calls, or calls from imposters trying to find out who your sources are. Caller ID will tell you the number of the phone from which the call is being made, and you can then reverse the number in the crisscross directory to find out the subscriber's name and address. (Note that in several localities automatic phone number reversal is being offered as part of the caller ID service.) Knowledge of the identities of such callers is not just good self-protection: It also can help you fill out the list of your subject's known associates. Some of them may later become sources (especially if you are investigating cults, an area in which today's true believer is tomorrow's defector).

Caller ID is also of value if you are dealing with an anonymous source who is not yet ready to tell you his or her identity. Learning the identity surreptitiously and then gathering a little background information will enable you to decide whether or not the person's information should be taken seriously.

The usefulness of caller ID is believed to be sharply limited by the fact that crank callers and other secretive callers often operate from pay phones and/or use per-call or per-line blocking. This perception is not altogether accurate. First, a person disturbed enough to engage in telephone harassment and/or play compulsive secrecy games may lack sufficient impulse control to use the blocking code and/or a pay phone consistently. Second, there is the laziness/ignorance factor: Surveys in several states have shown that call blocking is used in less than 1 percent of all phone calls. It would appear that most telephone users not only can't be bothered with memorizing the blocking code, but they aren't even aware that it exists (many are probably not even aware that caller ID exists).

Knowing a pay phone location (along with the time the call was made) can often be the first step in identifying a caller. If the phone is located near suspected caller X's home (and the call was made during hours when X is usually at home), or near X's workplace (during X's known lunch hour or immediately before or after his or her shift), or on the route X usually travels between home and work (and during X's normal commuting hour), you have a strong clue, although not proof, that X made the call. You can then call him or her at home, say "I know it was you," and see if he or she admits it.

An alternative to caller ID is call return, which allows you to call back automatically the last number from which you received a call. If you use call return after a mysterious or harassing call, the number will appear on your next phone bill (if it is a long-distance call) or will be available via a breakdown (or "detail") of your local calls that the phone company will provide you on request. As in the case of caller ID, this method won't work if the caller has used the per-call blocking code or has an all-call block on his or her line. And, obviously, you will have to keep a record of exactly when you made the return call in order to identify it in the phone company records.

For more on caller ID, see section 4.33.

4·

Finding "Missing" People

4.1 Overview

A major problem in many investigations is locating the seemingly hard-to-find source or witness. Usually such people are not deliberately hiding out (or at least not hiding out from *you*). Many prove willing and even eager to talk when and if you find them at their residence or place of employment. But what if you have only an outdated address for them? Or if all you know is that the person lived somewhere in the Boston area many years ago? Or if his or her phone has been disconnected and there's no forwarding number? Or if the new number is unpublished?

Difficulty in finding people stems partly from the high rate of mobility in the American work force. A 1984 University of Michigan study found that 30 percent of interviewees nationwide had lived at their most recent address for less than two years. An earlier survey estimated that 16.6 percent of all citizens of voting age had changed their place of residence within the previous year. The close-knit neighborhood in which folks sit on the front porch in the evening and everyone knows everyone else is largely a nostalgic memory.

This trend is paralleled by a growing desire for privacy, even a kind of secretiveness. By 1994, almost one-third of all Americans had an unlisted number (a number unpublished in the white pages and unavailable through Directory Assistance). In major California cities, the rate was well over 50 percent unpublished with a high of 64.7 percent in Sacramento. In addition, the percentage choosing to list their name and telephone number without their address (or with only a partial address or a post office box number) also rose sharply.

Such efforts to maintain privacy are relatively ineffectual in today's computerized society. Skip tracers, private investigators, and other professional finders—who for decades relied on marketing directories and pretext phone calls to track down people who had moved and/or didn't want to be found—today have at their command powerful electronic search techniques to supplement their traditional methods. So-called information brokers are providing them with routine access to giant databases compiled by credit-reporting agencies, mailing list vendors, and state and local governments; these databases track the overwhelming majority of American households. In addition, time-honored tools such as the crisscross directory are being used far more effectively today in an electronic format.

But databases are only as good as the information fed into them, and this information is often inaccurate or out of date. Some people contrive to drop out of the electronic information net temporarily, or they build a parallel database trail under a different name and at a different address. Their motives run the gamut: an ex-husband who wishes to evade child-support or alimony payments, the criminal suspect who has jumped bail, a deadbeat who owes thousands of dollars to department stores, a cult member who believes her parents are instruments of Satan plotting to have her tortured by deprogrammers.

People who don't want to be found use a variety of predictable tactics. For instance, they put their telephone or utilities in someone else's name, or they use a false Social Security Number (SSN) on job applications. But most such people are inconsistent in using these tactics. They may give a phony SSN at one job but forget and give their real SSN at the next. They may list their phone number in their girlfriend's name but list the utilities in their own name. Finding them just means searching systematically through the various records systems until you find the weak spot.

The problem is more difficult when your subject knows how to conceal his or her location and identity in a systematic manner and has the discipline to stick to it. Some of these people go to elaborate lengths to construct a false identity by obtaining a birth certificate and other ID in the name of a person who was born at about the same time as themselves but who died in childhood (this is called "paper tripping"). If the FBI can't always find such people, you probably can't either. But at least you can find most non–paper trippers with the techniques outlined below.

4.2 Important Search Tools

A variety of online, CD-ROM, microform, and hardcopy resources exist through which you can search for anyone anywhere in the United States or Canada, and eventually either locate them directly or locate relatives, friends, former neighbors, or ex-spouses who can put you in touch with them.

Electronic White Pages
This service is available to any telephone subscriber who has a computer and a modem. Essentially it gives you direct access to the database used by

Directory Assistance operators (all published telephone numbers and all daily updates reflecting the vast number of additions, deletions, and "moves" within the phone company's region). Unlike hardcopy directories and many CD-ROM directories, the electronic white pages tells you if a person has an unpublished number: the screen displays the subscriber's name with the letters "NP" (non published) when you request the number. This ability to confirm that subject indeed lives in (or at least has phone subscriber service in) a given area can be the first step in a successful trace.

For those who conduct searches on a daily basis, online access to the electronic white pages provides two key advantages over telephone access via Directory Assistance: (1) you can perform multiple-name searches at your leisure, e.g., you can search the entire list of Smiths in Anytown, Illinois, to figure out which of them are most likely to be the Smith for whom you are looking; (2) you are not dependent on an often harried operator (the percentage of erroneous answers from operators in some localities is extremely high).

The NYNEX Electronic White Pages gives you access to 14 million listings in New York State and the New England states. Although it does not include crisscross capabilities, it enables you to keep up with the vast number of "moves" in the NYNEX system.

AT&T offers combined access to the various regional white pages through Find America. The latter service, however, is far too expensive for journalists and other part-time searchers who, if they need an occasional search outside their own region, can use Directory Assistance and CD-ROM databases (see below) in tandem to get the information they need.

PhoneDisc and Other CD-ROM Directories
PhoneDisc Residential includes over 81 million U.S. residential listings that can be searched by surname or partial surname (thousands of cross-references are included so you can search alternate spellings of a surname). PhoneDisc Business includes 9.4 million alpha listings with reverse search (street listings and numerical listings) capabilities. Both are offered together in the PhoneDisc Combo Pack. However, PhoneDisc PowerFinder, which combines the business and residential listings with reverse search for both, is well worth the additional cost.

The chief drawbacks of PhoneDisc are (1) that it is only updated quarterly and (2) upward of one-fifth of the households listed in white-page directories nationwide are not included in PhoneDisc. On the other hand, PhoneDisc does include data on some households missing from the white pages, gathered mostly from postal change-of-address, driver's license, and mailing list databases.

Various regional telephone companies are also offering CD-ROM directories, although of a much more expensive (and supposedly more powerful) type. A good example is the NYNEX Fast Track Digital Directory, which offers nationwide listings not just from the white pages but also from outside vendors of non–telephone directory databases, especially direct-mail list compilers such as Metromail. Because of its high price, Fast Track is best consulted at the public library. Many libraries will have a noncrisscross white-pages-only version for their region (this is chiefly useful for filling in any gaps in PhoneDisc's coverage of the given region). However, some major research libraries that are heavily used by the business community will have the full high-powered-search version of Fast Track. Every budget-conscious journalist or investigator should find out the location of the nearest library with this version.

Finder Databases from Online Vendors

One of the most interesting products of this type is Prentice Hall OnLine's PeopleTracker. It is compiled from a variety of public records and commercial databases as well as from telephone white pages. It provides previous as well as current addresses of subject (with length of residency at each) and listings of subject's previous as well as current neighbors (again, with length of residency). It also includes subject's date of birth, names of other household members, median income of neighborhood, and so forth. This information, once available only from print directories (city and crisscross), can be invaluable in a difficult trace, as when the person has moved (or "skipped") from the latest address without providing a telephone recording or a postal change-of-address notice to help people reach him or her. Note that Prentice Hall OnLine provides searches per request for nonsubscribers, although only subscribers can obtain direct online access to the database.

A similar database is LEXIS/NEXIS's Person Locator Library, which covers 111 million individuals in over 80 million households; you can search the entire group file directory or individual state directories.

Phone*File is a directory available from CompuServe without the expensive subscription fees of LEXIS/NEXIS or Prentice Hall. Also compiled from telephone white-page directories and other publicly available sources of information, it covers 83 million households nationwide. You can search for a person by name with address, by surname with city and/or state, by surname with zip code, or simply by phone number.

If the above databases don't give you what you need, you can go to a search professional who has access to the full range of investigative databases and specializes in complicated electronic tracing. Or you can sign up with an investigative gateway service and do your own searching: You enter subject's name, SSN, and last known address, and search through the non-credit ("header") information in vast credit-reporting agency databases as well as public records databases to find subject's current (or at least a fairly recent) address.

Out-of-Town Phone Directory Collections (Hardcopy and Microform)

Major public libraries have collections of out-of-town directories. Although they are rarely complete or up to date, these collections can be useful if you are searching for people who basically stay put in one place (e.g., subject's parents in his or her hometown).

Searches of out-of-town phone books are best conducted via University Microfilms International's Phonefiche. This is a nationwide microfiche collection of 2,500 directories covering 50,000 communities (about 80 percent of the nation) which is available at many public libraries. Including both yellow pages and white pages, it can be bought in selective packages; thus, your public library may carry only the directories for your own state and for cities nationwide with a population of over 500,000. Phonefiche includes an annual printed cross-reference guide: You can look up any community in the United States, and the guide will tell you which multicommunity phone directory or directories cover that community or any portions thereof. Likewise you can look up any phone directory by title—say, the Grand Traverse Bay Area directory in Michigan—and get a list of all communities covered in whole or in part by it.

Social Security Death Masterfile
If you are searching for someone who has been missing for many years, or for a birth parent of an adoptee, check first if they are still alive. Several commercial CD-ROM versions of the Social Security Administration's death masterfile (with data added from other public records) are on the market. The least expensive, at $45, is the Social Security Death Benefits Index from Automated Archives, Inc. This version contains records on 52 million deaths, mostly since 1962 (the year reporting became mandatory). It provides the deceased's birth date, death date, state and zip code of residency at time of death, state in which the deceased's Social Security Number was originally issued, and the zip code to which the survivor's benefit was paid. (Once you have this information, you can get more from the SSA.) Another version is the Nationwide Death Index produced by CSRA. Although much more expensive than the Automated Archives' version, it is useful to journalists because it can be accessed via telephone ($8 per search with credit card) and also online ($1 per search after payment of $25 sign-up fee). The addresses of both the above companies are in the bibliography.

4.3 White-Page Directory Search Methods

Residential Listings
The following tips can help you squeeze the maximum information out of both the hard copy and electronic white pages:

- Never assume you have the correct spelling of a name; always check variant spellings. At the beginning of a list of same-spelling surnames, the white pages often will provide "see also" references to the variant spellings. For instance, in the Manhattan white-page directory, we look for Larry Kahn. At the beginning of the "Kahn" listings we find the notice, "KAHN SEE ALSO CAHN, CONN." Your directory may not always include such notices, however. And a notice, if given, may not include all variants (the *New Dictionary of American Family Names* is useful here).

- Familiarize yourself with the alphabetization and listing system of the particular directory you are using. For instance in the *NYNEX White Pages* for Manhattan we find that initials precede first names (e.g., "Jones, S.R." before "Jones, Samuel"); some abbreviations are listed alphabetically as if they were spelled out (e.g. "St. Michel, Jacques" is listed as if it were spelled "Saint Michel, Jacques"); and names with prefixes are usually treated as a single word regardless of whether the person spells it with or without spaces (e.g., "De La Cruz" and "DelaCruz" are listed in alphabetical order according to first name, with "DelaCruz, Amanda" before "De La Cruz, Anna").

- If you don't find subject under his or her surname, look under the spouse's birth name and under linked names, e.g., Mary Brown-Smith, Mary Smith-Brown, John Brown-Smith, John Smith-Brown, John & Mary Brown-Smith, and so forth. For more tips regarding such name variations, see section 7.1.

- If you cannot find subject's first name in the listings under his or her surname, check subject's middle name and nickname, if known. If you know only the initial for subject's middle name, call all listed first names in the same-surname list that start with that letter (if you were searching for William D. King, a freelance writer, this is how you would find him—listed under Dennis King). Also check other variations, e.g., John Morris Jones could be listed as J. Morris Jones, J.M. Jones, J. Jones, or M. Jones.

- If the same-surname list is a long one, study the entire list carefully—it is easy to miss the crucial name. For instance, Zebulon Smith's name may not be under "Smith, Zebulon"—it may be back at the beginning of the list under "Smith, *Albert* Zebulon" or "Smith, Albert Z." Also, subject's first name may be listed following the first name of his or her spouse in a joint listing, e.g., "Smith, Zelda & Henry" (if you don't know Henry's wife is named Zelda, you will miss Henry altogether unless you search all the Smith's to the very end).

- Never assume a number is unlisted, even if you think the person has some reason to need an unlisted number. On more than one occasion, I have been contacted by ace investigative reporters who complained about how many calls they had to make to get my number. When I asked them why they didn't just look in the Manhattan phone book (in which I am the only Dennis King listed) they told me that they just "assumed" I would have an unlisted number because I write about cults.

Business Listings

Always check under subject's name in the business as well as residential white pages. Millions of Americans, especially freelancers and self-employed professionals, have business listings under their own names. These names will usually be listed in the same format as in the residential directory, i.e., surname first, although alphabetized in sequence with corporate names and other nonpersonal names.

If you don't find subject listed by surname in the business white pages, search for the names of any corporate or other business entities that seem to include subject's name and/or his or her spouse's name in whole or in part. If subject John R. Simpson is operating a small home business he might call it Simpson Enterprises, John R. Simpson Enterprises, Robert (his middle name) Simpson Enterprises, or JRS Enterprises, among other permutations. Note that the white pages are often inconsistent in handling the article "the"; if subject Simpson runs a literary agency out of his apartment, he might call it The Simpson Agency but the phone directory might list it as "Simpson Agency, the" (or vice versa). In addition, you should watch out for possessives: Simpson's Design Shop may be listed as "Simpson Design Shop" (or vice versa). Also watch for inadvertent transposition of names in home business listings; for example, John Simpson Co. becomes "Simpson John Co."

If you have a good idea what kind of business your subject might be engaging in, you could conduct your search in part via the yellow pages. For conducting your business-listing search with maximum efficiency, however, use PhoneDisc or one of the other electronic business directories described in section 4.2.

Subject's Prior Telephone Number

If subject has recently moved but you don't know his or her new address, always call his or her old telephone number. Often there will be a recording that will tell you the new number. Or the old number may have been taken over by another member of subject's prior household (e.g., a roommate) who stayed when subject moved out, and this person may know the new number. Or the old number may now be listed in the name of a friend, relative, or sublessee of subject who moved in when subject moved out, and this person likewise may know how to contact subject.

The new holder of the phone number may stay in touch with subject for years, so if the last listing for subject in the local phone directory was 5 or 10 years ago, you should still call that number. At the least you may get a stranger who was reassigned the number and who may have received other calls from people trying to reach subject. If this new holder of the number is a gossipy type, he or she may have picked up some interesting information.

Sweep Searches

Unless you have information to the contrary, always begin your search with the localities closest to subject's last known address: The overwhelming majority of people who move their residence remain within the same metropolitan area or state. This means checking all area codes in the greater metropolitan area in which you think subject is located, including "exurbia" as well as suburbia. People nowadays commute longer and longer distances, especially those who can "telecommute" part of the time. In searching for the residential address of someone believed to be working in the New York City area, I would check eastern Pennsylvania as well as New Jersey, Connecticut, and downstate New York. To find the residence of someone who is said to be working in the Washington, D.C., area, I would check West Virginia, Delaware, and eastern Pennsylvania as well as Virginia, Maryland, and Washington itself.

If you lack access to the electronic white pages for the region in question, a sweep search is best begun via Directory Assistance. Only when this fails to find subject should you turn to CD-ROM directories that may be months out of date. Directory Assistance works best when you have the exact name and exact spelling under which subject is likely to be listed, and when the surname is an uncommon one. With Directory Assistance you can often search an entire area code via a single request, thus quickly covering an entire region. Directory Assistance will tell you if anyone with the exact name you are searching for has either a listed or an unlisted number (and how many listees with that name are listed), and it will give you each listee's address if you specifically ask for it before the operator switches you over to the automatic voice response system. If the operator you speak to fails to find the number you requested, always call back and try with another operator (this is essential because of the high rate of operator mistakes).

If you need to search a long list of same-surname names and numbers, you will have to use the CD-ROM databases or the phone book in the absence of online access to the Directory Assistance database. CD-ROM is preferable, but if you are using hardcopy or microfiche directories be sure to look at *all* the directories for the given metropolitan area. More than once, I've failed to find someone because I looked only in the New York City borough directories and the Nassau and Suffolk County directories—and was too lazy to reach up to the higher shelf for the Westchester and New Jersey directories.

Calling Lists

With the help of PhoneDisc PowerFinder, you can compile a same-surname calling list for any city, state, or region (or any zip code) that you think is worth searching. And you can establish priorities based on various permutations of subject's name and/or the spouse's name. If you are searching for George Morgan, you can isolate out all the Morgans that include "George" or "G." either as a first name or middle name or as part of a joint name. Even if you don't find *your* George Morgan, you may find an unrelated person with the same name who has received numerous phone calls in the past for subject and may know how to reach him or her. (This other George

Morgan may also recall news articles about subject, since his own friends and co-workers may have asked him, "Was that *you?*")

If you strike out with the Georges and Gs, don't give up. Try the various permutations for George's wife's first and middle names and also her maiden name. If this doesn't work, go to the full list of Morgans in localities in which relatives of George are most likely to be found, such as George's home city or state, other cities or states where he has lived for substantial periods (he may have moved there precisely because a relative was already there), and the area in which he lived most recently before dropping below the horizon.

Using this last method, you may find not only relatives of George but George himself: The number you call may be his own home with the phone listed under a middle name or nickname—or the name of another family member—that you didn't know about. If not, you may hit on a relative or ex-wife who will give you George's address and phone number on the spot.

If you're still stumped, try all the people with the same surname as George's wife prior to her marriage to him; you may find one of her parents or siblings, or her previous husband or previous in-laws.

4.4 If You Have a Number and Name, but Not the Street Address

Your subject may have chosen to list his or her phone number in the white pages without an address or with only a partial address (street but no number) or with a post office box number in lieu of street address. However, if you reverse the number in the crisscross directory you may find that another member of the household has a listing for that number with the full address included. Or, returning to the white pages, you may find a single listing (with address included) for a person having a different phone number from, but the same unusual surname as, your subject. Noticing that the first three digits of this person's number signifies a telephone exchange within the same exchange zone or central office service area (see below) as subject's, you hypothesize that this person is either subject's spouse or one of subject's teenage children. So you call *subject's* number and ask for the person listed at the other number; if the latter comes to the phone, you have just found subject's street address (*unless* the other person is a relative who happens to be visiting subject at the moment you call).

Sometimes a person who withholds his or her street address from the residential listings will provide that same address for a home business listing (see section 4.3). Although the white pages will not tell you whether or not the business telephone is actually located in subject's home, you can look in the crisscross directory to see if the business address is in fact in an exclusively residential neighborhood.

The street address (or the *full* street address) can also be obtained some-times by looking in a back edition of the phone directory. Generally, if the number listed in the old directory corresponds to the number in the new one, the address in the old will be the same as that deleted from the new (unless the person moved within the same telephone exchange and asked to keep the previous number).

Note that you can determine the exchange zone or central office service area of subject's phone service via the first three digits of his or her phone number. Your telephone directory should provide listings of these exchange numbers (not to be confused with the area code number) by which you can match them to the appropriate city neighborhood or suburban community. If this information is not included in your directory, you can obtain it from the phone company or your local public service commission. (In some lo-calities the Directory Assistance operator will tell you which community is served by a particular exchange zone number.)

This information can help to narrow your search: If you want to contact George Smith, and you believe he lives in a certain town in Nassau County on Long Island, and then if you find a "Smith, G." listed without an ad-dress, but with an exchange number corresponding to an eastern Suffolk County exchange zone, you can assign this listing a low priority.

Under some circumstances, the exchange number will not actually corre-spond to the exchange zone normally designated by that number; for in-stance: if a residential or business customer has a "foreign exchange" line that provides him or her with service from a central office other than the one that usually serves the given address; or if a customer pays a premium to obtain a customized number corresponding to letters that spell out a message.

If the telephone white pages lists a post office box number rather than a street address for subject, a skip tracer will call the given post office, com-plain that he or she purchased something by mail from that box number which never arrived, and ask for the name and address of the box holder.

4.5 If You Have a Number, but No Name or Address

For newspaper reporters this is important when they start getting calls from mysterious people and want to verify quickly that these people are really who they say they are. If the caller gives you his or her phone number (or if you get it via caller ID), look in PhoneDisc PowerFinder or in the numer-ical listing section of the appropriate crisscross or city directory. In some cit-ies, you can call the public library telephone reference service, and they'll look it up for you.

If the number is in Chicago, call the Chicago phone company's reverse di-rectory at (312) 796–9600. They'll give you both the name and address of the customer.

4.6 If Subject Has an Unpublished Number

Private investigators often have informants inside the phone company who will provide them with unlisted numbers. News reporters sometimes get a police officer or local politician to obtain a number for them. However, there are other ways to get an unlisted number, some of them almost ridiculously simple.

- When you call Directory Assistance, always ask for any business listing in a person's name as well as the residential listing. Often the former will be listed when the latter is not, perhaps even at the same residential address. (If you call the business number during off-hours, a recording may give you the unlisted residential number.)

- Just because one resident of the household has an unlisted number doesn't mean the others do. Check in the phone book for the names of other family members who may have separate listings or separate lines. (As noted repeatedly, the wife may be listed under her maiden name or a hyphenated name, while the kids from one or both spouses' previous marriages may bear the names of the absent parent.) And don't forget to check subject's spouse in the business listings for a possible home business line.

- Check any nationwide or regional locator database, which will often include unlisted numbers obtained from nontelephone company sources, e.g., from the noncredit "header" information in credit-reporting agency databases (see section 2.6). Even if such a search doesn't turn up the unlisted number, it may at least give you subject's address. Then you can check the street directory to see if any other members of the household have a listed number. Or you can call one of the neighbors and get the number from them on a pretext.

- If Directory Assistance tells you the number is unlisted, always look in the phone book. Subject may have obtained his or her unlisted number very recently. If subject has remained at the same address, you may find that the previously listed number is, in fact, the very number that is now unlisted (it costs less to unlist the old listed number than to get a new unlisted number). If not—and if subject obtained his or her unlisted number on the occasion of a move to a new address—you may get a recording at the old number that tells you the new one. (If the recording merely says the old number has been disconnected, try again in a few days—the new number reference may be missing simply because subject's telephone at his or her new residence has not yet been installed.)

- If there is no listing for subject in the current phone directory, look in your collection of back editions or in the Phonefiche backfile until you find a listing. The number unpublished for the past 10 years may have originally been subject's published number.

- Call listed numbers of all persons with the same surname in the white pages. If subject has several relatives nearby (especially in a smaller population center), this often produces quick results. You just assume you have the right number and say, "I'd like to speak to Marvin Klenetsky." They say, "Oh, you have the wrong Klenetsky; he's at . . ." and they give you the number automatically. Unlisted numbers are not exactly a deep secret; often the relative doesn't even know the number he or she is giving out is unlisted.

- The unlisted number may be found in a city directory. Unlike crisscross directories (which are based on the telephone white pages), city directories compile their information on each household via the survey method. The survey taker will ask the member of the household contacted to provide, among other things, the household's phone number. Only a very small percentage refuse to give out the number, even if it is unlisted in the white pages. (If they do refuse, the city directory will at least tell you the address of the family and possibly the place of employment of the head of household.) In most large cities, city directories have been discontinued for many years. However, if you know that your subject has lived in the same home for decades but has never been in the phone book, you might want to check the final edition of the city directory on microform at your public library. Subject's current unlisted number—its unlisted status maintained all these years—may be in that final 1962 edition. Of course, a person who has lived in one spot so long will probably be very well known to neighbors; thus, you might find it easier to call longtime neighbors listed in the current street directory to obtain the number.

- Check public records at the county courthouse or town hall (in some localities and for some records this can be done over the phone). The unlisted number may be included on, say, a license application.

- Subject may have a weekend or vacation home at the seashore or in nearby mountains. Although keeping unlisted the phone number of his or her main (weekday) residence, subject may not have thought to do likewise with the weekend phone.

- Some corporations distribute internal phone directories to their employees giving the home addresses and phone numbers of each. These directories will often include phone numbers and addresses not listed in the telephone company's white pages. Thus, if you know where your subject works or used to work, you might try to get the number and address from another past or present company employee who has a copy of the directory. Note that such directories are frequently obtained by personnel agency headhunters who use them to call around and see if anybody's interested in moving to a new job.

- If subject is a college student or a member of a college faculty or support staff (or the spouse of same), check the campus directory; the home number may be listed here even if unpublished in the telephone company's white pages. Campus directories are often accessible online via the Internet.

- If subject is an alumnus or alumna of a private school, university, or professional college, his or her home number will often be listed in the alumni directory. Subject may have consented to such listing because it never occurred to him or her that this directory would be used by anyone except old classmates.

- If subject has a personal computer and modem at home or work, you may be able to substitute e-mail communication for a telephone conversation. The e-mail addresses of over 100,000 individuals are listed in *The Internet White Pages*; additional directory information can be accessed via WHOIS servers on the Internet. (In some instances, the e-mail address will tell you what corporate, university, or organizational computer network subject's computer is linked to.)

- You can send a letter to subject at his or her last known address, with a request that he or she call you collect. If the letter is forwarded to subject, and he or she does call collect, and you accept the call, you can afterward call back the operator and find out the number from which the call was made. If subject calls you, but not via a collect call, you may still find out the number from which he or she is calling via caller ID or call return (see section 3.8). Note that the switching technology on which caller ID is based does not distinguish between listed and unlisted numbers.

4.7 If the Phone Number Is in Another Name

As we have seen above, a male subject's phone number may be listed under his wife's maiden name. It may also be in the name of another family member, a live-in lover, or a roommate. This may be simply for convenience—Janet agrees to handle the phone bills while Harold takes care of the utilities. Or it may be that Harold is ducking bill collectors, in which case both phone and utilities may be in Janet's name. It also may be that when Harold and Janet moved from their previous address, Harold owed the phone company hundreds of dollars. Getting the phone in Janet's name is thus a tactic to evade that bill and also avoid paying a deposit on the new phone service. In general, finding Harold under these circumstances will be a serious problem for tracers only if Harold met and became involved with Janet *after* skipping out on his last address (otherwise, one of Harold's previous friends, neighbors, or co-workers could be induced via a pretext question to describe her and/or give you her name).

Sometimes people will list their number under a variation of their name which you would not easily recognize, or even under a fictitious name.

Using such a name means that a searcher cannot verify through Directory Assistance that subject is living within the given area code (which *can* be determined if subject has an unpublished number in his or her own name). However, if the account name (the name of the person who is billed) is nevertheless subject's real name, you may be able to find him or her through a source inside the phone company. If not, subject can often be found by going to various public records—such as tax assessment or voter registration lists (see section 4.22)—where subject's real name may be listed. If you get the address from one of these lists, you can then go to a crisscross directory and find out the name and telephone number listed for that address. Chances are this will be either the fictitious name subject is using or else subject's wife's maiden name. Call the answering machine and see what name, if any, is given with the message.

If subject is living under a false identity, tracing him or her via telephone and crisscross directories and county courthouse records will become extremely difficult if not impossible. For finding such people, see section 4.32.

4.8 If Subject's Listed Address Is Not His or Her Real Address

Phone customers who use a telephone answering service and/or a mail-receiving service may list the address of this company as their own address in the white pages or other directories. If you cannot visit the address, look in the crisscross directory to see if the neighborhood is residential or business, and also to determine if the particular building includes both businesses and apartments or is exclusively an office building (of course, an answering service or mail-receiving service might operate out of someone's private home, depending on the local zoning laws). You should also check the yellow pages to see if any of the local answering and/or mail-receiving services are located at this address. If there is indeed such a service at the given address, note that subject may have chosen it because of its proximity to his or her real home or place of work (in some parts of Manhattan, mailbox rental services are located on street level every few blocks).

A residential telephone customer may also have a phone line at and a directory listing for a private home where he or she doesn't really live or spend any time. This could be done for a variety of reasons. For instance, Mrs. Smith may get a telephone installed in her own name at a friend's house in a neighborhood with good schools as part of a scheme to make her kids eligible to attend those schools rather than the blackboard jungle in her own neighborhood. (If she's going to be careful about this, it means putting her *real* home phone in someone else's name.)

Another example would be Mr. and Mrs. Jones, the yuppie co-op owners who are temporarily renting their apartment to Ms. Price without the knowledge or permission of the co-op board, while themselves living at another address. The Joneses maintain the phone in their own name at the co-op while listing the number at their real place of residence under Mrs. Jones's maiden name. Ms. Price uses the phone listed under the Jones's name as her own phone (giving the number to her friends, for instance) but if anyone from the building management or the co-op board calls she says she's the cleaning lady.

If you need accurate information about a residential address, never rely solely on the white pages. Crosscheck the address against other records systems.

4.9 If Subject Has No Phone

Almost 6 percent of American households lack telephone service. This includes about 200,000 Americans in isolated rural areas. It also includes low-income people in urban areas: A 1993 survey found that 20 percent of the homes in New York City's poorest neighborhoods were without phones. In some cases this may not be simply because of poverty: Illegal aliens often don't apply for phone service because of fear of the Immigration and Naturalization Service and also because their need for phone service for overseas calls to family members is adequately served by the many storefront phone parlors that have sprung up in immigrant communities in recent years.

Often, people without phone service in urban areas can be found through databases inclusive of the poor: voter registration lists, landlord/tenant court index, and so on. Those without phones in isolated rural areas may be found through the county tax rolls, Department of Motor Vehicles records, and hunting license rosters, as well as voter lists.

4.10 Postal Change-of-Address Notices

Most people, when they move, file a change-of-address notice with the post office so that their mail can be forwarded. Even skips (people who have moved out leaving many unpaid bills) often file such notices, blithely unaware that skip tracers can easily obtain the information included on the notice.

Until 1994, you could send your request for a person's forwarding address, together with a money order for $3, to the postmaster of the station responsible for mail delivery at subject's old address. This method has been suspended, at least temporarily, because of pressure from privacy advocates. However, an alternative method is still available: You can mail an empty envelope to subject at his or her old address with the words "Do Not Forward—Address Correction Requested" on the front of the envelope.

Although change-of-address notices are kept at the local post office only for a limited period, the data is not destroyed. It goes into the U.S. Postal

Service's National Change of Address System, a database that contains permanent change-of-address information on more than 25 million relocating customers. Although you cannot just call up Washington and get this information, the Postal Service does sell the tapes and frequent updates to more than a dozen mailing list companies, who use the data to keep their own lists up to date. Information brokers then buy these mailing list databases, add their own software, and offer skip tracers and private investigators access to the National Change of Address System!

The Post Office is still reviewing its policy on change-of-address information. There is a good chance that people who request mail forwarding will be allowed to opt out of the databases provided to mail-order vendors as well as opting out of any method that remains for private individuals to obtain change-of-address information. But the address changes already safely ensconced in the brokers' databases will still be useful for years to come in tracking people; while many future movers can be expected *not* to opt for privacy when filing change-of-address notices (there is a certain convenience in being "easy to find"). In addition, the already existing information-broker change-of-address databases are being merged with credit-reporting agency "header" databases, voter registration databases, magazine subscription change-of-address databases, and others that will take up the slack.

In using any past or future system for tracing people via postal or magazine subscription (or any other) change-of-address notices, be aware that the address you receive may not actually be subject's new address but rather that of a closed-mouthed friend or of a mail drop or mail-forwarding service.

4.11 Searching for Subject via His or Her Previous Address

A person can't always have been in hiding. If you believe subject previously lived in your city, check the back editions of the local phone directory (see above). Start with the most recent editions and work backward (or with a long-ago address and work forward). Remember to follow the procedures used with the current phone book (wife's maiden name, parents' names, etc.). If subject appears in a recent or not-so-recent back edition, call the number and see who answers.

If you need to search backfile directories in another city, use Phonefiche's nationwide backfiles of thousands of telephone directories dating back to 1976 (these will be available for the cities in your own region, at least, at the public library). If you do high-volume searching in your own metropolitan area, you might consider buying the local Phonefiche backfiles. These cost $25 per directory per year, but if you want all the directories for a given metro area, you can get a substantial discount. Of course, you will have to buy a microfiche reader as well (which costs about $200).

City directories and crisscross directories are often essential in tracing a person via his or her past addresses. Although CD-ROM products have in part replaced these directories as a source of reverse information about current households, the print directories are still indispensable for searching back through the years as well as for certain specific details about households. The back editions may be available at the public library or the local historical society, sometimes in microform. In addition, some directory publishers have a call-up number for obtaining information from back editions (see section 2.3).

Essentially there are three methods for using back directories in finding people: first, find out who lived with subject at his or her last listed household, track them down at their current address(es), and persuade them to give you subject's current address (or, at least, a more recent address); second, contact the current residents of subject's former house or apartment and see if they know anything (we touched briefly on this method in section 4.3); third, question subject's former neighbors and/or the shopkeepers in his or her former neighborhood. Note that these techniques are valuable not only in finding people but also in compiling detailed background or security clearance reports and in writing biographies of celebrities.

Finding Former Household Members

If the given locality was covered by a city directory at the time subject lived there, the directory may list all members of subject's former household and provide information that will help find them today, such as their occupations and/or former places of employment. If the given locality was not covered by a city directory, you can still find some of the names of household members via the crisscross directory:

- The numerical section in back editions of the local crisscross directory can be used to find any multiple listings (both same-surname and different-surname) under subject's former phone number; in addition, it can be used to spot instances of duplicate service (two people sharing the same phone number but with lines in different apartments or houses within the same telephone exchange) and instances in which a person who shared the phone chose to list an address other than the actual household's (for instance, a P.O. box) or no address at all.

- The street listings in the crisscross directory back editions can be used to find the name of anyone in the household who at any point had his or her own separate telephone account/line with a listed number (unless that person chose not to give an address or gave an alternate address in the listings).

The record of who lives where can only get more detailed now that phone companies are offering such services as NYNEX's Ringmate, by which you can add up to two separate incoming numbers to your telephone line, each with its own distinctive ringing pattern and its own directory listing. Since this service is an inexpensive way to relieve parents from having to answer the phone when Todd calls Lisa, a vast expansion of telephone directory listings for teenagers can be predicted.

Besides the presence of teenagers in a household, separate phone numbers or multiple directory listings for a single phone number may occur under the following circumstances (among others): married women retaining their premarriage names for professional reasons, roommates sharing an apartment, adults living with their parents (or vice versa), renters or sublessees who live in the home while the owner or primary tenant is away, and businesses being operated out of the home (note that 20 million Americans operate part-time or full-time home businesses today). In addition, a separate phone account under a different surname at a private home may be that of the family that rents the basement apartment or of an individual who rents a room in the house.

As crisscross directories do not include people with an unlisted number—or household members with no separate listing or separate number—you may want to supplement your search with other types of street listings that do not have this limitation. Your board of elections may maintain street listings of all registered voters (in New York City, there is a computer printout volume for each assembly district). These may list any member of a household who is old enough to vote and has bothered to register. Likewise, if you can access the state Department of Motor Vehicles database, you can obtain a list of every licensed driver or car owner at the given address. (If these latter records are unavailable in your state, try the local parking violations bureau index for a list of every scofflaw at subject's former address.)

The New Residents of Subject's Former Home

If no one was listed at the previous address except subject—or if none of the former household members will talk—it's time to go to the second stage of your crisscross/city directory search. Obtain from the street directory the name and phone number of the new occupant of subject's previous home and also of the closest neighbors on the block.

First check out the new occupants of subject's former home, since (1) they may be renting or subleasing from subject (with a new telephone number in their own name, of course); (2) they may have bought the house or co-op apartment from subject and have a current address for him or her; (3) they may have bought the house from a third party who acquired it from subject and who knows subject's current address; (4) they may be renting from the same landlord from whom your subject rented. In this last case, ask them to give you the landlord's phone number (or the number of the rental office or managing agent, in the case of an apartment house). If subject skipped out owing several months' rent, the landlord may provide you with information from subject's rental application form—or from a credit check the landlord once ran on subject—in the hope you will reciprocate by giving landlord the new address when you get it.

New Residents of Subject's Former Apartment

Often the new tenant of an apartment will know nothing about his or her predecessor. Sometimes, however, the new tenant is a friend of the previous one and obtained the apartment on the latter's recommendation. Indeed, the current tenant may be subleasing from the previous one. Or if the apartment is a co-op or condo, the new tenant may be directly renting from the old tenant, who is now the apartment owner (of course, in this case you can probably get his or her new address from the co-op board or the building management).

Crisscross directories often do not give the apartment numbers but only the phone numbers for residents of large apartment buildings. Sometimes this information is available, however, on PhoneDisc (and certainly via some of the more expensive online people-finding databases). Another way to find out which tenant now occupies subject's former apartment is to ask the super. (The super usually lives in the building; just call any tenant at random and ask for the super's name.) If the super won't help you, go back to the crisscross directory, which tells the number of years each telephone number has been listed. Call up all tenants who moved in around the time subject moved out. (Note that this will work only if the new tenant of subject's former apartment has a listed phone number.)

Former Neighbors

Next try subject's former neighbors. The latest crisscross directory will tell how many years each telephone number has been listed at a given address, so you can figure out which neighbors were around at the same time as subject. Start with the next-door neighbors and also those directly across the street (the latter might be the most likely to have noticed the name of the moving van company). If these all moved in after subject moved out, start with the nearest neighbors who resided on the block at the same time as subject.

If a former neighbor of subject had or has an unlisted number, you will not find him or her in a crisscross directory (on a residential street of single-family homes, a missing number in sequence in the street listings may be your tipoff to an unlisted number). In such cases, however, you might find the neighbor's name and address if not phone number in PhoneDisc and/or other special databases. You also can find it in the voter registration lists, property tax rolls, and other public records arranged by street address.

The crisscross directory listing system breaks down for our purposes when subject lives at an intersection of two or more streets. How do you find the name, address, and phone number of subject's next-door and across-the-street neighbors whose houses face on the other streets? And how do you identify subject's backyard neighbor, who may have known subject better than the next-door neighbors did? If you're searching in your own city, you can just pull out your city street map. But if you frequently search for people in other cities, invest in Street Atlas USA, a seamless CD-ROM map of virtually every street and every road in the entire country.

If you encounter a gossipy former neighbor of subject's, let him or her talk awhile. You never know what clues you'll pick up. For instance, the neighbor may recall that subject had a serious weight problem. Later, when you get a tip that subject is living in Portland, you might want to check with weight-loss clinics in the Portland area.

If most of the current residents on subject's former block are people who moved in after he or she left (a frequent problem in neighborhoods that are rapidly changing their ethnic character), you will have to use a back-issue crisscross directory to identify residents who lived on the block at the same time as subject. These people can then be looked up in the local telephone directory and/or PhoneDisc at their new addresses.

Neighborhood Stores

You can find businesses of various types in subject's former neighborhood by using PhoneDisc and the Street Atlas USA in tandem. As there may have been a high turnover rate in small retail businesses in that neighborhood, you will also want to check the back-issue crisscross directory for subject's last known year of residence there. (This will not only save you unnecessary calls to businesses that did not yet exist when subject lived there, but it also may help you identify local businesses—or the offices of local professionals—that later moved to other locations.) Based on what you've previously learned about subject, you can decide which businesses or professionals are most likely to remember him or her. If subject had pets, call up the nearest vet's office. If subject's wife is especially fashion conscious, check with neighborhood boutiques. You might also try local auto dealers, video stores, bookstores, and dry cleaners. Business establishments that are centers of local gossip, such as beauty parlors, should always be called.

If subject left town owing money to a local merchant, there are two possibilities. First, subject later paid by mail, in which case the merchant may remember the address on the check or the return address on the envelope. Second, subject never paid up, in which case the merchant may cooperate by making inquiries for you among customers and other store owners.

Checking with merchants may be a long shot in areas where most shopping is done in vast malls; still, there is usually an equivalent of the old corner store (or country store) for convenience shopping.

4.12 Tracking a Person via His or Her Family, Friends, and Ex-Spouse(s)

Most people have a hometown (or, at least, a town or city where they spent a considerable period of time during their early years), and most stay in contact throughout adult life with one or more members of their family, who often have remained in the hometown. Likewise, most people establish families of their own; these family units may not remain intact, but even the worst reprobate usually maintains some kind of contact with his or her children.

Finding a Person's Hometown and Members of His or Her Family

When attempting to track subject through former next-door neighbors (see above), always ask if they recall where subject grew up. If they don't, you can find this information or clues to it in various records. For instance, the name of subject's high school—and sometimes subject's place of birth—will be included on job applications. Credit-reporting agency databases will often also have the place of birth and may have a string of addresses for subject going back to his or her hometown days. In addition, you can try old Selective Service records, military discharge papers, and driving (moving violations) records, while subject's Social Security Number may be the best clue of all: It is coded to reveal the state of issuance (see section 7.4), which probably is a state in which subject lived as a teenager or young adult.

If subject has listed himself as "John R. Doe III," you could search national or regional telephone databases (see section 4.2) for the father or grandfather, getting printouts of all listings under "John R. Doe," "John R. Doe, Jr.," "John R. Doe, Sr.," "J.R. Doe," "J.R. Doe, Jr.," "J.R. Doe, Sr.," and various other permutations. In addition, if subject has a very unusual surname, or a very unusual spelling of a common surname, you might compile a complete list of everyone with this surname or spelling via PhoneDisc. And if you know which state is subject's home state, you might generate a list of every telephone subscriber in that state with subject's surname, even if it's a rather common one.

When you call the same-surname people cold, begin with those in subject's hometown if you know it. Start with persons with the same first name and middle initial (subject might be a "Jr." without you knowing it). This method is not guaranteed, but there is a good chance that, with a few calls, you will find someone who is at least a cousin of subject and will be able to steer you to the immediate family.

If you know subject's mother's maiden name (sometimes found on loan applications or in credit-reporting agency records), you might also call people with that surname in subject's hometown or home region to find maternal grandparents, aunts, uncles, and cousins.

You may find that subject's family left the area long ago and that they are apparently scattered throughout the country. Nevertheless, the hometown records may give you their names and perhaps clues to where they live now. Back-issue city directories may tell you the names of everyone who lived in the household while subject was growing up—his or her siblings, parents, perhaps a grandparent. (The city directory may also have information from that period on the households of aunts and uncles.) As described above, back-issue crisscross directories and white pages can also be used to gather the names of at least some former household members.

Society-Page, Obituary, and Other Clippings

You might also obtain clips filed under subject's name at the hometown newspaper morgue (see section 6.9), as well as clips relating to the other household members who were listed in the city directory and clips on other local people with the same surname as subject. The clips may include information about the arrest of one family member and the winning of a lottery by another, but you will be looking mainly for an overview of the family. A society-page article about subject's marriage will provide the names of his or her parents (possibly including subject's mother's maiden name) and other family members. An article about a sister's wedding will give her married name, and the list of guests may fill in gaps in your own list of family members. An article about the parents' silver wedding anniversary may also be useful. In addition, an obituary notice about a parent or other family member may provide the names of all subject's siblings (including the married names of his or her sisters) and their cities of residence at the time of the funeral. It may also list subject's surviving aunts and uncles on the deceased parent's side.

If a daily newspaper does not have a general index, it may at least keep a card file of the obituaries it has printed. Large metropolitan dailies generally do not print obituaries on ordinary citizens, but you may find a brief mention in the paper's vital statistics column; also, an ordinary person's death may be mentioned as a news item if the death was a murder, auto accident, drowning, etc. Obtaining the date of death from such news items (or from the Social Security Death Benefits Index), you could then look for an obituary in a suburban daily or an ethnic or neighborhood weekly. The city directory will have told you the occupation of the father and/or mother and possibly where they worked; you could thus search for an obituary in a local or statewide trade, professional, or labor union newspaper or in the house organ of the company where the deceased worked. Finally you could look for a death notice placed in any of the above publications (including the metro daily) by grieving family members, friends, or co-workers and listing the names and cities of residence of the survivors, or a thank-you notice from the family in a newspaper issue following the funeral.

If the deceased family member is a college alumnus or alumna, the alumni association's newsletter may have published an obituary. Also, an obituary may have appeared in the class anniversary book of the deceased's college class.

CD-ROM and Microfiche Records and Indexes at Local Genealogy Centers

You will most easily find what you need in old newspaper files if you first get the dates of family members' births, marriages, and deaths from county or state vital statistics indexes. Often microfiche of these indexes is available at the county historical society or the public library. In many localities, the best resource is the local Family History Center (FHC) run by the Mormons. These centers, located throughout the country (2,000 world-wide), are listed in the white pages under Church of Jesus Christ of Latter-day Saints. Each FHC has a CD-ROM system called FamilySearch, which includes:

- The Family History Library Catalog, which covers the holdings of the Mormons' Family History Library in Salt Lake City, Utah. The catalog gives a breakdown by locality of 1.7 million microfilm rolls of local records, including birth, marriage, and death indexes; wills, deeds, and land records; church records (e.g., baptismal records) from churches of all denominations; and over a million books and maps pertinent to genealogical research. Each local FHC will have the microfilm records for its own locality; microfilm for other localities can be borrowed from Salt Lake City for your viewing—it's one way to search old courthouse records in Oregon if you're stuck in New Jersey.

  The catalog also includes a comprehensive list of family name histories and genealogies (this list can be supplemented by *Genealogies in the Library of Congress* and *Complement to Genealogies in the Library of Congress*). Not every name in the library's records is provided, but the catalog does list the major families included in each family history (thus, you should look not only under subject's surname but also, if you know it, under wife's maiden name, subject's mother's maiden name, etc.).

- The International Genealogical Index (IGI), which lists more than 147 million living and deceased people in the United States and overseas. Similar surnames are grouped together in the IGI under standardized spelling, with entries providing the event type (B for birth, M for marriage, etc.) and the year/place of the event.

- The Social Security Death Index (this is a version of the SSA death masterfile; see section 4.2).

- The Ancestral File: An index to millions of names extracted from pedigree charts or family group sheets and filed by genealogy enthusiasts around the world.

- The Military Index: Data on almost 100,000 American soldiers who died in Korea and Vietnam.

Biographical Dictionaries and Obituary Indexes

Another quick way to get information about subject's family is to look in the same-surname listings in the *Biography and Genealogy Master Index* (*BGMI*) (see section 5.2). Your subject may be an obscure person, but he or she may have a notable father, mother, or sibling who is listed in a half dozen biographical dictionaries (including *Who Was Who* for a deceased family member). All it takes is one notable in the family, and you've got a wealth of information—including the hometown—for family backgrounding purposes. (If subject's father is listed, then the entry may include the names and dates of birth of all subject's siblings, as well as the name of the mother and/or stepmother.) For obituaries of notable persons, see the *BGMI* and the *New York Times Obituary Index* (the latter includes 353,000 names from 1858 to 1968). For full indexing of *Times* obituaries up to the present—and for indexing of *Times* articles on deaths from accident or murder—see the *Personal Name Index to the New York Times Index* (described in section 6.8).

Probate Court Files
Another way of getting information about subject's family is through the local probate court, which administers estates, trusts, and guardianships and includes the office of the registrar of wills. Here you may find detailed information about the family and its finances. For the names of subject's children (as well as of subject's siblings), look especially at the wills of the grandparents. Also check if subject or any of his or her siblings ever filed a motion for conservatorship over an elderly parent's affairs (this is handled by the state district court rather than the probate court in some jurisdictions). In an investigation several years ago, I discovered such an action in New York State Supreme Court, listed under my subject's name as plaintiff. In the microfilm records, I found the names and addresses of all six of subject's siblings (his copetitioners), most of them in the metropolitan area. This proved invaluable in tracing subject's real estate dealings under straw names.

Miscellaneous Records That Identify Family Members
Securities and Exchange Commission filings will list stock that subject controls, as an insider owner, on behalf of his or her spouse, children, grandchildren, and other family members. U.S. Department of Labor Form LM-30 may list business dealings of a labor union official's family members. Department of Motor Vehicles records will list all owners of cars at a given address; this may include a son or daughter who owns one of the family cars in his or her own name. Board of Elections rosters will include all registered voters at an address, which may include subject's spouse and any children 18 or older (you can search these rosters going back decades on microfilm, either at the city or county archives or at the board itself). Limited partnership filings may list several family members as owners of shares in a particular partnership and/or may include records of a transfer of shares from subject to a son, daughter, parent, or other family member or to a trust established on their behalf.

Tracing Subject Through His or Her Ex-Spouse
The full premarriage name of subject's ex-spouse may be found in the marriage index in the county where the marriage took place, and possibly in the marriage column of a local newspaper (along with the names of subject's former in-laws). In addition, you can learn the names of ex-spouses (including

an ex-wife's maiden name if listed as a middle name or as part of a hyphen-ated surname) via back-issue city, crisscross, and white-pages directories for the period in which the couple lived together. You also will find ex-spouses' names in the divorce and annulment index at the county courthouse and in the "header" material in credit-reporting agency databases. Furthermore, if you look in the court plaintiff and defendant indexes under subject's name, you may find a child custody or other case in which subject and ex-spouse are listed as adversaries. You may also find cases prior to the divorce in which subject and former spouse were jointly sued by a neighbor or indicted together for growing marijuana in the backyard.

If a subject's first wife has not remarried, she may be listed in the phone directory under either her maiden name or her ex-husband's sur-name. If she has remarried and is using her new husband's name, but you don't know what it is, you can often contact her through her di-vorce attorney, whose name and address will be in the court file. You may also try to contact her through her parents, whose names were in the hometown newspaper marriage clippings. If she and her new hus-band have a teenage child from her previous marriage living with them, that child may have a separate telephone listing under subject's surname. In addition, the remarried spouse may have retained her previous mar-ried name within certain record systems (e.g., a department store credit card or driver's license) simply because it was too much bother to change it. And if she reverted to her maiden name temporarily before remarry-ing, she might retain this name for some of the same records systems *after* her remarriage (or for *all* records systems after her remarriage if she's become a feminist as a result of the first marriage's unpleasant as-pects). Generally, however, the records systems will have her new address regardless of what name she is using.

If you are having trouble finding an ex-wife's maiden name (as when the marriage was a common-law one and there is no marriage license on file), check the following possibilities:

1. She and your subject may have lived together before they adopted the same last name. During that period she may have had a separate list-ing for their telephone under her maiden name or a previous married name. Or subject may have moved in with her in an apartment where the phone was previously in her maiden name.

2. A teenage child may have adopted a hyphenated name (mother's maiden name/father's surname) even if the mother never did so. Look for a separate listing of the previous household telephone number (or a separate number at the same address) under the child's name.

3. Couples may use hyphenated names temporarily or on isolated occa-sions for various reasons; you may spot some public record in which subject and/or his wife did so.

In searching for subject's ex-wife, don't be blinded by male chauvinist assumptions. Although subject is an obscure person, his ex-wife (indeed, his current wife) may have become quite a successful person. Look for her under both her married and maiden names in *BGMI* and in *Biography Index* (if this search succeeds, you will get from the cited biographical dictionary entry or biographical article the names of her children). If she is a professional or a businessperson, you may find her in one or more professional or trade directories or rosters (see section 5.5).

Tracing Subject Through His or Her Children

If subject's children are grown, check for current local telephone listings under their names. Note that after the split-up of their parents and the remarriage of their mother, these children (if they ended up living with the mother) might have adopted their stepfather's (or mother's same-sex domestic partner's) name, their mother's maiden name, a hyphenated version of their mother's/stepfather's (or mother's/domestic partner's) name, or a hyphenated version of their mother's/real father's name (see section 7.1). If the children had lived primarily with their father, of course, they might have chosen yet other variations.

Contacting Former Spouses and Relatives

Note that a subject hiding from the police or from bill collectors often has left a string of legal or common-law marriages and children in his or her psychopathic wake. However tragic this might be, it makes the investigator's job easier: Bitter ex-spouses are excellent sources of information, especially if subject has skipped out on child-support payments or just skipped out period, leaving his or her erstwhile partner to raise a houseful of kids alone. However, not all marital breakups are like this, and some divorced couples even remain close friends. The ex-wife or ex-husband you contact may be quite loyal to subject. Even if not, the "ex" may refrain for the sake of the children from providing any information harmful to his or her former spouse.

Before contacting *any* relative, ex-spouse, son, or daughter of subject, plan carefully what you will say to them. If your reason for finding subject is benign, and if subject is not in hiding, a relative may either give you subject's number or pass along a message that you wish to speak with him or her. But if subject is hiding out, you may have to employ a ruse to obtain the information you need.

Subject's Close Friends of Years Past

If you can't find family members, you can still possibly trace subject through childhood or early adulthood friends with whom he or she might have kept in touch. High school or college yearbooks will give the names of classmates; by noting who was on the same sports team or in the same fraternity or sorority with subject, you can compile a list of classmates most likely to have kept in touch with him or her. College and prep-school classmates will be easily traceable through the school's alumni directory; for public and parochial high school classmates, see the telephone directory of the town in question.

A clipping from the local newspaper's society page will give you the names of the members of the bridal party at subject's wedding. In addition, the clipping may tell where both bride and groom were employed at the time of the wedding; employees at those firms may still be in touch with them.

4.13 Local Churches and Other Organizations

Check with the church secretaries at local churches of subject's denomination—they may have records regarding a transfer of membership. If you want to contact members of subject's former congregation who might have known him or her well, ask the church office to send you a copy of the membership mailing list. Churches will often tell you just about anything about congregation members except their sins.

Make similar inquiries with subject's former civic club or fraternal lodge and any other organizations to which subject or other members of the household belonged. You might even check with the scoutmaster of subject's son's former troop.

4.14 Former Employers and Co-Workers

Subject's former place of employment can sometimes be found in a listing for subject in a back-issue city directory or in the Federal Election Commission's databases (see section 10.10). Try calling the firm's personnel office to see if they have a recent address for subject. If they can't help you, go back to the city directory and see if anyone on subject's former block worked at the same firm during the same time period. Such a neighbor/coworker might have known subject fairly well. Even if this person doesn't have subject's current address, he or she may at least remember some potentially useful personal trivia, such as whether or not subject has a dog, and the name, color, and breed of the dog. (This can be useful in finding subject if he or she is living under an assumed name with an altered personal appearance; you identify subject by the dog's appearance—and by whether or not the dog still answers to its old name.)

Sometimes the city directory or the FEC records only tell you subject's occupation without giving any place of employment. In such cases, you can look in the electronic yellow pages (searching by Standard Industrial Classification [SIC] code might be helpful here) and *Thomas Register of Amer-*

ican Manufacturers to find the names of area firms most likely to employ people in subject's job category.

4.15 Professional, Alumni, and Other Types of Directories

Professional and trade organizations, college alumni associations, and the reference book industry publish thousands of directories each year for the purpose of helping people with mutual interests find or keep in touch with one another. These works give current or recent addresses for tens of millions of Americans.

To use these resources you will need a little background information on your subject; for instance, his or her occupation or profession, college alma mater, hobbies, and so forth.

Check every heading in *Directories in Print* that might pertain to your subject. Then call your public library's telephone reference service and ask them to look in the most likely volumes. If your library doesn't have a certain volume, call a library in another city.

Is your subject a full-time or part-time college teacher? The three-volume *National Faculty Directory* lists over 600,000 college teachers at more than 3,800 American and Canadian junior colleges, four-year colleges, and universities. Always check the annual supplement, which includes tens of thousands of new and updated listings. If subject has retired or quit teaching, you may still find him or her in a back issue.

Is subject a lawyer? The 27-volume *Martindale-Hubbell Law Directory* gives the business addresses of over 800,000 lawyers and law firms in the United States and Canada, divided according to town, city, state, and province.

Is subject a physician? The AMA's *Directory of Physicians in the United States* gives the address of virtually every licensed medical doctor and doctor of osteopathy in the United States.

The variety of such directories is extraordinary, covering even very obscure professions, trades, and hobbies; I suggest that you spend some time browsing through *Directories in Print* to get an idea of the possibilities.

If the comprehensive national directory for a given profession does not include your subject's name, look in *Directories in Print* for the names of local, regional, or special-focus directories for subject's profession. For instance, nonpracticing law graduates (especially those who never passed the bar) are not listed in the massive *Martindale-Hubbell*, but some of them may be found in such works as the *Directory of Women Law Graduates and Attorneys in the U.S.A.* (more than 25,000 names).

The United States's college alumni associations are probably the largest source of directory-type listings. Virtually every college and university has an alumni directory that gives the names and current addresses of most living alumni as well as annual listings of recently deceased alumni. Alumni associations need alumni addresses for fundraising purposes and often pay search agencies to find missing alumni and keep the rosters up to date.

If you know which college subject attended, simply call the alumni office on campus and ask them to look up subject's address in the latest directory. If they don't have a recent address, you might try the national office of subject's fraternity or sorority. (To find out which fraternity or sorority this is, you'll have to persuade the librarian at the campus archives to dig out the yearbook for subject's senior year; see section 11.1.)

Note that many alumni directories list not only graduates but also matriculants who dropped out, flunked out, or transferred. Thus, if Jane Doe is not listed (or is listed at an out-of-date address) in the alumni directory of the state university from which she received her bachelor's degree, you may still find her current address (or at least a more recent address than you started out with) in the directory of the community college she attended during her first two undergraduate years. And if she's not in either of these, she may be in the graduate student alumni directory of the university where she studied for her master's degree. Alumni associations vary widely in their commitment to keeping their mailing lists up to date; thus, the more colleges or universities subject has attended, the greater your chances of finding a current address.

If you find that subject's current address is not in the latest published directory, the alumni office might be willing to check its update files for you.

Most prep schools also have alumni directories; check these if you don't find what you need in the college directories.

4.16 Electronic Business Directories

Dun's Electronic Business Directory, available on DIALOG, provides directory information (updated quarterly) on over 8.9 million businesses and professionals throughout the United States. You can use it to search for business names that include subject's name or subject's spouse's name in some form (see sections 4.3 and 8.27) and also to find the office addresses of almost 2 million doctors, lawyers, veterinarians, and other professionals.

Much of the same information can be obtained via PhoneDisc Power-Finder (see section 4.2).

4.17 Membership Rosters

If you have sufficient information regarding subject's occupation and interests, you can seek help from trade, professional, labor, charitable, religious, hobby, or sports organizations to which he or she might belong. Thousands of these organizations maintain membership rosters (although perhaps not in the form of a directory sold to the public) as well as mailing lists of financial supporters.

Two library reference works that will orient you to the vast world of membership rosters and membership/contributor mailing lists are the *Encyclopedia of Associations* and the *National Trade and Professional Associations of the U.S.* For the really offbeat groups, see *Organized Obsessions* by Deborah Burek and Martin Connors.

Even if an organization does not give out members' addresses, they may be willing to forward a letter in which you ask subject to contact you (see section 4.30).

4.18 Subscription Lists

A former neighbor of subject recalls that subject played the fiddle and often attended bluegrass conventions. You go to the *Standard Periodical Directory* and look under the subject category "Music and Music Trades," where you find the *American Fiddler News*. If you can get someone at this publication to check the mailing list, it might include subject's current address. (Also, you might ask them to check the membership roster of the American Old Times Fiddlers Association, which publishes *American Fiddler News*.) Note that some information brokers offer searches of change-of-address databases that include magazine subscription address changes.

4.19 Licensing Agencies and Certification Boards

In any locality of the United States, the city, county, and state governments license hundreds of professions, trades, and types of business activity. The roster of license holders is a good place to search for your subject if you can figure out which licenses he or she is likely to have. For a full discussion of licenses, see sections 10.11 and 10.12.

4.20 Department of Motor Vehicles Records and Other State Records

An abstract of a person's driver's license (see section 10.2) will give you his or her address at the time of license issuance or renewal. To access this license information by mail or over the phone, you may need to provide subject's Social Security Number.

If you think that subject has moved out of state, the Department of Motor Vehicles may have records of license transfers that will tell you the state to which he or she moved. You can then request from the latter state an abstract of the new license, which will include either subject's current address or a more recent address than the one you started with.

Note that many people who don't know how to drive or whose licenses have been revoked will apply to the Department of Motor Vehicles for a nondriver's state I.D. card. The information on their application for this card, including address and SSN, may be publicly available in your state.

In 1994, Congress passed the Driver's Privacy Protection Act which provides individual auto owners and drivers a limited veto over public access to personal information about themselves in DMV files (see section 10.2). Ironically, Congress had earlier passed a bill that allows people to register to vote when they apply for a driver's license (the "motor voter" law). Thus, many of the driver's license applicants who choose to keep the information on their license private will at the same time be helping to create a new publicly accessible record on themselves. Voter registration information is currently being compiled into commercial databases across the country by public records providers (partly to offset the new privacy restrictions on DMV records). Also, any driver's license information downloaded into information brokers' computers nationwide prior to when the new law takes effect will be useful for many years to come in tracking people by their past addresses.

In addition to automobile and truck drivers' licenses, you might check licenses for the operating of recreational vehicles and motor boats and also hunting and fishing licenses.

4.21 Abandoned Property Lists

In New York State, about 5 million names and addresses are on these lists, maintained by the state's Office of Unclaimed Funds. Updates are published twice a year and are available at municipal offices and public libraries. Although the majority of addresses are outdated, the address listed for your subject may be newer than the one with which you began your search. (Even if it's an *older* address than the one you have, it may turn up a former neighbor who has kept in touch with subject through the years.)

4.22 Miscellaneous Local Government Records

If you've narrowed your search to a single locality, you can check various public records at the county clerk's office, the municipal building, the register of deeds office, and so on. Your options may include the tax assessment rolls, the county water commission's roster of accounts, the roster of sewer charges, and the "grand lists" (the latter are lists of persons paying taxes on valuable personal property such as autos, boats, and airplanes). You also might check the judgment docket, the wage garnishment index, the Uniform

Commercial Code (UCC) filings, the federal tax lien index, the courthouse plaintiff/defendant indexes, and the roster of municipal employees.

If your subject is a low-income person, the voter registration lists may be your best bet. (The Democratic party registers millions of welfare recipients and other impoverished people every presidential election year.) You can often find noncitizens this way, since those with children in the public schools are eligible to vote in school board elections in some localities.

To find both low- and moderate-income persons, check the county or municipal civil court (claims for under $10,000). Certain plaintiffs (such as finance companies and hospitals) may each have filed cases against thousands of people over the years. If the index lists cases only by plaintiff, the defendants may be listed in alphabetical order under the plaintiff's name. (Note that in some cities, there will be a separate index of hospital liens.) Also, if a large percentage of your city's residents are apartment renters, try the housing court index. Look under subject's name and also his or her spouse's name (including maiden name) or live-in lover's name. To search housing court indexes for an entire metro area or state, check with the tenant-screening services used by landlords; a list can be found in *The Sourcebook of Public Record Providers.* (One screening company in California claims to have records on more than 2 million tenants.)

The scofflaw index is a marvelous tool for finding people of all socio-economic brackets. In New York City, every car owner who has an unpaid city parking ticket is listed, together with the address on his or her car registration at the time the ticket was issued. I have often used the multivolume computer printout indexes at the county clerk's office in Manhattan; these include separate volumes for scofflaws who received their tickets in New York City but reside in New Jersey, Connecticut, or elsewhere. There are back files available, so even if subject has paid up you can find a listing.

The backfile of scofflaw index volumes, if such exist in your city, may be located in the municipal archives. Although the addresses may be years out of date, even in the current index, they at least will give you a place to start.

For journalists in a central city, scofflaw indexes are a quick way to locate residents of the suburbs and exurbs who have unlisted phone numbers. A large percentage of these people work in the city, and many others come into the city to shop or dine, getting parking tickets in the process.

Skip tracers recommend looking at the county roster of dog owners. In many localities you can obtain a copy of the entire roster for a small fee.

A good rule of thumb is: Begin your search with the records systems that list the largest numbers of local residents on a citywide or countywide basis with addresses updated annually (the tax rolls, for instance). Work your way down to the narrower and often harder-to-search records systems.

For further description of the various courthouse and municipal records, and their larger uses in compiling background reports, see Chapters Eight, Nine, and Ten.

4.23 Mail Drops and Mail-Forwarding Services

As noted in section 4.8, subject's supposed home address may turn out to be a mail drop located in an office building. If so, the mail drop may also be a mail-forwarding service that forwards subject's mail to just about anywhere in the world. You can determine if the company in question provides mail forwarding either by looking at its advertisement in the yellow pages or by a pretext phone call. You might also look in the *Directory of U.S. Mail Drops* (see bibliography), which includes over 1,200 such companies and is widely circulated among individuals with a secretive bent. Be aware that a small number of these mail drops/mail-forwarding services are actually run by, or sell their forwarding address lists to, firms specializing in skip tracing. (The latter do reverse traces on the mail drop customers, find out to whom they owe money, and then sell the forwarding addresses to the creditors.)

4.24 Trailer Rental and Moving Companies

If your subject has recently moved, ask the neighbors (or the doorman or super, if it's an apartment house) what they remember. Did subject hire a small van or U-Haul–type trailer and do the moving with the help of friends? Or did he or she hire professional movers? Did the movers arrive in a panel truck or in a large moving van? If no one remembers the rental company or mover's name, you'll have to start calling the various companies in both categories listed in the local yellow pages.

4.25 Locating Present, Former, or Retired Military Personnel

Each military branch has a locator service that will tell you the military unit and installation to which subject is currently assigned. You should provide subject's full name, date of birth, SSN, and any other basic data you have gathered.

To find those on active duty in the Army, write: U.S. Army World Wide Locator, EREC, Ft. Benjamin Harrison, Indiana, 46249. For those in the Army Reserve or Inactive Reserve—and those retired from U.S. Army active duty, the Army Reserve, or the Army National Guard—write: U.S. Army Reserve Personnel Center, 9700 Page Boulevard, St. Louis, Missouri, 63132. For current members of the Army National Guard, write the State Adjutant General of the given state.

For those on active duty in the Navy or in the Navy Active Reserve, write: Chief of Naval Personnel, Bureau of Personnel, 2 Navy Annex, Washington, D.C., 20370 (the Navy will provide the U.S. land-based unit location only). For personnel retired from active duty or from the Navy Reserve, and those in the Individual Ready Reserve and the Inactive Reserve, write: U.S.

Navy Reserve Personnel Center, 4400 Dauphine Street, New Orleans, Louisiana, 70149.

For those on active duty in the Air Force or in the Air Force Reserve or Air National Guard, or retired, write: AFMPC-RMIQL, 550 C Street West, Suite 50, Randolph AFB, Texas, 78150. (The Air Force will not provide the location of overseas personnel.)

For those on Active Duty in the Marines or in the Marines Selected Reserve, write: Commandant, U.S. Marine Corps, HQMC, MMSB–10, 2008 Elliot Road, Room 201, Quantico, Virginia, 22134. For Individual Ready Reserve and Fleet MC Reserve/Inactive Reserve, write: U.S. Marine Corps Reserve Support Center, 10950 El Monte, Overland Park, Kansas, 66211. For Marines retired from Active Duty or the Reserve, write: Commandant, U.S. Marine Corps, MMSR–6, 2 Navy Annex, Washington, D.C., 20380.

For those on active duty in the Coast Guard or in the Coast Guard Reserve, write: Commandant, U.S. Coast Guard, Locator Service G–PIM–2, 2100 2nd Street S.W., Washington, D.C., 20593. For those retired from either Active Duty or the Reserve, write: Retired Military Affairs Branch G–PS–1, U.S. Coast Guard, 2100 2nd Street S.W., Washington, D.C., 20593.

Once you know the base or post at which subject is stationed, you can check with the locator at that facility, who may provide subject's unit or ship assignment and work phone number. A directory of military bases and other military facilities in the United States, with zip codes, telephone information numbers, and base/post locator numbers, is included in Lt. Col. Richard S. Johnson's *How to Locate Anyone Who Is or Has Been in the Military: Armed Forces Locator Directory* (see bibliography).

For overseas personnel, the servicewide locators provide unit location by post office zip code only. Johnson's book provides a list of zip codes matched to overseas base/post (this information is also available in the *National Five-Digit ZIP Code and Post Office Directory*).

The service locators will forward letters to current armed forces members at home or abroad. To take advantage of this service you must provide the basic identifying information described above. If you already know the base/post where subject is assigned, you can send the letter care of the local base/post locator.

Records on all personnel discharged from Active Duty or Reserves (all services) are kept at the National Personnel Records Center (NPRC), 9700 Page Boulevard, St. Louis, Missouri, 63132. The NPRC will not give out addresses. Under a few circumstances (such as a financial institution attempting to collect a debt) the NPRC will forward correspondence to the last known address. The NPRC will not forward correspondence for persons seeking lost family members; for this you must go to the government locator services described in section 4.29.

You can locate some war veterans through a private organization, Information Up, which has 150,000 addresses in its database and access to national locator databases. Write: Information Up, Veterans Locator and Resource Center, 4614 Hamlet Place, Madison, Wisconsin, 53714. Or, if you are looking for a former war buddy, send a letter to the locator column and/or reader exchange section of such publications as *Army Times* and *The Retired Officer*.

For other methods of locating discharged military personnel, see Johnson's book, which should be in every investigator's library.

4.26 Locating Licensed Pilots

You can obtain the address of a Federal Aviation Administration (FAA) licensed pilot by writing the FAA Airmen's Certification Branch, AVN–460, P.O. Box 25082, Oklahoma City, Oklahoma, 73125.

4.27 Locating the Homeless

The Salvation Army operates a locator service for finding homeless people. It will help only those searchers who have a positive motive, such as those searching for lost family members. The Salvation Army will not tell you where the homeless person is but will pass on the message that you wish to contact him or her. The regional addresses for the Salvation Army Missing Persons Service are:

- Eastern United States: 440 West Nyack Road, P.O. Box C–635, West Nyack, New York, 10994

- Central United States: 10 West Algonquin Road, Des Plaines, Illinois, 60016

- Southern United States: 1424 N.E. Expressway, Atlanta, Georgia, 30329

- Western United States: 30840 Hawthorne Boulevard, Rancho Palos Verdes, California, 90274

The sharp rise in the number of homeless since the late 1970s has led to a plethora of private and local government agencies providing health care and counseling as well as soup kitchens and shelters. To a great extent these agencies have taken over the Salvation Army's traditional role. To find the appropriate agencies in your locality, look in the local community resources directory at your public library. In New York City, you can look in *The Source Book*, the *Directory of Community Services*, or the *Directory of Alcoholism Resources and Services*. The social service agencies listed in such directories are your most practical means of communicating with the homeless population if the Salvation Army can't help. (You might fax each of these agencies a photograph of subject, with a request that they make copies for circulation among their staffers and clients and/or to post on bulletin boards.)

4.28 Finding the Addresses of Celebrities

Avid fans often want to find out the home addresses of celebrities of stage and screen. This is not very difficult. Numerous tourist maps show the homes of movie stars in Hollywood and Beverly Hills. For East Coast celebrity fans, Larry Wolfe Horwitz has written *New York City Starwalks*, which includes the addresses of about 1,000 stars of screen, stage, and TV, plus information about the restaurants and clubs where they hang out, the hair salons they visit, etc. Horwitz found 5 to 10 percent of his targets by looking in the current phone book; they were often listed under their last names with only an initial for the first name. Horwitz's main tactic, however, was simply to walk around the trendiest neighborhoods in Manhattan and talk to shop owners, pizza and grocery delivery persons, building maintenance employees, and also neighborhood residents who had seen this or that celebrity walking the proverbial poodle.

Garbologist A.J. Weberman searched in old phone books for his celebrity targets. He found that many had been listed before they became famous. They later obtained unlisted numbers to fend off the fans and tabloid journalists, but they did not move to new apartments. Instead (like many other well-to-do but thrifty New Yorkers), they remained in their rent-controlled digs.

The home addresses of some entertainers can be found in biographical dictionaries and directories such as *Who's Who in Entertainment* or *Christensen's Ultimate Movie, TV & Rock 'N' Roll Directory*. The addresses of famous people in journalism, politics, and literature can very often be found in similar biographical works (for writers, see *Contemporary Authors* and *Contemporary Authors New Revision Series*).

Most famous people first achieved listing in a dictionary or directory when they were still only moderately well known. By the time they became sufficiently celebrated or notorious to cherish their privacy (and fear stalkers), their home address was already easily available in numerous reference works.

Home addresses of the more secretive celebrities (including their vacation home addresses) often can be found via property tax rolls, condo ownership rosters, voter registration lists, and Department of Motor Vehicles (DMV) records. Note that in California DMV records are not available to the general public, in part because of concern over stalkers.

4.29 Government Locator Services

The Social Security Administration (SSA) has one of the largest government databases of names and addresses. You can try reaching your subject through the SSA Letter Forwarding Service, Office of Central Records Operations, 300 North Greene Street, Baltimore, Maryland, 21201. To use this service, you must give a humanitarian reason, such as a search for a lost family member, or else you must be attempting to notify the person that money is due them (as from an inheritance). The SSA will not provide the address to you, but will forward a letter to the person you are seeking care of the employer who filed the last quarterly earnings report for them, or care of the address at which they are receiving Social Security benefits. You should provide the locator office with subject's full name, date of birth, and any other identifying information you have. The letter you wish forwarded must be sent to the SSA unsealed, but you can include a return address.

The Internal Revenue Service (IRS) will also forward a letter to someone if you have a compelling humanitarian reason. You must provide the SSN, which is also the person's taxpayer identifying number.

The Department of Veterans Affairs (VA) will forward a letter to any of the 5 million veterans listed in its files, that is, any veteran who has ever applied for VA benefits. Call the VA regional office nearest you to find out where to send your locator request. Then mail an envelope to that address enclosing: (1) an unsealed, stamped envelope *without* your return address and with subject's name and VA file number or SSN on it; (2) your letter to subject; and (3) a letter to the VA requesting that the letter to subject be forwarded and providing any information to help locate subject's records (e.g., full name, date or year of birth, approximate dates of military service, etc.).

You can also have a letter forwarded to a retired federal civil servant. Write: Office of Personnel Management, Employee Service and Records Center, Boyers, Pennsylvania, 16017.

The Federal Bureau of Prisons will locate a federal prison inmate for you; call (202) 307–3126.

4.30 Locator Form Letters and Mailings

If you are an adoptee searching for a birth parent, or if you are searching for a long-lost relative, try sending a form letter to a broad array of government agencies, private organizations, and periodicals that might have the person in their files and/or on membership, mailing, or subscription lists. Explain in the letter your humanitarian need to reach subject and provide any identifying information you have, such as full name, physical description, date and place of birth, SSN, mother's maiden name, spouse's name, and previous known addresses. State that you have enclosed a stamped envelope with a personal letter to subject inside it and ask the organization or agency to either forward the letter or otherwise contact subject on your behalf. Urge the organization or agency to write you or call you collect if they have any questions about your request.

Make plenty of photocopies both of this letter and of a handwritten appeal to the person you are trying to find, and buy stamps and envelopes.

Go to the public library and sit down with the *Encyclopedia of Associations, Washington Information Directory, Standard Periodical Directory,* and other relevant reference books. Address your mailing to any and every organization, agency, or periodical that you think might have a past or present address for subject. Be sure to send the form letter to the circulation departments of the highest circulation general interest magazines as well as to specialty publications that might attract subject's interest (e.g., if your lost brother is a biker, you obviously would send the letter to motorcycle magazines).

With the exception of the official government locator services (see above), it's difficult to predict how any of these third parties might react. They may have a fixed policy regarding such appeals, or it may be up to the person who opens the letter (or his or her supervisor) to decide on the spot. Even if the organization usually ignores such requests, your letter might touch the heartstrings of the person opening the letter. Obviously a lot will depend on the care with which you word your appeal.

Unless told not to (as by the Department of Veterans Affairs), always include your return address on the envelope of the letter to be forwarded. If the third party forwards it to the address in its files, and the Post Office returns it to you marked "moved," you are one leg up: You now have a prior address for subject and can use the crisscross directory and other resources to eventually find a more recent address for subject or possibly the current one.

Another type of mailing could be sent nationwide to people listed in PhoneDisc and/or other locator databases who have the same surname and given name as subject. If the surname is an uncommon one and/or if you have narrowed your search to a manageable geographic area or areas (say, the state in which subject was born and grew up, and the state in which he or she was last sighted), you might also send the letter to everyone with subject's surname regardless of their given name. Tell them you are looking for subject and provide any identifying information you have collected (such as date of birth). Ask them to get in touch with you if they happen to be the person you are looking for or know how to contact that person.

4.31 "Missing" Posters on the Internet

The television show "America's Most Wanted" has helped law enforcement catch many fugitives. You can use the same tactic on a smaller scale, not to search for violent desperados but to find a missing teenager, an adoptee's birth parents, or the genial Romeo who absconded with your elderly aunt's life savings. You can do this by circulating information about the person you are seeking on computer bulletin boards nationwide via CompuServe, the Internet, Ziffnet, etc.

The National Center for Missing and Exploited Children has dramatically increased its recovery rate of missing children by this method, which targets a potential audience of millions of people. The center uses imaging technology to "age progress" photographs of the children to show what they might look like now, as opposed to when they were first reported missing.

Adult sons and daughters looking for the father who walked out on the family 20 years ago could also circulate age-progressed pictures. Obviously such an effort would not get the same level of cooperation from the online networks that a missing children's center receives; still, the searchers could place their appeals for help on bulletin boards frequented by those computer users who, because of their special interests or their geographical location, would be most likely to have encountered subject.

4.32 Reverse Traces

As noted in section 4.1, many Americans are living under false ID, often as fugitives from the law. When the police or the FBI want to find one of these paper trippers badly enough, they first identify through database searches everyone who appeared for the first time in certain key public records systems (for instance, the motor vehicles bureau records of the state where subject is rumored to be hiding) within a certain time frame following subject's disappearance. Next, they narrow this list to include only those who, according to their driver's licenses and other available data, share certain physical characteristics of subject (e.g., race, height, approximate age).

You don't have to be a police officer to use this method. If you believe the person you are looking for moved to a certain city two years ago and is now living there under false ID, examine that city's roster of water connects (and other utility connect records if available) and compile a list of names of all persons who had utilities turned on during the weeks following subject's disappearance from his or her previous address. Then crosscheck those names against the local crisscross directory and/or back-issue white pages to identify those who were prior telephone subscribers at other addresses in the same locality and those who are new-to-the-directory subscribers. (Prentice Hall Online's PeopleTracker may also be useful for this purpose.) Next, obtain abstracts of the driver's licenses of all those who were listed both as new water connects and new-to-the-directory telephone connects and cross off those whose physical characteristics don't fit. If you now go to visit (or conduct surveillance on) the homes of the remaining people on your list, you may find that one of them is in fact your subject living under his or her new identity. (Of course, a highly intelligent paper tripper would have prepared his or her disappearance carefully, either by purchasing or renting a new home and getting the utilities turned on months in advance, or else by waiting a couple of months after his or her disappearance before getting any new utilities under any name whatsoever. In addition, he or she would have avoided getting a telephone listing in the white pages, precisely in order to keep out of local and national crisscross directories.)

4.33 Caller ID

If you are calling around to find people who don't want to be found, they may hear about you from a former neighbor and become curious or angry. They may call your number just to hear what your voice sounds like and then hang up without saying anything. Or they may call pretending to be someone else and try to pump you for information. Or they may call anonymously with threats, obscenities, or heavy breathing. Caller ID will tell you the number from which the call was made. If you call back immediately and ask for subject, he or she may break down and talk to you. If you reverse the number in the crisscross directory, you may find that it's a residential number listed under a name you've never heard of (perhaps subject himself under his assumed identity, or perhaps a friend with whom subject is staying), a business number (perhaps subject's new place of work), or a pay phone (at least you now know which city subject is in). (For more on Caller ID, see section 3.8.)

4.34 If You're Completely Stumped

Consider the following:

- Subject may be in an institution. According to the 1990 census, over 3.3 million Americans (more than 1 in 100) are in a prison, old-age home, long-term care facility, juvenile detention center, mental hospital, etc.

- Subject may have moved overseas.

- Subject may be dead, but there may be no record of the death in the Social Security death masterfile (this would be the case if subject was murdered and the body buried in a swamp).

- Subject may be living in a rural commune or a totalitarian cult, completely cut off from the outside world.

5.

Backgrounding the Individual—Biographical Reference Sources

5.1 Overview

Millions of Americans are included in one or more "who's who"–type biographical dictionaries or other reference works containing biographical data. There are thousands of such works: Never assume a person is not listed, no matter how humdrum his or her life might be.

Biographical dictionaries generally contain one-paragraph entries with noncontroversial basic information such as date and place of birth, names of parents, schooling, military service, job history, awards and other honors, names of spouse(s) and children, membership in professional or fraternal societies, published writings, hobbies, and current office and/or home address.

Such information provides a springboard for further investigation. The date of birth may help you in ordering driver's license abstracts and other public records concerning subject. The name of a parent or former spouse may lead you to court papers regarding a divorce or probate of a will. Information about subject's educational background may guide you to college yearbooks, a master's thesis, or a doctoral dissertation.

As the biographical dictionary information on living persons is usually provided by the subjects themselves, some of it—even in the prestigious *Who's Who in America*—may be false or misleading. Indeed, since a subject will rarely wish to advertise his or her warts, most "who's who"–type profiles will be slanted toward the positive. The late Teamster leader Jimmy Hoffa never described himself in a biographical dictionary questionnaire as a "labor racketeer." Nor did he ever list, under awards and honors, his multiple indictments in federal court. Nevertheless, most subjects tell the truth about noncontroversial basic facts such as when and where they were born, and this provides leads for further investigation and a chronology around which you can organize your research findings.

5.2 Biography and Genealogy Master Index

Always begin with Gale's *Biography and Genealogy Master Index* (*BGMI*), which indexes over 8 million biographical sketches from 2,000 editions and volumes of 700 source publications, both current and retrospective. Names of over 3.5 million living and deceased individuals are in this index. It lists not only each biographical work in which there is an entry for your subject, but also all editions in which the entry appears. Thus, you can trace the changes in subject's entry from year to year, and you can glean from old editions information excised from the current one, such as former addresses and the names of former spouses.

The core of *BGMI* is an eight-volume base set published in 1980. Since then, annual updates have been cumulated every five years into subsidiary sets (1981–85 and 1986–90); there are now 20 volumes in all, with almost half a million citations being added each year. There is also an abridged version that covers 115 of the most widely available source publications. (Since the full version is easy to find in libraries, you should not restrict your search to the abridged version.) Note that the entire *BGMI* is available on microfiche (under the name Bio-Base), on CD-ROM, and online from DIALOG.

Some of the *BGMI* source publications may be hard to find, especially the cited back editions (smaller libraries often discard them once the new edition is cataloged). If a publication is not available at your local library, get the research librarian to order the volume (or a photocopy of the cited entry) through interlibrary loan.

5.3 Marquis Who's Who Index and Search Service

The annual one-volume *Index to Marquis Who's Who Publications* (first published in 1974) is available, like *BGMI*, in most research libraries. It will direct you to biographies of almost 330,000 persons in the current editions of most regional and professional Marquis Who's Who publications as well as *Who's Who in America*. The Marquis publications are also covered by *BGMI*, which provides (unlike the Marquis *Index*) cumulative indexing of past editions. The only advantage to the Marquis *Index* is that it provides indexing of current Marquis editions several months earlier than *BGMI* does.

In 1994, Marquis released The Complete Marquis Who's Who Plus, a CD-ROM product that enables you to cross-search and instantly retrieve the contents of all the books listed in the Marquis *Index*. (For details see section 5.9 below.)

Marquis offers a same-day search service that may be useful for paralegal researchers who have to gather background information quickly for an upcoming deposition. Marquis staff researchers will search the Marquis databases, which are updated daily, and fax you what they find (no charge if they fail to find anything). The researchers draw on their company's 2,500 volume collection of biographical dictionaries as well as its files of professional résumés and other research materials compiled for upcoming biographical sketches. Although they will not send you copies of materials from other publishers' dictionaries, they can provide you with information from various sources as they add it to the Marquis databases.

5.4 Biography Index

BGMI indexes only biographical dictionaries. For other types of books and for periodical articles of a biographical nature, you should consult the H.W. Wilson Company's *Biography Index*, a cumulative work going back to 1946. *Biography Index* issues quarterly indexes, interim annual cumulations, and permanent two-year cumulations. It covers every biographical-type article (including interviews and obituaries) in over 2,700 periodicals, together with more than 2,000 works annually of individual and collective biography. In addition, it includes autobiographies, memoirs, journals, diaries, letters, bibliographies, and biographical information from otherwise non-biographical works.

Biography Index tells you if an article or book contains a photograph of your subject. It also includes cross-indexing by profession or occupation (I usually do a quick search to see if any of subject's colleagues or business associates are listed). Many public libraries have *Biography Index* from mid-1984 to the present on CD-ROM. It is also available online from mid-1984 via CompuServe.

5.5 Biographical Material Not Listed in the Master Indexes

As vast as *BGMI*'s range is, it skips over many important biographical reference works. Indeed, there is a vast unindexed universe beyond *BGMI*. Start with Robert B. Slocum's *Biographical Dictionaries and Related Works*. This is a standard guide describing 16,000 source publications. Even if you find your subject in *BGMI*, you might check in Slocum's (based on what you know about subject's background) to see if there are other books in which he or she is likely to be included. Slocum's describes many obscure local who's whos (many of them are from decades ago, but they might include subject's parents), society registers, vanity registers, state government handbooks, works of collective biography, genealogical works, and bio-bibliographies.

Among the thousands of titles that can be used to supplement the standard biographical dictionaries, certain types stand out as being especially useful for journalists and private investigators:

- Society registers provide a means of tracing the marriages, divorces, re-marriages, yacht club memberships, and Ivy League academic credentials of America's upper crust. Preeminent is *The Social Register*, which, together with its supplement, the *Social Register Summer*, reports annually on the most prominent families nationwide. *The Social List of Washington* (the so-called Green Book) covers society and officialdom in our nation's capital. Social registers have also been published for various states over the years (e.g., *The Social Record of Virginia*).

- State government handbooks (often called "blue books" or "red books") may contain detailed biographical sketches of state legislators and officials. Back editions and current editions of these handbooks nationwide contain upwards of 50,000 sketches of living Americans who are now or who have been in state government.

- College class anniversary directories (usually published on the 15th, 25th, and/or 35th anniversary) may include autobiographical sketches provided by the class members themselves. Such sketches can be quite elaborate, providing data available from no other published source; reading between the lines, you can often figure out which of your subject's classmates will be most likely to talk freely with you.

  To find out if your subject's class has published such a directory, call the college archives or alumni association. And also check if subject's prep school or parochial or public high school class has held a reunion and published an anniversary book.

- "Vanity" directories solicit biographical information from ordinary people and charge them a flat fee to be included (the fee may be disguised as the advance purchase price of a deluxe, gold-embossed copy). At any given moment, there are about 200 vanity directory publishers soliciting from the American public (often the mailings come from a British address to provide an aristocratic touch). Typically, such publishers will produce one or two editions of a work before replacing it with a new title. Thousands of such works have been published in the English language over the past century. They are of interest to an investigator for two reasons: first, they include people who would never get into a legitimate directory on their own merits; and second, they often devote a relatively long entry to a local person who would rate only the briefest of entries in a legitimate who's who. Unfortunately, research libraries rarely buy vanity directories. Your best hope is that the proud listee has donated a copy to his or her local public library or the library of the college from which he or she flunked out in 1948. If you find a copy, the self-written entry on your subject may include the fact that he or she previously appeared in another vanity directory (as if this were an honor of the highest distinction). By going from one to the other, you may notice odd variations in subject's life story that warrant further probing. The largest collection of vanity directories is at the Library of Congress.

- Local history buffs may have produced a biographical directory for your town, county, or state. Check with your county or state historical society.

- Family name books sometimes contain biographical dictionary–style entries on various living family members as well as their antecedents (e.g., the Doe family, which emigrated from England in 1801). These books, also called genealogy books, are often self-published in very small editions by a family genealogy enthusiast for circulation mostly among his or her relatives or the members of a particular family name association. Many family name books are listed in the Mormon's Family History Library Catalog (see section 4.12). Others can be found in *Genealogies in the Library of Congress* (look in the supplements as well as the base volumes) and *Complement to Genealogies in the Library of Congress* (the latter lists volumes that are *not* in the Library of Congress). In searching these reference works, be sure to look under John Doe's mother's maiden name as well as under the Doe surname.

  To find the right family name volume (if the surname is a common one), you may need the help of an expert. Consult the *Directory of Family Associations* and also the *American Family Records Association—Member Directory and Ancestral Surname Registry*. These volumes match the names of hundreds of genealogists and family historians with the thousands of surnames they have researched.

  Once you find the right family name volume, it may turn out to have only genealogical lists and charts. This of course is useful information, but you were hoping for a collection of biographical sketches. In such cases, contact the author—he or she may have files containing very detailed biographical data. (If the volume includes biographical sketches, I would still contact the author to see if he or she has additional data.) You might also contact other members of the relevant family name association.

  Although your chances of finding a biographical sketch of your subject in a family name book are not great, it's worth a try. You could end up with a wealth of material about subject and his or her children, parents, siblings, grandparents, aunts, uncles, and cousins. If subject still lives in his or her hometown, surrounded by these relatives, information about the extended family could be quite important in researching subject's business affairs.

- A vast amount of biographical material is contained in professional, organizational, or alumni directories or rosters. The *BGMI* does not index them (nor does Slocum's list them) because the amount of biographical detail per entry is usually too sketchy. Yet, if you can find from such a directory where a person lives and works (and, from back issues, where they used to live and work), their year and place of birth, their college and year of graduation, and their spouse's name, you will have made a good beginning. There are a vast number of such directories—thousands are published each year by college alumni associations alone. I have found that although each volume listing your subject may contain only one or two facts not included in the others, the amount of information builds up when you go through volume after volume. One individual I was tracking was listed in two alumni directories, two national faculty directories, a law directory, and a directory of consultants. By the time I finished looking through these, I had almost as much material as from a brief *Who's Who* entry. Such directories can also be useful in finding sources who will tell you their recollections of your subject: professional colleagues, fellow faculty members, former classmates, and others. In addition, some professional directories may contain full-blown biographical sketches of selected persons: For instance, *Martindale-Hubbell* includes sketches on about 40,000 attorneys along with its roster of over 800,000.

  In searching a professional directory or roster, don't just look at the entry for your subject; the volume may contain other gleanings as well. For instance, take the annual directory of the Special Libraries Association, a national organization. As well as having an alphabetical roster of member librarians and their work addresses, it lists members by city or state chapter and subject specialty division, which could help you identify members who might be close colleagues of the librarian you are backgrounding. Furthermore, the directory includes lists of SLA charter members, honorary members, Professional Award and Special Achievement Award holders, Special Citation recipients, SLA Hall of Fame members, SLA past presidents, current officers (both nationally and for each chapter and division), SLA committee members and officers, SLA representatives to other professional organizations, and a name index with page citations for each listing of each member's name. On top of this—should you wish to engage in personal surveillance of your subject librarian—the directory even gives you a list of upcoming meetings and the city and hotel at which each will take place. (It also gives you subscription information on the SLA's monthly newsletter, *SpeciaList*, which might have much more detailed information about subject's career in its backfiles.)

- Major corporations and law partnerships sometimes publish inhouse biographical works. For instance, LeBoeuf, Lamb, Leiby & MacRae, a

New York law firm, publishes an attorney biographical book that includes a half-page sketch on each of several hundred partners and associates (both in New York and in its regional and overseas offices) with a picture of each attorney.

- The annual bulletins of medical, law, and divinity schools often contain biographical sketches on all or selected faculty members and administrators.

- Boards of elections and/or nonpartisan citizens' groups such as the League of Women Voters will often publish voter guides at election time that include biographical sketches of all candidates for local, state, or federal office who will appear on the local ballot in the given primary or general election. In addition, the Reporters' Resource Center of the Center for National Independence in Politics in Corvallis, Oregon, provides profiles on candidates for state and federal office.

5.6 Back Editions of Biographical Dictionaries

If you have found an entry on subject in the current edition of a biographical dictionary, don't neglect the entries for past years in this and other dictionaries. As noted above, the earlier sketches may provide you with past residential and business addresses and the names of former spouses that are not included in the most recent entry. By going to these earlier sketches in the library stacks, you may be able (if subject is consistently included) to use the back editions almost like a city directory.

Although *BGMI*'s indexing of back editions dates back only to 1974–75, a few standard reference works have their own cumulative indexes covering earlier years. For example, *American Men and Women of Science*'s index to its first 14 editions (1906 to 1979) includes over 270,000 living and dead scientists. In searching most biographical dictionaries prior to the mid-1970s, however, you will have to check each edition separately in the library stacks.

Often a subject who is not included in any current biographical reference work was included years ago because of a government appointment, electoral candidacy, or some other factor that temporarily qualified him or her. To find sketches not indexed in *BGMI*, look in *Directories in Print* and Slocum's for works in which subject's name might have appeared given what you already know about his or her past. For instance, let's say you are backgrounding John Doe, a local public relations consultant. You know from the rather meager press clippings that he was a congressional staff aide for a brief period in the early 1970s for the late Congressman Mark Grouch. Looking in *Directories in Print*, you see a listing for the annual *Congressional Staff Directory*. Finding it in the public library, you note that it includes in its current issue 3,200 biographical sketches, many of them rather detailed. You also note that it has been published since 1959. If you can get the back editions for the early 1970s from the library stacks, you will probably find a sketch of Mr. Doe.

5.7 Parallel Backgrounding Using Biographical Reference Works

Information that your subject has failed to provide to the compilers of a biographical work may be contained in a sketch of one of his or her relatives, business partners, or close friends. In an investigation of a local attorney, I found biographical sketches that contained virtually nothing about what I was interested in—his connections to the Arab world. Then I found a sketch in a biographical dictionary about his closest friend from college days, who was described as a lobbyist for Arab governments and a partner in a Mideast trading firm, the name of which included subject's surname. I was later able to confirm that subject was indeed connected to this firm.

To utilize parallel backgrounding to the maximum, I suggest you keep a list of names of your subject's associates and relatives as you find them. Periodically check the biographical indexes again to see if they include any of the latest names you've collected. Also, as you search the indexes, develop a roster of persons who have the same surname as your subject (or as a married woman subject or male subject's wife prior to marriage). When you check any biographical dictionary that has an entry for your subject, always look at the surrounding same-surname entries. And if your subject comes from a successful, highly educated family, always check the same-surname entries in *Who's Who in America*.

Parallel backgrounding works best when you find what I call a "high-yield" biographical dictionary—one that specializes in a category of people likely to include a high percentage of subject's cronies. Once I was looking into the background of a Harlem businessman. The world of black New York politicians and businesspeople is unusually tight-knit—everyone has dealings with everyone else, and, since they live in the city that has long been the cultural center of black America, a large percentage of them are included in *Who's Who Among Black Americans*. I found myself returning to this book again and again.

If I were backgrounding a prominent New York corporate attorney, *Who's Who in American Law* and *Who's Who in America* would be high-yield books sure to include many of his or her colleagues, friends, and clients. In addition, if the attorney was from an old-money family I might use *The Social Register* to ferret out the more subtle interrelations.

Of course high-yield dictionaries are most useful (and the usefulness of lower-yield dictionaries can be enhanced) by full-text and other advanced search capabilities available online or on CD-ROM (see section 5.9).

If one or both of your subject's parents were professionally prominent, Marquis's retrospective work, *Who Was Who in America*, will be invaluable for parallel backgrounding purposes. Available both in book form (12 volumes) and on CD-ROM, this reference work includes every deceased individual who appeared previously in *Who's Who in America*. You can use it not only to get data on the prominent parent but also to get the other parent's name (including mother's maiden name), the names of siblings, and information about where the family lived during subject's childhood and youth. If neither parent is found in this book, look for them in other regional, local, or professional biographical works from years past.

5.8 The Clues Hidden in Biographical Sketches

The fact that the information for biographical sketches is provided by the sketchees themselves (in effect, is subject to censorship) can be turned to your advantage. Study the sketches for clues inherent in the facts as presented. For instance: Are there any glaring or subtle contradictions among the versions of subject's life that he or she provided to different directories (or to the same directory) at different times? Are there any unexplained time gaps? Does subject list himself or herself as a board member of a corporation, bank, or foundation that you can't find in any business directory? Does he or she claim a degree from a college that is not listed in the directories of accredited institutions? Does he or she list attendance at a college without claiming a degree? (If so, what happened?) Does he or she claim personal achievements that sound dubious on the face of it (e.g., an alleged Rhodes scholarship for someone whose life before and after does not fit the pattern)? Note that some legitimate directories try to verify such claims; others let them pass unless they are embarrassingly obvious.

Politicians occasionally get caught listing exaggerated or false information in their campaign bios. You may find that your subject has done likewise in his or her biographical dictionary entries (which is one reason you should develop an efficient filing system and/or a computer hypertext for the background information you collect).

5.9 Biography Database Searches

Biographical dictionaries/directories currently available online from DIALOG include *Who's Who in America* (82,000 records of current top professionals in many fields); *American Men and Women of Science* (more than 125,000 entries on active scientists and engineers); *Standard & Poor's Register of Corporations, Directors and Executives* (over 68,000 entries on key corporate executives and directors); *Who's Who in American Politics* (about 26,000 sketches); and *Who's Who in American Art* (over 11,800 sketches). ORBIT Search Service offers the online version of *Who's Who in Technol-*

ogy (almost 38,000 entries). The LEXIS/NEXIS People Library offers a vast full-text compendium of biographical information, including (among others) the *Almanac of American Politics*, Associated Press Candidate Biographies, *BNA Labor Relations Reporter* Arbitrators' Biographies, BASELINE Celebrity Biographies, Congressional Member Profiles, Gale Biographies (which includes *Who's Who Among Black Americans* and *Who's Who Among Hispanic Americans*), *Martindale-Hubbell*, and the *Directory of Bankruptcy Attorneys*, as well as biographical stories from the *New York Times*, *Los Angeles Times*, *Washington Post*, and *People* magazine. Beyond this, hundreds of thousands of biographical articles from the online back-files of a vast array of newspapers and periodicals can be accessed via the various database vendors (see Chapter Six).

You can greatly enhance the usefulness of online biographical dictionaries and other biographical databases via full-text cross-searching. *Who's Who in America* is especially useful in this respect: Prominent people tend to associate with other prominent people, and thus any person listed in *Who's Who in America* is almost guaranteed to have ties to other listees. Do you need sources for an article about Mr. Doe? Search for listees who are the same age as Doe and come from the same hometown, or who attended the same university as Doe during the same years, or who worked at Corporation Y while Doe was an executive there, or who today live in the same city as Doe and belong to some of the same professional or fraternal organizations, or who married women with the same maiden name as Doe's wife (this may help you find Doe's brother-in-law). If you are a reporter doing a friendly feature story on Doe, probably the majority of these people will be willing to talk to you. If you are an investigative reporter, your search may turn up Doe's bitterest enemy.

Beyond the online who's whos, an excellent source of online biographical data is the vast number of prospectuses, annual reports, and other securities documents filed each year with the Securities and Exchange Commission (SEC) (see section 8.14). Recent SEC filings are available directly from the SEC's inhouse database via the Internet. Filings back to 1987 are available via DIALOG and LEXIS/NEXIS. These filings include tens of thousands of career summaries (along with personal financial information) on corporate executives, members of boards of directors, investment advisors, and broker-dealers. (Note that a portion of this data is included in the online and print versions of *Standard & Poor's Register of Corporations, Directors and Executives*—see above.)

A new source of biographical information is the employment-oriented online directory. For instance, the Journalism Forum on CompuServe includes a directory of freelance writers and photographers available for assignments. Each listing contains a brief biographical sketch as well as information on the listee's publications, awards, experience, areas of interest, and so forth. CompuServe also offers access to résumés (updated weekly) of thousands of jobseekers nationwide via the Career Placement Registry: If the subject of your investigation recently lost a salaried job—or is a new college or professional school graduate hunting for his or her first job in a given field—you may find the résumé here (the résumés are kept on file for six months). In addition, you can find on the Internet several registries for people seeking jobs in computer science. As cyberspace expands, the number and variety of these freelance and job-placement registries will inevitably increase dramatically. (See appendix.)

To supplement online searches, try the CD-ROM databases at your local research library. Here the new blockbuster is The Complete Marquis Who's Who Plus, which integrates the current *Who's Who in America*, 14 regional and professional Who's Who directories, and the most recent volumes of *Who Was Who in America*. Providing profiles on over 400,000 persons, this CD-ROM product enables the user to retrieve information using any of more than 40 searchable characteristics.

Other biographical directories and dictionaries available on CD-ROM include *Martindale-Hubbell*, Marquis's *The Official ABMS Directory of Board Certified Medical Specialists* (over 435,000 entries), and Gale's *Contemporary Authors* (more than 100,000 detailed entries). In addition, one can find on diskette and mag-tape, although not yet on CD-ROM, several of The Taft Group's annual biographical directories on wealthy Americans; see, for instance, *Who's Wealthy in America*, which provides data on over 103,000 potential givers to charity.

Look for many more biographical reference works and other biographical sources to become available online and on CD-ROM in the next few years. To keep up to date on this, subscribe to *Link-Up* (see bibliography).

6 ·

Backgrounding the Individual—Newspaper and Periodical Searches

6.1 Overview

If your target is a celebrity or an elected public official, newspapers and periodicals are the obvious place to start your search. But newspapers, especially local dailies, can also provide a wealth of easily accessible data about tens of millions of noncelebrities, from stockbrokers to panhandlers. The back issues of America's newspapers and periodicals—and the knowledge and working files of the vast number of journalists working for these publications and for wire services—are a potential intelligence resource to rival the combined assets of the CIA and the former KGB.

The searching of newspapers and periodicals is done most easily by computer. An ever-increasing number of publications are available online. You can search the entire contents of every issue of a newspaper for, say, the last five years, finding every mention of subject and his or her associates. Indeed, you can do full-text global searches of hundreds of publications at once via large database networks such as LEXIS/NEXIS.

The vast majority of newspapers and periodicals are not yet included in the electronic information net, however, and of those included most are available online only for issues dating back less than 10 years. If you need to search a relatively obscure publication that is not online or an issue of an online publication that precedes the publisher's adoption of an electronic news storage system, you will have to use traditional low-tech resources. These include printed or microform indexes and abstracts (although some of these are online for the more recent years), newspaper "morgues," archival clippings files, and microform or bound volume backfiles. The online databases, however, may show you where to look. An online article will often refer to a pre-online incident that the reporter read about in old newspaper clips while preparing his or her own article. Usually the reporter will give the date or at least the year of the prior incident/article; you can then find the article on microfilm and perhaps learn from it about a still earlier incident/article.

6.2 Serial Directories and Catalogs

In backgrounding a prominent Midwest businessperson, you may decide to search the daily newspapers in his or her state as well as local and national business and trade publications. But how do you find out which publications are online and from which vendors? And what if you want to search smaller dailies (and weeklies) in subject's locality that are not online? Or pre-online issues of the major local daily? Or the backfiles of the latter's now defunct rival? The following directories and catalogs are available in most research libraries:

- *Fulltext Sources Online*. This directory, updated every six months, lists over 4,500 journals, newspapers, newsletters, and newswires available online. It includes vendors, coverage dates, database codes, lag times (between date of publication and date available online), title changes, and whether the coverage is selective or complete.

- *Gale Directory of Publications and Broadcast Media* (formerly *Ayer Directory of Publications*). This three-volume set (with an interedition supplement) enables you to identify quickly by city and state/province about 43,000 newspapers and periodicals in the United States and Canada. It includes every type of publication except newsletters, house organs, publications issued less than four times a year, and publications issued by primary and secondary schools or houses of worship. Defunct publications are removed from the main body of entries and listed as "ceased" in the master name and keyword index. (For further listings in a given city, see the local yellow pages.)

- *Standard Periodical Directory*. This includes annotated entries on 75,000 periodicals in the United States and Canada, divided into 250 major subjects and featuring a title index and cross-index.

- *Newsletters in Print*. This includes over 12,000 newsletters arranged under 33 subject headings.

- *Newspapers in Microform*. This cumulative Library of Congress reference set (with annuals between cumulations) includes religious, collegiate, labor, and other special-interest papers, as well as general news dailies and weeklies. It also covers defunct and merged papers. Under the current title of a paper will be listed its previous names and the names of papers that merged with it or split from it, with the dates of each change; for example, if you look under the *Anytown Courier-Herald* you will find that it is the successor to the *Anytown Courier* and the *Mist County Herald*, which merged in 1949. *Newspapers in Microform* tells which libraries, archives, or microform companies in the United States or overseas have copies of the given newspaper; it also indicates partial or badly broken runs.

- The *Union List of Serials* and *New Serial Titles*. These multivolume sets, available in major research libraries, include many obscure and long-ceased serials that are not listed anywhere else. They will tell you which libraries in your region have a particular serial.

- University Microfilms International's *Serials in Microform*. This is a biennial catalog that lists over 18,000 periodicals and 7,000 newspapers (with years available and price). The major public or university libraries of the locality in which a given publication is or was published will probably have the microform backfiles, and you should be able to obtain the issues you need through interlibrary loan.

6.3 Full-Text Searching

Database searches are conducted via key words or phrases supplied by you; for example, the full name of the person you are researching, or the names of businesses he or she is associated with, or the names of his or her closest cronies. The database vendor's mainframe computer will search through every word of every text in the entire database or any portion thereof and transmit to your computer—for screen display or a printout—the title, date of publication, and source of each article in which the key word or phrase appears.

The most obvious advantage of newspaper database searching is that you avoid the tedium of going through indexes and microfilm. Equally important, database searching enables you to find articles in which your subject is only mentioned in passing—those obscure, unindexable references that so often furnish a researcher with the best leads but are found only by sheer luck when one is perusing the headlines on microfilm.

Full-text-search capabilities also facilitate research into your subject's associates and business interests. Let's say you are compiling information about Moe G., a Midwest racketeer. Your search of the database that includes the leading daily in Moe's city (online since 1981) turns up six articles, from which you learn that Moe owns a trucking company and a nightclub and that he is alleged to control a Teamster local. The articles also tell you the name of the lawyer who won Moe's acquittal in a 1984 extortion trial and the names of Moe's codefendants. You then search the database for every article mentioning Atlas Trucking, the Starlite Lounge, IBT Local

4294, or any of the individuals mentioned in the six articles. You find 12 additional articles via this second search. Some have no probable connection to Moe (i.e., an article about the death of Moe's lawyer's mother in a nursing home). Others spark your interest—for instance, the article about the Atlas driver arrested for armed assault in 1982. You can take your search through additional cycles if you believe the results will warrant the expense. (Understand that this example of a search restricted to one newspaper is somewhat simplified; in reality you would be doing a global search of other publications in the database along with the local daily. You might also enter another database from another vendor that carries the city's rival daily. And you would surely search a variety of nonnewspaper databases— for instance, the Dun & Bradstreet databases for Moe's trucking business and the computerized indexes of the local courts for all names connected to Moe.)

6.4 Newspaper Databases

Online Full-Text-Search Newspaper Databases

The number of newspapers searchable online is constantly growing. As of 1994, major database vendors were offering over 250 daily papers from every region of the United States and Canada. The *Gale Directory of Databases* and/or *Fulltext Sources Online* will tell you which vendors offer which newspapers. If the paper you need is not listed in either of these volumes, check the online version of the Gale directory, which is updated daily.

Four database vendors dominate the market for full-text newspaper searches:

- DataTimes provides about 130 daily newspapers, mostly beginning in the late 1980s or early 1990s. Its coverage ranges from big-city papers such as the *Houston Chronicle* to dailies in medium-sized cities (e.g., the *Des Moines Register*) to those serving smaller cities (e.g., the *Greensboro News & Record* in North Carolina). The DataTimes databases can be accessed through CompuServe and other gateways.

- Dow Jones News/Retrieval offers the DataTimes newspaper databases and those from other sources for a total of over 200 dailies; these range from the major national papers through small hometown papers such as the *Jonesboro Sun* in Arkansas.

- DIALOG—the online network most widely available at public libraries and on college campuses—offers via its "Papers" file almost 60 newspapers, from the *Anchorage Daily News* to the *Wichita Eagle*.

- Mead Data Central's LEXIS/NEXIS offers over one hundred U.S. and foreign newspapers. These include the *New York Times* (since 1980), the *Washington Post* (since 1977), the *Los Angeles Times* (since 1985), the most important regional U.S. newspapers, and business and law newspapers such as *American Banker, Computerworld, Legal Times,* and the *National Law Journal.*

LEXIS/NEXIS, unlike its competitors, cannot be accessed through gateway services, and a direct subscription is too expensive for most individual PC users. You can gain access, however, at a local research library or via a student or faculty member at a college or law school which has an account with Mead. In addition, Mead offers an express service through which non-subscribers can order LEXIS/NEXIS searches by Mead's inhouse researchers (you are given a cost estimate before the search begins; the results are faxed or mailed to you).

Note that there may be differences in the amount of text from a given newspaper offered by different vendors. Not all vendors offer the complete electronic backfiles; nor do all vendors offer every single edition (city and final, all suburban editions, etc.) or even the full representation of a single edition (the vendor may have only the stories with the newspaper's byline). If full coverage is important to you, question the customer service representatives of the different vendors to find out who offers the closest approximation.

The *Washington Post,* the *Chicago Tribune,* and other major dailies are now offering interactive online editions through inexpensive gateways such as Prodigy and America Online. In some cases, these interactive editions offer material not included in the print edition or in the traditional electronic backfiles available via NEXIS or DIALOG. Such supplemental materials may include the portions of important articles that were cut from the print edition because of lack of space, expanded neighborhood news, expanded local business news, the full texts of press conferences and speeches, and various types of background reports.

With the development of electronic information nets on college campuses, student daily newspapers as well as administration weeklies are gradually coming online, offering outsiders access to backfiles as well as current editions via the Internet (see appendix). Look for a vast expansion of campus electronic journalism before the end of this decade.

Full-Text-Search Newspaper Databases on Compact Disk

The backfiles of many newspapers are now available on CD-ROM. Although updated less frequently than their online counterparts, and usually offering less-than-full coverage of the news text of the editions included, CD-ROM databases can be searched for free at your local public library. Newsbank, Inc., is currently offering the full text of seven national and regional newspapers: the *Atlanta Journal/Constitution* (from 1983); *Boston Globe* (from 1985); *Chicago Tribune* (from 1985); *Christian Science Monitor* (from 1982); *Dallas Morning News* (from 1984); *Los Angeles Times* (from 1985); and *Washington Post* (from 1986). UMI's ProQuest offers the *New York Times,* the *Wall Street Journal, USA TODAY,* and the *Washington Post.* DIALOG OnDisc offers CD-ROM versions of the *Boston Globe, Detroit Free Press, Los Angeles Times, Miami Herald, Newsday* and *New*

York Newsday, *Philadelphia Inquirer*, *San Francisco Chronicle*, and *San Jose Mercury News*.

The "Hidden" Newspaper Databases

Many of the online newspaper databases offer full-text coverage back only to the middle or late 1980s; very few provide coverage for issues prior to 1981. However, a given newspaper might have earlier issues stored electronically that have not been offered for sale through an online vendor because the demand is not sufficient. Also, some newspapers have had electronic storage for years but have not yet signed an agreement with a vendor to sell even their most recent issues.

If you need access to any of these "hidden" databases, call the newspaper's library. They may occasionally do courtesy searches for serious researchers. Some publications have a reader call-up service, linked to the inhouse database, through which you can get at least the date of the article you need.

You can also try contacting the staff reporter whose beat corresponds most closely to what you are working on, get him or her interested in your research, and obtain printouts from the electronic library—and photocopies from the clippings morgue that predates the electronic library—in return for news tips or a promise of access to the fruits of your investigation.

Full-Text-Search Newswire Databases

Most people think of the wire services as organizations with correspondents in Washington and Moscow who cover the Big Picture. But the wire services' state and regional bureaus, and their stringer correspondents, generate a vast amount of news at the grassroots. United Press International (UPI) has full-time staff in every major U.S. metropolitan area, as well as overseas, and a network of over 1,000 stringers. The Associated Press (AP) employs more than 3,000 staffers in 143 domestic and 93 overseas news bureaus; as a news cooperative, it also draws on the resources of its 1,800 newspaper members and 6,000 radio-television members.

Wire service databases can be accessed through LEXIS/NEXIS, including AP and UPI's world, national, business, and sports wires (since 1977 and 1980 respectively), UPI's state and regional wires (since 1980), Canada NewsWire (since 1992), Southwest Newswire (since 1984), States News Service (since 1984), Central News Agency (since 1984), Gannett News Service (since 1989), and the Jewish Telegraphic Agency (since 1991). LEXIS/NEXIS also offers foreign wire services, such as Reuters, and several publicity, business, financial, and government newswires. DIALOG offers AP News (since 1984), UPI News (since 1983), Federal News Service (since 1991), BNA Daily News (since 1990), and several other wire services.

Online and CD-ROM Newspaper Abstracts and Indexes

The Information Bank, produced by the New York Times Company and available through LEXIS/NEXIS, offers abstracts of *New York Times* articles from 1969 (as well as the full text of the *Times* from 1980 on). It also selectively abstracts dozens of other national and regional newspapers.

University Microfilms International (UMI) selectively indexes and abstracts 29 national, regional, and ethnic newspapers. Online coverage since 1989 is included in UMI's Newspaper and Periodical Abstracts (formerly Courier Plus) database, which also includes over 1,600 periodicals. For 1984–88 coverage, see UMI's Newspaper Abstracts database. Both are available through DIALOG. UMI also offers Newspaper Abstracts Ondisc (coverage of nine newspapers since 1989 on CD-ROM).

The National Newspaper Index, available on DIALOG, provides front-to-back indexing of the *New York Times*, *Christian Science Monitor*, and *Wall Street Journal* from 1979 on, and selective indexing of the *Los Angeles Times* and the *Washington Post* from 1982 on.

NewsBank Electronic Information System and NewsBank Library

The NewsBank Electronic Information System provides selective indexing of newspapers in over 450 U.S. cities, including the state capital and largest city of each state (for NewsBank's coverage of periodicals, see section 6.5 below). The system is offered on CD-ROM back to 1981 with microfiche coverage back to 1970. All articles included are locally written; the index does not include wire service or syndicated articles. Issued concurrently is the NewsBank Library, which offers the full text on microfiche of over 2 million of the indexed articles dating back to 1970. A CD-ROM version of the NewsBank Library, with over 40,000 full-text articles per year, is available back to 1991 only.

NewsBank's research tools can extend the range of your search significantly beyond the current limits of online databases. The system is available at over 6,000 libraries nationwide.

6.5 Periodicals Databases

Online and CD-ROM Full-Text-Search Periodicals Databases

LEXIS/NEXIS offers over 2,000 general-interest, business, and trade periodicals online. Most of these can be searched full-text via the LEXIS/NEXIS News and Business Library (you can either search the entire library or narrow your focus to a particular type of publication or region of the United States). In addition, the LEXIS specialized law libraries (e.g., the Environmental Law Library) include relevant titles from the News and Business Library.

The LEXIS/NEXIS News and Business Library also includes hundreds of newsletters, mostly in business and technology. For more comprehensive coverage of newsletters, see NewsNet's databases, which offer the full text of over 700 newsletters and other news and information services in dozens of subject categories.

Magazine ASAP (available from DIALOG) selectively provides the full text of over 100 general-interest magazines from 1983 to the present.

Some magazines have developed online interactive editions; for instance, *Time* is now available on America Online. Via such editions you can not only search the text but you can also send letters to the editor and messages and queries to the writers and to other online readers. Most significant, the online edition is able to include (as in the case of *Time*) entire articles or portions of articles that were cut from the print edition because of lack of space (some on-line magazines, however, offer *less* text than is found in the print edition).

In 1993, *Newsweek* became the first general-interest magazine to publish on CD-ROM. It offers a quarterly cumulation of its weekly editions with multimedia additions to the text (for instance, recorded radio interviews with people whose activities were a major focus in the articles). Other major magazines will be available on CD-ROM soon; check with your public library.

Another new development is the Internet electronic serial (or e-serial); examples range from scholarly and scientific journals through science fiction fanzines. Some of these serials are exclusively electronic; others have a print version as well. Eric Braun's *The Internet Directory* lists almost 300 e-serials as well as several of the electronic archives (e.g., the Internet Wiretap On-line Library) that store e-serial texts.

Online Periodicals Abstracts and Indexes

Over 1,600 general-reference, professional, and scholarly periodicals are indexed and abstracted in UMI's Newspaper and Periodical Abstracts database back to 1988 (with selected titles dating back to 1986). UMI's ABI/Inform offers abstracts and indexing for over 1,000 business-oriented titles with coverage of some back to 1971. Both of these databases are available via DIALOG. Note that there is an overlap of titles, so if you need a pre-1988 search of a Newspaper and Periodical Abstracts title always check ABI/Inform.

Magazine Index, an Information Access Company product available through DIALOG, covers more than 500 general-interest and consumer magazines, with some records dating back to 1959. All citations from 1992 to the present, except those for short articles and reviews, are accompanied by a brief abstract. (See also Magazine ASAP, discussed above.)

The online version of *Readers' Guide to Periodical Literature* (dating from 1983) and *Readers' Guide Abstracts* (from 1984) are available on WILSONLINE and CompuServe. These databases cover 240 popular magazines; the abstracts, averaging 125 words in length, cover every article indexed in *Readers' Guide*.

Numerous other indexes and abstracts are available through DIALOG and other database vendors (see section 11.3 for scholarly and scientific periodicals and section 13.2 for business periodicals). If the index in question does not include personal names, a search of appropriate subject listings may turn up articles in which the person you are backgrounding is mentioned.

CD-ROM *Periodicals Indexes and Full-Text Retrieval*

UMI's Periodical Abstracts on CD-ROM is an index/abstract to 1,600 periodical titles dating back as far as 1986; you can also check the CD-ROM version of UMI's ABI/Inform, covering about 1,000 business titles (some records date back to 1971). Through UMI's ProQuest databases, you can get electronic page images, cover to cover, of hundreds of these publications back to 1988.

The NewsBank Electronic Index to Periodicals, available in many public libraries, is a comprehensive CD-ROM index of 100 general-interest magazines beginning with the January 1988 issue. NewsBank also offers cover-to-cover microfiche and CD-ROM editions of selected periodicals from this list.

CD-ROM versions of Magazine Index as well as of *Readers' Guide to Periodical Literature* and *Readers' Guide Abstracts* are also available at many public libraries.

Diskette Indexes

A crucial resource for investigative journalists is NameBase, an index of over 159,000 citations to 73,000 personal, corporate, and organizational names that have appeared in thousands of pages of periodical articles since 1973 (as well as in over 400 books since 1962) dealing with national security, the CIA, narcotics trafficking, corporate white-collar crime, and similar topics. All titles are annotated. (See appendix.)

6.6 Full-Text Copy Services and Interlibrary Loan

If the index/abstract you are using does not offer direct microform or optical disk retrieval of the cited article, you may find it in bound volumes of the publication or on microform from another publisher at your public library. If not, you can obtain the microform or the bound volume (or a photocopy of the particular article) through interlibrary loan.

Another option—if you need the article quickly—is to go through a commercial copy service. You can order virtually any article indexed by DIALOG through an online service called DIALORDER, which will route you to the appropriate company (one of about 80 full-text copy services) for copies of articles from the periodical or newspaper in question. This company will send you the copy by mail or fax.

If you are using a non-DIALOG index, contact the vendor or publisher regarding such services (hardcopy indexes may include a copy service telephone number in the front of the book). Note that UMI will provide copies, through its Articles Clearinghouse, of articles indexed in UMI databases covering over 1,000 periodicals.

6.7 Using Database Searches to Identify Relevant Hardcopy Files

An article found in LEXIS/NEXIS may be based on another article from a paper that is not included in any database or print index. But even with no citation, you can often figure out where to look. For example, if the *New York Times* publishes a short article on the antics of a right-wing extremist group in Iowa, the *Times* stringer has probably just followed up on a much more detailed story or series in a local Iowa paper. To decide where to look, keep in mind the following:

- A major local or regional story, although covered in major newspapers in other regions, will usually be treated in greater detail in the newspapers of its own region.

- A local story will often be treated in greater detail in a small local daily or weekly than in a major metropolitan daily 50 miles away.

- A local daily may be taking its story from a rival local daily or from a local weekly that treated the story in greater detail.

- Newspapers rarely give proper credit to each other.

6.8 Print Indexes to Newspapers and Periodicals

The New York Times Index
This is the grand old lady of newspaper indexes. Much larger and more detailed than any other index, it provides coverage back to 1851 and has been published in roughly its present index/abstract format since 1913. If your subject has been prominent in a part of the country distant from New York, don't automatically assume his or her name is not included. The *New York Times* is America's newspaper of record—truly national in scope—with bureaus or stringers in every region.

The *Times Index* is an annual, with monthly supplements cumulating quarterly. Unless you access it via database (or use the personal-name print index described below), you must search the volumes one by one. I find it chiefly useful in parallel and indirect backgrounding (see sections 1.3 and 1.4). Indeed, its hierarchical, topic-oriented mode of organization and its chronological abstracting of articles on each topic will give you a unique sense of your subject's interrelations with the people and institutions surrounding him or her. Let's say you are backgrounding a Teamster official and you want to know about his rise in the union in the 1970s. Irrespective of whether there is any mention of him in the *Times Index*, I would suggest you photocopy everything under the headings for Teamsters Union and Organized Crime for every year during that period. Take the material home for careful study because it is likely to contain a wealth of leads to unindexed articles, old court files, and subject's former associates or opponents. (As you learn more about subject, you should consult these photocopies again from time to time to see if you've missed anything.)

Personal Name Index to the New York Times Index

Searching for references to an individual (or his or her associates) in the annual volumes of the *New York Times Index* can be tedious. Entries for individual names merely refer you to subject entries, and you thus have to look up a name at least twice within each annual index. You can find personal name references quickly, however, via a remarkable reference work, the *Personal Name Index to the New York Times Index*. The base set is 22 volumes covering 1851 to 1974. A supplemental set brings things up to the present and also corrects errata and adds names missed in the base set. Both sets are organized alphabetically by personal name—you only have to look in two volumes (one for the base set, one for the supplemental set) to find every listing of your subject's name.

The *Personal Name Index* lists each reference to a person's name in chronological order, providing the year and page in the *Times Index*. To find out more you must go either to the *Times Index* volumes or (beginning in 1979) to the online National Newspaper Index. Then you must decide whether to access further information either from the microfilm (back to the *Times*'s beginning) or from the online abstracts (since 1969) or from the full text online (since 1980). If there are only a couple of references to your subject and you're in the library anyway, you'll probably just go to the microfilm. Although the *Personal Name Index* is *not* an index to the full text of the *Times*, skillful use of it can help you find articles in which unindexed references to subject (or mention of his or her activities without mention of his or her name) occur. Simply look under the names of subject's closest associates, especially those who are better known than subject (or were better known during the years in question). For instance, I decide to background New York City Councilman X. I know that in the early 1960s he was an aide to Congressman Y. I do not find him in the *Personal Name Index* for those years, but I do find Congressman Y. Checking in the *Times Index*, I find that several of the articles on Congressman Y concern a bribery scandal. I then look at the text of the articles on microfilm and discover that the future Councilman X's name was mentioned several times in connection with the scandal. This stimulates me to try to learn more about this all-but-forgotten incident.

Print Indexes to Other Daily Newspapers

UMI offers print indexes of the following newspapers: *American Banker* (since 1971); *Atlanta Journal & Constitution* (since 1982); *Boston Globe* (since 1983); *Chicago Sun-Times* (1979–82 only); *Chicago Tribune* (since 1972); *Christian Science Monitor* (since 1945); *Denver Post* (since 1976);

Detroit News (since 1976); *Houston Post* (since 1976); *Los Angeles Times* (since 1972); *Minneapolis Star & Tribune* (1984–85 only); *Nashville Banner & Tennessean* (since 1980—only on microfilm); *New Orleans Times-Picayune* (since 1972); *St. Louis Post-Dispatch* (since 1975); *San Francisco Chronicle* (since 1976); *USA Today* (since 1982); *Wall Street Journal* (since 1955); and *Washington Times* (since 1986). These indexes are not as detailed as the *New York Times Index* (which is also available from UMI). If your subject is not listed, look under the subject headings with which his or her name is most likely to be linked, then search the most promising articles on microfilm.

For other indexes to daily papers, check Scarecrow Press's three-volume *Newspaper Indexes: A Location and Subject Guide for Researchers*. Many of the listings in this set are of interest only to historians and genealogists, but contemporary newspapers are also included. You will find that many of the indexes only offer spotty coverage or coverage of a single brief period. Some are listed as unpublished inhouse indexes or as being in preparation. Some are little more than obituary card files. *Newspaper Indexes* is incomplete in many respects, so if you don't find a particular newspaper listed you should check with the paper's librarian (or the local historical society if the paper is defunct).

If your library does not have the microfilm backfiles of a newspaper whose index you have searched, you can obtain the microfilm reels through interlibrary loan or photocopies of specific articles via an article delivery service (see section 6.6).

Indexes to weekly newspapers specializing in investigative journalism are covered in section 6.13.

Print and Microform Magazine Indexes

Magazine Index (see section 6.5) is available on microform at many public libraries; its coverage dates back to 1959. For earlier coverage, consult the *Readers' Guide to Periodical Literature*, which has indexed the nation's most important weekly, monthly, and quarterly general-interest magazines since early in this century. It is an annual work with cumulative supplements between volumes, and today it covers 240 periodicals. Although it is available online dating back to 1983, you must search the annual volumes for previous years. *Readers' Guide* can be useful in filling in the gaps in what you find in *Biography Index* (see section 5.4).

The rather stodgy list of publications in *Readers' Guide* is supplemented by *Popular Periodicals Index* (about 35 magazines), *Access: The Supplementary Index to Periodicals* (about 120 magazines and weekly newspapers), and *The Left Index*. These works include a number of publications specializing in investigative and advocacy journalism.

Print Indexes of Business Newspapers and Periodicals

Described in section 13.2, these indexes are rich in biographical data about individuals in all fields, not just business.

6.9 Morgues of Local Dailies

Morgues (systems of cross-referenced and cross-filed clippings files) are kept by most daily papers. In recent years many papers have turned to computer databases to replace clippings files. Many of these databases are then leased to vendors who sell online access to the general public. So, in essence, when you perform a full-text search of a newspaper database you are accessing its "electronic morgue." But such databases rarely date back more than 15 years. For earlier material, reporters must rely on the old-fashioned clippings files. The best of these will contain every mention of your subject, his or her business firm, and so forth, going back many decades.

Even if there is an index to your local paper, access to the morgue is of great value. First, it will save you the tedium of going to microfilm at the public library. Second, a morgue that has a really thorough system for clipping the daily editions will be much more complete than any index. Third, the morgue may contain court papers and other documents gathered by reporters in the course of their investigations. Fourth, it may contain clippings from the local weekly, ethnic, or "underground" papers (which usually can't afford their own morgues) as well as from rival dailies in the city and surrounding region. Fifth, the newspaper may have obtained the clippings files of defunct local dailies and merged these files into its own.

Some newspapers will allow limited morgue access to scholars, freelance journalists working on books, or researchers from public-interest organizations. If not, contact one of the newspaper's staff reporters or part-time stringers (or a freelancer who often writes for the paper's weekly magazine or Op-Ed page). Interest him or her in your investigation and arrange an exchange of information, including morgue clippings.

6.10 If There's No Index or Morgue

Don't despair. A longtime reporter may remember an article on your subject and the approximate date. Or you may learn through one of subject's former neighbors or a biographical dictionary the approximate date of an event in subject's life that might have been reported (for instance, subject's marriage or the marriage of one of his or her children). In these cases, you will have to do some searching through the microfilm or bound copies, but at least you've narrowed your search within reason.

An event covered by an unindexed local paper may also have been covered by a larger, regional paper that does have an index. Learning the date of the event from the indexed paper, you then go to the microfilm or bound volumes of the unindexed paper.

Federal, state, and local court indexes will tell you about civil and criminal cases involving subject that may have been reported in the press. The press coverage of such cases is crucial because it may touch on matters that

the rules of evidence, rulings by the judge, and the prudence of the opposing parties kept out of the court record. A particular case may drag on for
years, but the most important news articles usually appear at predictable
times. In a nonsensational criminal case, this will be the newspaper issues
immediately following the arrest, the grand jury indictment, the trial jury
verdict, and the sentencing. If the case was a high-profile one, you will have
to search through the newspaper issues for the entire period from arrest to
sentencing, but look especially for articles regarding the opening arguments
and the summations (and don't forget the post-trial appeals process!).

For civil cases, news coverage is most likely to come when the case is first
filed (especially if the plaintiff calls a press conference) and thereafter either
when the jury announces its decision or the parties to the action announce
an out-of-court settlement. To find these dates, examine the docket sheet at
the courthouse.

If the above methods fail to turn up any articles, consult a local muckraker's clippings files (see sections 6.24 and 14.1).

6.11 Suburban News

Your subject may work in the city but live in a suburban community (or a
smaller nearby city) that has its own daily newspaper. Suburban papers,
such as *The Record* in Hackensack, New Jersey, are gradually becoming
available online. They are often the best source for news about subject's social life, civic activities, and grassroots involvement in electoral politics.

An area's major metropolitan daily may produce special editions for various suburbs to compete with the suburban-based dailies. Generally, a
major metropolitan paper's article on a suburban event that you find in the
paper's index or through a database search will have been treated at greater
length in the edition for that suburb than in the metropolitan edition or in
editions for other suburbs. Indeed, it may have appeared *only* in the given
suburban edition. Although you will be able to find the article in a properly
organized morgue, you may not find it (or may not find the full version) on
the microfilm or in the database if these only include a single edition.

6.12 Defunct and Merged Dailies

The importance of newspapers in the United States has declined steadily
since the advent of television. If you are backgrounding a prominent person
of middle age in any medium-sized or large American city, it is quite likely
that at least one local daily newspaper—a newspaper that might have reported on your subject's activities—has gone out of business or merged with
another since your subject became an adult. Indeed, a local daily may have
gone out of business or merged with another since your subject's rise to
prominence (say, within the last 10 years). To find the names of defunct and

premerger papers, check *Newspapers in Microform* and *Serials in Microform* (see section 6.2.). For papers not in microform, check the back issues of *Editor & Publisher Yearbook, Ayer's* (now the *Gale Directory of Publications and Broadcast Media*), and/or the local yellow pages. The microfilm or the bound volumes of a defunct newspaper may be available in the public library of the city in which it was published, or in the library of a surviving local daily, and there may be an index of some kind. In addition, the defunct paper's morgue may have been sold to a surviving daily or donated to the local public library or county historical society.

6.13 Local Weeklies

In every metropolitan area, you will find flourishing weeklies, both of the free-distribution variety and of the paid subscription/newsstand type, aimed either at the entire city or at a particular city neighborhood or suburban community. You will also find weeklies specializing in ethnic or alternate-lifestyle news.

A few weeklies will have excellent clippings files organized like those of the dailies. Most weeklies lack this, but they may keep files on ongoing local political conflicts or the paper's most important investigative pieces through the years. In addition, the editor may remember an article on your subject and be willing to dig out the back issue in which it appeared.

Never underestimate the weeklies, including the smallest. Major investigative pieces by large dailies frequently are based upon spadework performed by the weeklies, and the latter may treat a story in much greater detail (and with much less pulling of punches) than any large daily would.

The *Alternative Press Index* and *Access: The Supplementary Index to Periodicals* cover feisty metropolitan weekly newspapers such as New York City's *Village Voice*, as well as defunct or still-existing counterculture newspapers that, in their heyday, uncovered vast quantities of scandalous (and still relevant) material about people in high places. (Most of the counterculture papers have been put on microform by UMI; a few of those not covered in the two indexes mentioned above may be found in *The Left Index*.) If you are investigating a crooked politician, landlord, or businessperson, the alternative press is often the best place to start. Note that its investigative function is also performed to a lesser extent in some localities by city magazines, such as *Boston*, and state magazines, such as *Texas Monthly*. You can find profiles of hundreds of such periodicals in *Regional Interest Magazines of the United States*.

6.14 Ethnic and Minority Weeklies

Virtually every ethnic group in the United States has its own weekly or weeklies. African-Americans alone have about 300 newspapers (mostly weeklies) throughout the country. Jews also have at least one weekly for each metropolitan area in which there is a significant Jewish population. Smaller ethnic groups may have one or two papers giving nationwide news; for instance, the New York–based *India Abroad* has regional editions in Chicago, Toronto, and Los Angeles and reports in detail when any member of the Indian-American community wins a civic award or gets convicted of a crime. (Note that *India Abroad* has a very well-organized clippings morgue dating back to the early 1980s.) Native American communities also publish a number of newspapers, such as *The Tundra Times* serving the 80,000 Eskimos, Aleuts, and Athabaskans in Alaska.

Nine African-American newspapers, mostly weeklies, are covered by the *Black Newspaper Index* (1979 to present). Selective abstracts from these newspapers can be accessed via UMI's Newspaper Abstracts database (1984 to 1988) and UMI's Newspaper and Periodical Abstracts database (1989 to present), both available on DIALOG.

In 1992, SoftLine Information introduced Ethnic NewsWatch, a CD-ROM product that offers full-text articles, editorials, and reviews from over 75 publications of all ethnic and minority groups. (General categories include African-American, Asian/Pacific, European/Eastern European, Hispanic, Jewish, Arab/Middle Eastern, and Native American.) An online version of Ethnic NewsWatch is available via NEXIS.

6.15 Professional and Trade Publications

Articles that feature or mention your subject may have appeared in a professional or trade publication. If it's an interview in a publication read only by subject's colleagues, he or she may have spoken far more freely than if being questioned by a reporter from the major media. To find the most likely publications, look under the appropriate topic headings in *Associations' Publications in Print, Standard Periodical Directory*, and *Newsletters in Print*. Also check *Ulrich's International Periodicals Directory*, as subject may have talked most frankly of all to a foreign trade publication.

To find additional trade and professional publications, look in the *Encyclopedia of Associations* and the *National Trade and Professional Associations of the U.S.* If an association is listed, it probably has, at the least, a newsletter for its members. Simply call the association's research director and ask for the names of its local, regional, and national publications and where library backfiles might be located.

The most important trade and professional newspapers and periodicals are indexed in works such as the *Business Periodicals Index* or can be accessed online via major database networks. Others must be searched issue by issue, unless they include an annual index at the end of each year. Fortunately, many have a short section in each issue devoted to news about members. If your subject is prominent in his or her trade or profession, it may be worth your while to spend an hour or so going through back issues.

Even if you don't find any direct information about subject in a professional or trade periodical, you will at least find the names of many people in subject's field who will know subject either personally or by reputation. In addition, you may find articles about the company for which subject works or about one or more of his or her closest colleagues or associates.

6.16 House Organs

The inhouse publications of companies or nonprofit organizations for which subject has worked may include noncontroversial background information on his or her career. For instance, such publications may tell about job promotions or professional honors that subject has received. Possibly there will be a section of personal news in each issue telling about marriages of employees, births of their children, and so forth. (If not in the house organ, this material is often included in a staff newsletter produced by the personnel department.) Equally important, house organs will give you the names of many of subject's past and present co-workers.

The *Magazines and Internal Publications Directory* (formerly the *Gebbie House Magazine Directory*) describes over 1,200 of such publications. Note that current issues of a house organ can sometimes be obtained from a company or nonprofit organization's public relations department, while the backfiles will usually be available in the inhouse library. (Nonprofit organization libraries are usually open to the public, while corporate libraries can often be accessed by a college business major preparing a term paper.) For backfiles in public libraries, check the *Union List of Serials* and *New Serial Titles* or one of the online union catalogs.

6.17 Alumni Newspapers and Magazines

If you know what college your subject attended, contact the editor of the alumni paper at the alumni office on campus. Many of these papers maintain clippings files of back-issue articles. As boosters of their school, they are happy to furnish copies of any article that shows what high achievers their alumni are. Even if they don't have clippings files, the editor may recall an article on your subject. You should also try the university archives, which may have clippings files more comprehensive than those at the alumni office.

In searching the bound volumes of an alumni magazine, note that brief biographical notes and obituaries are often organized under class headings. If subject is a member of the class of 1956, you can quickly search through the listings for that class in each issue.

6.18 Trade Union Publications

In the United States and Canada, there are hundreds of labor union newspapers, magazines, and newsletters published by international unions, by state or local AFL-CIO councils, or by individual unions on the district or local level. In some unions, each local will have its own publication. District councils (the locals of a given union within, say, a given metropolitan area) may also have a publication. The backfiles may have valuable information on your subject if he or she is a union officer, an active rank and filer, or a management figure who has clashed with the union.

Don't neglect the dissident newspapers put out by rank-and-file groups at odds with the union bureaucracy. For instance, *Convoy Dispatch*, the Teamsters for a Democratic Union monthly, is an excellent source on the misdeeds of old-line Teamster officials on every level.

Collections of trade union newspapers can be found in university libraries, especially if the university has an industrial relations department. To find the nearest library with back copies of a particular publication, see the *Union List of Serials* and *New Serial Titles*.

6.19 Sports, Hobby, and Other Specialty Publications

Is subject a collector of ancient coins? A breeder of prize-winning dogs? A rock climber? An ardent participant in bridge tournaments? Look in *Associations' Publications in Print* as well as *Standard Periodical Directory* for periodicals relevant to subject's field of interest. Investigative journalist Steve Weinberg found interesting material for a biography of billionaire Armand Hammer in publications as obscure as *Arabian Horse World*.

6.20 Publications of Fraternal, Civic, and Charitable Organizations

If a biographical dictionary lists subject as holding membership (or a volunteer or paid position) in any fraternal, civic, or charitable organization, look in *Associations' Publications in Print* for the name and address of that group's newsletter or bulletin. If no publication is listed, inquire directly from the association's national or local headquarters. Note that many associations (e.g., the Boy Scouts) have state or regional as well as national publications; always check out the one for subject's locality.

6.21 Religious Publications

There are a huge number of religious newspapers and periodicals in the United States. For example, American Catholics have no less than 155 diocesan newspapers. If subject is in the clergy or is a lay person active in church affairs, his or her activities are almost certain to have been covered in denominational publications on some level, whether national, regional, state, or local.

Weekly church bulletins handed out at the Sunday services often include news about members of the congregation, such as births, marriages, participation in a mission-work team, election to the church governing board, or appointment as a Sunday schoolteacher. If one of subject's children is being baptized or confirmed on a particular Sunday, that too will be in the bulletin. For many blue-collar families, these publications may be just about the only place they are mentioned in print. Church bulletins are usually on file in the church office, often going back decades.

For news of the clergy and prominent lay persons active in the church, you might check the online church news services. These include the Religious News Service (with its daily news reports), the Lutheran News Service, the Episcopal News Service, United Methodist Information, ChurchNews International, and the Catholic News Service, all available via CompuServe and/or NewsNet.

See also Religion Index (on DIALOG), which covers scholarly religious journals and book reviews from 1949 to the present.

6.22 Genealogical Periodicals and Indexes

If there is a periodical devoted to persons with subject's surname or subject's mother's maiden name, it may contain biographical information about subject or some of his or her relatives. *The Directory of Family One-Name Periodicals* lists 1,600 of these publications. Many other genealogical periodicals are indexed (by individual as well as family name) in the *Periodical Source Index* (PERSI), which also covers local history periodicals; always check the *PERSI* supplements as well as the base set.

6.23 The Reporter—His or Her Sources and Files

The main object of searching through newspapers and periodicals is not simply to compile more and more clippings; rather, it is to find live sources: the people behind the news stories who know the things that didn't get printed.

Clippings will lead you to basically four types of people: the reporter who researched and wrote the article; the people mentioned in the article as participants in the reported events; the people whom the reporter quotes as sources (whether participants, eyewitnesses, or experts with background information); and the reporter's unnamed informants.

If the reporter is an expert on your subject (for instance, the longtime reporter on the labor beat who has written several articles about the carpenter's union official you are investigating), get whatever background information and advice he or she is willing to provide and, if possible, gain access to his or her private clippings files and a referral to his or her chief sources. (Contrary to the TV depiction of reporters, most are not jealous of their files and sources unless a major scoop is involved. In approaching them, remember that it's in their interest to cooperate with you if your research can fill in gaps in their own work.)

Sometimes the reporter may not know very much, as, for example, when an article was only one of many hurried pieces written on a tight deadline. In such cases, you may want to see whatever documentation the reporter has retained, but your main objective will be to get the telephone numbers of the sources who provided most of the information.

6.24 The Amateur Muckraker

This is the freelance writer or citizen-researcher devoted to gathering all the scandalous clippings (and gossip) on everyone in town (or at least on particular groups or individuals who have incurred his or her wrath). At their best, muckrakers can be an almost miraculous source of information on evildoers, and you should urge local reporters to put you in contact with them. For a full discussion, see section 14.1.

6.25 Library Clippings Collections

Hundreds of libraries around the United States have newspaper or periodicals clippings files donated to them by private researchers or compiled by library staffers. A good example of the treasures you might find is the vast collection of news clippings in the North Carolina Collection at the University of North Carolina's Wilson Library in Chapel Hill. The library staff began collecting these clippings from newspapers across the state in the 1920s. Photocopies of all clippings through 1975 have been compiled into 364 volumes, which are divided into biography and subject collections. The biography volumes, organized alphabetically by name, contain clippings on thousands of North Carolinians. They include profile articles, interviews, and obituaries as well as news articles centered on the individual's activities. You can access further information on an individual by looking in relevant subject files. The library staff is currently completing a second set of volumes to cover the years 1976–89; the biographical section (99 volumes plus index) is already on the shelves.

To find similar collections elsewhere, see *Prospect Researcher's Guide to Biographical Research Collections*, which lists more than 1,000 genealogical, biographical, and other special libraries (cross-referenced by subject and geographical area) that maintain files on individuals. See also the tips given in section 11.2 on archival collections and in section 14.4 on the clippings files of nonprofit organizations.

6.26 Broadcast Transcripts, Abstracts, and Indexes

Two companies, Journal Graphics and Burrelle's Information Service (see bibliography), dominate the broadcast transcript field, offering wide coverage of national television and radio news programs, public affairs programs, and talk shows. To find the transcripts you need, consult the indexes published by both companies (Journal Graphics's index is cumulative back to 1968), and then have the transcript sent to you by mail or fax.

Journal Graphics transcripts (from 1990 on) are available online from LEXIS/NEXIS, together with transcripts from several other sources; Burrelle's transcripts (from 1994) can be accessed via DataTimes.

Broadcast News, a CD-ROM database, provides over 44,000 full-text transcripts annually from more than 50 broadcast news and public affairs programs.

Abstracts of the transcripts from about 90 TV programs are included in UMI's Newspaper & Periodical Abstracts database, available on DIALOG.

The multivolume *Television News Index and Abstracts*, found in many research libraries, covers the national evening news on all three networks back to 1972 (or, in microform, back to 1968). This remarkable reference work is also available on the Internet (see the appendix). It includes an item-by-item description of each program—you can then order a videotape copy of a given segment or the entire program from Vanderbilt University's Television News Archive.

7·

Collecting the Basic "Identifiers"

To conduct a thorough background check, three items are most important: first, subject's full name correctly spelled, including full middle name and correct generational designation (e.g., "Jr.," "III"); second, subject's date of birth; and third, subject's Social Security Number (SSN). Without the first, it is sometimes difficult to follow the paper trail even on the simplest level (especially if the name is a common one). Without the second and third, it is difficult to find public records filed according to these identifiers.

7.1 What's in a Name?

Without any deceptive intent, many individuals leave a confusing paper trail because of marital name changes or informal name variations. When you first see your subject's name in a newspaper article or phone directory or on a mailbox, you should not assume that this is the full name under which most records regarding subject's past are filed. Indeed, there may be no one form of his or her name that covers most of the available documentation.

Middle Names, Nicknames, and Aliases
Your subject may be commonly known by his or her middle name, a nickname, or a shortened form of his or her first name (e.g., "Dell" for "Delmore"), and your subject may give any of these as the first name in a telephone listing or when introducing himself or herself. John Quincey Public may receive utility bills as Quincey Public, receive MasterCard statements as John Q. Public, sign his name on checks as J. Quincey Public, and be listed in the phone book (and also be known to most acquaintances) as Quince Public. In searching through phone or crisscross directories and county courthouse indexes, this might be only a minor annoyance since

"Public" is such an uncommon surname. But if your subject's last name is Smith, you will have to get things clear. This is all the more necessary if subject has more than one middle name and varies their use according to whim, for example, John Gerald Wellington Marshall Smith, who is always one step ahead of the bill collectors!

To make matters even more confusing, some people don't have a middle name; and others may use only a middle initial, as did Harry S Truman.

In your earliest interviews with persons who know subject, find out whether he or she is usually called by first or middle name, what his or her past and present nicknames are, and whether he or she has ever used any pseudonyms or aliases. Also note carefully any evidence of name variations in newspaper clippings about subject.

Generational Designations

Confusion may arise when father and son have the same first and middle as well as last name. This is supposed to be cleared up by the use of "Jr.," "III," and "IV." But your subject and those with whom he shares the name (grandfather, father, son, or grandson) may not use the generational designations consistently. For instance, if the father and son live in different cities, the son may not bother to include "Jr." or "III" in his telephone listing. Or he may drop the "III" because it sounds pompous. Someone searching for the son may see "Jr." after the father's name in the phone book and thus mistake father for son. Confusion may also result when father and son live in the same household and the telephone listing for one or the other lacks the proper designation.

Maiden Names, Married Names, and Other Variations

If a married woman uses her husband's surname, you will still need her previous name or names. Records from before her marriage will be listed by her maiden name and/or previous married name, and she may still use her maiden or previous married name in her professional career. (Note that her maiden name is not necessarily her birth name; she may have taken it from her stepfather when her mother remarried.) If subject is her husband, he may be using her maiden name (or the name of one of her parents) as the "straw name" to conceal his ownership of a real estate parcel.

In this era of frequent divorce and remarriage, joint custody of children, two-career households, and legally recognized gay and lesbian partnerships, name variations can become extremely complicated.

▪ Wives frequently use hyphenated surnames, and the practice has been adopted by some husbands. Although this can sometimes be convenient for genealogists and skip tracers, it can also be quite confusing. The wife may put her name first, the husband may put his first, she may put his first, he may put hers first, both may put his first, both may put hers first. In addition, either or both spouses may vary the usage according to the situation or their mood. In filling out a job application, for instance, the husband may drop the hyphenated name to avoid appearing flaky.

- The husband may give up his own surname for his wife's.

- Husband and wife may choose an entirely new surname to share, which can be an amalgamation of syllables from both names or an entirely new name with a shared symbolic meaning.

- The wife may retain her maiden name for all purposes, social and business, and may be listed in the phone book *only* under that name. Or she may use her maiden name for professional purposes (especially if she was established in a profession such as medicine or law prior to her marriage) and her husband's name for social purposes. Or she may use both names *without* a hyphen, e.g., Hillary Rodham Clinton. Or she may shift from maiden name to married name (or vice versa) for certain narrow purposes such as establishing an alternate credit history if she has a bad credit rating under the other name.

- When a teenage child is living with a mother who has remarried, the mother may use her new husband's surname while the teenager continues to use (and has a telephone listing under) the father's surname. Or the teenager may use the father's name in some situations and the mother's new husband's name in other situations (for other variations on this, see section 4.12).

- Parents may choose for a child, at birth, a surname in the maternal line, a hyphenated surname with either husband's or wife's name first, or a surname that is an amalgamation of the parents' surnames. This has become an increasingly common practice since the early 1980s.

- Parents may choose a surname at random for their child. According to the *Wall Street Journal*, February 11, 1987: "Parents are making use of little-known laws that allow them to bestow on the children the surname of their choice. Short of a curse word or a series of numerals, the choice in most states is unlimited."

- When an unmarried couple is living together, the woman may use the man's surname or a hyphenated version of the two names in certain social situations or in signing an apartment lease (hence ensuring that the "married" name will appear in the building lobby's directory). But she may continue to use her maiden name or the name of the husband from whom she is separated or divorced in other situations. In the case of one couple I tracked, this was complicated by the fact that both were using "political" surnames at meetings of and in their writings for an extremist sect. Over a 10-year period, the woman used, interchangeably, her lover's political surname, her lover's real surname, her ex-husband's surname, her own previous political surname, and her maiden name.

Common-Law and Statutory Name Changes

If you are tracing subject's name backward in old telephone books and the trail runs out, it could be that subject has changed his or her name. Emigrants of earlier generations often "Americanized" their names. African-Americans often abandon their "slave names" for Arabic, West African, or Swahili names. Cult members (such as the Hari Krishnas) change their names on the instructions of their guru. Persons who have suffered public disgrace change their names to facilitate building a new life. Actors adopt names that will enhance their box office appeal. And some people change their names on a whim.

The laws regarding name changes vary from state to state. In New York, the right to change one's name for nonfraudulent purposes is a common-law right, which can be exercised by simply beginning to use the new name in all transactions and having it recognized by friends and associates. This right, which includes that of the mother of an illegitimate child to adopt the name of the putative father for herself and the child, does not require court permission. However, the law provides for statutory name change (by order of a court) as an affirmance of the common-law right. This process is distinct from name changes pursuant to marriage, adoption, divorce, or annulment.

Court-approved name changes are typically recorded at the county courthouse in a ledger book that gives both old and new names. The number of name changes per year is usually quite small.

Whether a person uses the court method or the common-law method, he or she will have to notify various ID issuing agencies, his or her bank, and so forth. When a person notifies the Social Security Administration of a name change, that change is recorded but the person keeps the same SSN as before. The SSN thus becomes a convenient means by which an investigator can establish (via credit-reporting agency "header" records) the link between subject's old and new names.

Note that some people who adopt a new name (especially those who do so via the common-law use method) may only selectively notify public and private record-keeping agencies, thus continuing to use the old name in various transactions. Even if a person does notify the most important agencies, there will be a time lag before the new name fully replaces the old.

If you can't find any record of a name change, the person with the suspiciously short paper trail may be using a false identity based on fraudulently obtained ID (see section 7.5).

Finding Subject's Previous and Alternate Names

College alumni directories and class anniversary directories (and similar directories on the secondary-school level) give both the maiden and married names of their alumnae. Society guides (such as *The Social Register*) also provide both names, as do family name books, genealogy charts, and the biographical dictionary entries for women. Biographical dictionary entries for men often give the maiden names of their wives.

Alumni directories, class anniversary directories, high school and college yearbooks, and newspaper clippings may provide subject's former or present nicknames.

The judgment docket at your county courthouse sometimes lists a/k/a's beside a person's name. These may include personal aliases as well as business names and property ownership "straw" names.

Criminal court records and newspaper crime articles often give the aliases and nicknames of persons charged with crimes.

Making Sure You Have the Right Person

In the early 1980s, Edward H. Heller of Brooklyn practiced law at 230 Park Avenue in Manhattan. Meanwhile, another Edward H. Heller, also of Brooklyn, practiced law at 250 Park Avenue. When the former was convicted of grand larceny and disbarred, the latter wrote a letter to the *New York Law Journal* to clear up the confusion, signing his name "Edward Harris Heller."

The innocent Mr. Heller's problem was no different in essence from that of the many Americans who are mistakenly arrested each year—or denied credit—because of name confusion in databases rife with small errors that are really big errors.

Never assume you have the right person unless (1) the middle name (not just the middle initial) fits; (2) the address (including street number) fits; (3) the date of birth and SSN fit (the latter are especially important in avoiding mistakes in generational designation, as when the John Smith of 221 Elm Street, arrested for indecent exposure, turns out to be John Smith, Jr., the emotionally disturbed son who lives in John Smith, Sr.'s basement).

If you are writing for publication and are making your own assertions rather than relying on an official statement from police or prosecutors, always call the person about whom you are writing to verify his or her identity.

7.2 Obtaining the Birth Date

"Real" Versus Operative Birth Date

In following a person's paper trail, you can become confused if you don't distinguish between "real" birth date and operative birth date. The "real" date is that found on the birth certificate. (I have put "real" in quotation marks because, prior to the sexual revolution of the 1960s, dates on birth certificates were often fudged to disguise the fact that a child was born less than nine months after his or her parents' wedding). By contrast, the operative birth date is that used in adult life as an identifier. The two are frequently different because there are so many reasons to deliberately misreport one's age. The initial misreporting may occur early on, as in the case of teenagers who added a year to their age in order to join the Marines during World War II. More often, people misreport their age later in life to avoid age discrimination when applying for a new job, to retire or qualify for benefits early, to delay retirement, or simply for vanity's sake. Often, the "new" birth date may become operative in one set of records but not in another (say, employment applications for successive jobs, but not applications for new credit cards). If the "new" date is used on a credit application, it may be part of an attempt (also involving a shift from married to maiden name, the listing of a new address and phone number, etc.) to set up an alternate credit history.

The operative date of birth is therefore best defined as that which is recognized by any particular records system as an identifier for subject's records. Below, unless we are speaking of the birth certificate, date of birth will be used in this sense.

Getting the "Real" Birth Date

In the county courthouse of the county where subject was born, there may be a birth index that you can look through to find the date of birth. This birth index may also be on microform in the genealogy division of the local public library or the Mormons' local Family History Center. The New York Public Library's genealogy division, for instance, has the city health department's annual birth indexes from 1917 to 1982.

If you know the state but not the county in which a person was born, contact the state's bureau of vital statistics (usually part of the state health department). In many states, you can get the birth records searched and obtain a copy or abstract of the birth certificate. For more information on how to deal with county and state vital statistics registrars, see section 10.1.

A subject's "real" date of birth may also be found in church baptismal and christening registers, which are usually open to the public. Many church registers from all parts of the country have been collected on microform by the Mormons.

Credit-Reporting Agency Databases

The operative birth date is header material on credit files and as such should be readily available from credit-reporting agency databases via an information broker.

Biographical Dictionaries and Professional Directories

Although some of these works provide only the year of birth, others provide the full date. For instance, *American Men and Women of Science* generally includes the date of birth in its 123,000–plus entries. *The Martindale-Hubbell Law Directory* gives only the year of birth in its roster listings but includes the date of birth in biographical sketches of about 40,000 attorneys.

Note that with the year of birth alone you can still search many records systems (for instance, some military personnel records); it's just a bit more difficult. Depending on the system being searched, secondary identifiers such as place of birth and mother's maiden name may compensate for the lack of a more precise date.

Miscellaneous Public Records
A subject's date of birth may be found on his or her marriage license and in Motor Vehicles Bureau and voter registration records.

Military Rosters
Date of birth is included in the annual registers of Army, Air Force, Marine, Coast Guard, and Army National Guard officers. The Navy register gives only the year of birth.

Applications for Jobs, Loans, and So Forth
A date of birth, accurate or not, will be on every application subject has ever filled out for a job, loan, rental of a house or apartment, or admittance to a college. A landlord or former employer may be willing to dig out such an application from his or her files.

Date of Birth: No Great Secret
Some investigators will call a subject, claim that they want to include him or her in an occupational directory (or register him or her for a lottery prize), and get various basic items of personal information (including birth date) in a few moments. This type of deception is not recommended for journalists. I simply want to illustrate the point that, because date of birth is so commonly asked for, most people are not secretive about it.

7.3 Finding the Social Security Account Number

As header material on his or her credit file, subject's SSN is readily available from credit-reporting agency databases via an information broker. The broker may need to check multiple database systems to find it; the price for this can be as much as $35 depending on how many databases are searched. In many cases, however, you won't need to pay a broker—you can easily obtain the SSN while checking various public or private records that you would check anyway. What follows are some of the places the SSN might be found.

Driver's License Abstracts
In some states, the SSN is always the same as the driver's license number or is listed on the driver's license in addition to the driver's license number. In other states, the use of the SSN is optional (for instance, in Massachusetts, where about 15 percent of drivers request a non-SSN number), or it is not used at all.

Voter Registration Records

In some localities the SSN is included on voter registration cards as a safe-guard against vote fraud. Voter registration records are kept at the local board of elections and are almost always open to the public. The use of the SSN for this purpose has declined in recent years, so look in older records if available.

Court Records

The SSN may be found in civil court records; for instance, when an apartment rental application is attached as an exhibit to a motion or affidavit in a landlord/tenant case. If subject has ever been convicted of a crime, you may find his or her SSN in the criminal court file. If a person has ever filed for personal bankruptcy, the case file will include his or her SSN.

Income Tax Records

The SSN is the same as a person's TIN (taxpayer identifying number). Thus whenever tax records of an individual are made public (see section 8.13), one will find his or her SSN.

Disclosure Statements and Other Filings

The SSN may be included in financial disclosure statements required from elected and appointed public officials, high-ranking civil servants, and candidates for public office.

In addition, you may find the SSNs of officers of nonprofit corporations on the 990 forms filed by their organizations with the IRS.

Applications for Jobs, Housing, and So Forth

The SSN, like the date of birth, is required information when a person opens a bank account, rents an apartment, or applies for a job, loan, mortgage, or credit card. If you are investigating an obnoxious local cult, you may find that local landlords or businesspersons will give you access to cult members' apartment rental or job applications.

Discarded Personal Records

The SSN is sometimes found on health insurance bills (here the number may be divided into three sets of three digits each, rather than the SSN's 3–2–4), brokerage account statements, and so forth. Canceled checks may have the SSN (or driver's license number including the SSN) scrawled on the back if subject had to show ID in cashing the check. The SSN will also be on all correspondence received from the IRS. Subject may routinely throw such things out with the garbage. The use of garbology as a research technique is described in section 11.4.

Military Records

Present, former, and retired members of the Armed Forces, Reserves, and National Guard are identified by their SSN. Although the Privacy Act of 1974 prevents the government from giving out the SSN when you request someone's service record, you may find the SSN on discharge papers filed at the county courthouse.

Until the mid-1970s, the SSN was listed beside each officer's name in the register of officers for each service. The Army National Guard register included SSNs as late as 1980. Back issues of the service registers may be found at your nearest federal depository library.

Multiple SSN Holders and Other Special Problems

Under Social Security regulations any SSN holder may change his or her SSN by applying to the Social Security Administration and showing good reason. Some people do it because of suspicion that their SSN and name are being used by someone else for fraudulent purposes. Others do it to put distance between themselves and negative credit information held in databases. Militant trade unionists in past decades did it to avoid blacklisting. But after a person obtains the new SSN, the old one does not disappear suddenly from non–Social Security Administration records. For instance, if the old SSN was already established as the identifier on subject's health insurance policy, it could continue as such indefinitely.

The problem of tracking people by their SSN is compounded by the many deceptive practices involving this so-called universal identifier. Some people will switch the digits on their SSN or make up a fictitious SSN if they are opening a new bank account that they don't want bill collectors or the IRS to know about. Others will list SSNs taken from stolen or forged Social Security cards (illegal aliens frequently do this). Con artists have been known to expropriate a stranger's identity and SSN (as by learning the SSN and other identifying information through a telephone ruse, then applying for a new card in the victim's name), so that John Doe who has an impeccable credit rating in Connecticut becomes John Doe the deadbeat in Oregon. Participants in the so-called underground economy may utilize a false identity (and an SSN issued in that name) for certain banking transactions while continuing to use their real identity and SSN on other occasions. These are only a few of the possible deceptions and frauds that make it difficult to track people by their SSN alone.

7.4 Making Use of the SSN Code

Have you been unable to find out where subject grew up? Do you suspect that subject has given false information about his or her past? The SSN may be a key to unraveling the mystery.

The nine-digit SSN is divided into an area number (first three digits), a group number (middle two digits), and a serial number (last four digits). Both the area number and the group number are useful for our purposes.

Area Number

The Social Security Administration assigns the area number based on the zip code of the mailing address shown on the SSN application. The area number will fall within one or more consecutive series of numbers that identify the state in which that mailing address is located. With the single exception of area numbers 232–234 (see below), no two states share the same range of area numbers. The higher series of area numbers assigned to some states following a nonadjacent lower series are the result of population growth—the given state simply ran out of numbers within the originally assigned series.

The majority of today's adult native-born Americans obtained their SSN in high school or shortly thereafter. Thus, subject's area number quite likely indicates the state in which he or she grew up. (Subject's family may have moved one or more times during his or her childhood, but most families that move tend to stay within the same state or region.) If you lack any information about subject's past except for this one clue, you might look in PhoneDisc for persons with subject's surname who are currently residing in the state in question. One or more of them may be related to subject.

(Note that beginning in 1987 federal law required parents to obtain SSNs for any child five years old or older if they wished to list that child as a dependent on their income tax returns. In 1992, this requirement was extended to children one year old or older. The inferences you might draw from area numbers should be adjusted accordingly.)

Even if you don't want to bother with investigating subject's childhood, the SSN may at least give you an indication of whether or not subject is being minimally truthful about his or her past. If subject claims to have grown up and attended college in Hawaii, but the SSN is coded for North Dakota, you have definite grounds for suspicion.

Note that area numbers have been assigned only within two ranges: 001–649 and 700–728. Any area number outside these ranges represents a fictitious SSN.

The following is a list of area numbers and the states to which they correspond:

001–003 New Hampshire	235–236 West Virginia
004–007 Maine	237–246 North Carolina
008–009 Vermont	247–251 South Carolina
010–034 Massachusetts	252–260 Georgia
035–039 Rhode Island	261–267 Florida
040–049 Connecticut	268–302 Ohio
050–134 New York	303–317 Indiana
135–158 New Jersey	318–361 Illinois
159–211 Pennsylvania	362–386 Michigan
212–220 Maryland	387–399 Wisconsin
221–222 Delaware	400–407 Kentucky
223–231 Virginia	408–415 Tennessee
232–234 North Carolina,	416–424 Alabama
West Virginia	425–428 Mississippi

429–432 Arkansas
433–439 Louisiana
440–448 Oklahoma
449–467 Texas
468–477 Minnesota
478–485 Iowa
486–500 Missouri
501–502 North Dakota
503–504 South Dakota
505–508 Nebraska
509–515 Kansas
516–517 Montana
518–519 Idaho
520 Wyoming
521–524 Colorado
525 New Mexico
526–527 Arizona
528–529 Utah
530 Nevada
531–539 Washington
540–544 Oregon
545–573 California
574 Alaska
575–576 Hawaii

577–579 District of Columbia
580 Puerto Rico, Virgin Islands
581–584 Puerto Rico
585 New Mexico
586 Guam, American Samoa,
    Northern Mariana Islands,
    Philippines (i.e., former and
    present Pacific territories)
587–588 Mississippi
589–595 Florida
596–599 Puerto Rico
600–601 Arizona
602–626 California
627–645 Texas
646–647 Utah
648–649 New Mexico
650–699 Unassigned
700–728 Assigned prior to 1963 to
    railroad workers covered under
    the Railroad Retirement Act,
    irrespective of the state in which
    the worker applied.
729–999 Unassigned

Note that the California area/group numbers 568-30 through 568-58 were issued to Vietnamese and other Southeast Asian refugees between 1975 and 1979, as were SSNs within 574 (Alaska), 580 (Puerto Rico and Virgin Islands), and 586 (Pacific territories).

Group Number

The fourth and fifth digits—the group number—can sometimes give you an indication of when the SSN was issued. This will help you pin down the time during which your subject resided in the state identified by the area number. It also may suggest that the individual is using false ID or that something odd has been going on in his or her life: If subject is a man in his mid-fifties, why should he be using an SSN issued no earlier than 1972? If this is his first number, how was he able to get and keep jobs earlier in his life without having a number? If he obtained a new number to replace the old one, what was his motive?

The assigning of group numbers is a complicated matter that cannot be explained properly in a few paragraphs. The National Employment Screening Services' *Social Security Number Guide* (see bibliography) explains how to figure out if a job applicant has listed on his or her application an SSN that includes a group number not yet issued by the SSA. The pamphlet provides a Social Security Number Table that enables you to check instantly even if you don't understand the system. The chapter on SSNs in the SSA's *Program Operations Manual System* (*POMS*), available at your nearest SSA office, will tell you such esoterica as how to spot an SSN that was issued prior to 1972 (the year in which SSN issuance by field offices was replaced by a system of central issuance from headquarters in Baltimore).

7.5 How to Detect a False Identity

If records of subject's past go back only a few months or years, it may be that he or she is "paper tripping," that is, using a false identity based on the birth certificate of a dead person. Paper trippers will usually pick the identity of someone who died in infancy or early childhood and whose date of birth, sex, race, eye color, etc., as recorded on the birth certificate, fit the imposter. The imposter obtains a copy of the birth certificate and uses it to obtain a Social Security card, a driver's license, and other ID. This is possible in many localities because applicants for birth certificates are not required to show proof of identity and also because there is no cross-register of birth and death certificates.

Careful paper trippers will select the identity of a dead person who was born in one state and died in another; this ensures them against being unmasked as a result of any future statewide correlation of birth and death records. To guard against accidental discovery (as by an encounter with a sibling of the dead person), they may search through old newspapers to find reports of accidents in which entire families perished (e.g., an auto crash or a household gas leak or fire) and then adopt the identity of one of the victims. Note, however, that such accidents are relatively rare, and law enforcement authorities have caused the relevant birth records to be "flagged."

One indication that a person might be an imposter is if his or her SSN does not fit plausibly with his or her reported age (e.g., the man in his fifties who has an area number that was assigned to his state only within the past decade). Of course, a person can obtain a new SSN legitimately at any point in his or her life (see section 7.3). But if he or she does so, credit-reporting agencies will have a record of it, and there will be other evidence of a paper trail for that person predating the new SSN's issuance.

Another tip-off is if subject received a driver's license for the first time at an age older than usual (this is generally the second piece of ID a paper tripper accumulates). One might then look in the white pages and/or crisscross directory backfiles to determine if subject's name first appeared in the directory only around the time he or she received the delayed driver's license.

In tracking an imposter, always check the central death index in the state in which he or she claims to have been born. Although (as noted above) many paper trippers prefer to use the identity of a child who was born in one state and died in another, this is not always easy to do (the majority of

families who move from one town to another stay within the same state).
Your subject may have been careless about this.

Next, try to find the parents and/or other relatives of the presumably dead
child. Once you have the child's date and place of birth (which may be on the
imposter's driver's license abstract or in credit-reporting agency header material), simply check the birth register or obtain your own copy of the birth
certificate to find out the parents' names (see section 10.1). Track them down
(or track down surviving siblings or other relatives) using the techniques described in section 4.12 and solicit their help in exposing the imposter.

Some users of false ID are too lazy to adopt the paper-trip method. They
prefer to just steal a Social Security card or purchase a stolen card for short-
term use. In such cases, you can simply check the name and SSN in online
databases that include credit-reporting agency header material to find the
address of the real holder of the SSN.

Another short-term alternative to paper tripping is the forged card. Forg-
ers (or the purchaser of the forgery) may pick a nonexistent area number.
Or, if they know enough to get the area number right, they may pick a group
number that has not yet been assigned to anyone or that is otherwise suspicious (see above). If they pick a number that has already been assigned, you
can locate the person to whom it really belongs via the header databases
(see above). If they pick a number that was assigned to a person who is now
deceased, you can determine this fact via the Social Security Death Benefits
Index.

8 ∎

Credit and Financial Information

8.1 Credit-Reporting Agencies and Other Database Sources

The amount of information collected by credit-reporting agencies is staggering. TRW's Updated Credit Profile database, alone, has information on 170 million people, including data on their credit card payment history, lines of credit, and secured loans. It also has public record information on tax liens, judgments, and personal bankruptcies. Equifax and Trans Union Corporation, the two other major national agencies, have equally vast consumer files; Equifax's include gossip from a subject's neighbors as well as arrest and conviction data. Regional or local credit bureaus (about 1,300 nationwide) often have more detailed files than any of the Big Three on individuals and small businesses in their locality.

The Fair Credit Reporting Act restricts the dissemination of credit information about individual consumers. To obtain such information, a client of a credit-reporting agency must have a "legitimate business need." Banks, department stores, insurance companies, credit card issuers, employers, and landlords fall into the category of clients with legitimate needs. Permission of the consumer is required only in Vermont and notification of the consumer only in Rhode Island.

Private investigators and skip tracers routinely obtain credit information on a debtor from the company that extended the credit. Creditors are regarded as having a legitimate business need for data about their debtors as long as the debt is outstanding, and once a creditor has obtained a report from a credit-reporting agency it can show it to anyone it chooses.

Investigators sometimes engage in illegal information trading with people in the credit-reporting industry or else purchase the data from middlemen who have themselves purchased it under a pretense of legitimacy (e.g., for direct-mail purposes) from the credit-reporting agencies. These middlemen, or information brokers, will resell the data to a private investigator (PI) for the ostensible purpose of checking out a prospective employee of the PI's firm (such firms occasionally do have an inhouse need to check out job applicants, but *most* of their inquiries are made pursuant to an investigation for a third party). The Federal Trade Commission has issued a few cease-and-desist orders in recent years regarding this practice, but, given the fact that so much credit-reporting data has been downloaded into the computers of so many information brokers around the country (each of which has hundreds if not thousands of subscribers and is daily engaged in purchasing similar downloaded data from or selling its own data to numerous other brokers), it is doubtful if this problem can be easily brought under control.

Be aware that under the Fair Credit Reporting Act anyone who knowingly obtains information on a consumer from a credit bureau under false pretenses can be fined up to $5,000 and imprisoned for up to one year. Several states also provide stiff criminal penalties. In addition, anyone caught obtaining a consumer credit report illegally can be sued by the consumer.

Also be aware that credit reports from the major credit-reporting agencies are rife with error. According to a 1991 Consumers Union report, almost 50 percent had one or more inaccuracies, and almost 20 percent had errors that could seriously impair a consumer's ability to obtain credit. Typical errors in credit files include the mixing of data from the files of two people with the same name and the inclusion in a consumer's file of data reflecting the fraudulent use of that person's identity and SSN by an imposter.

8.2 Alternatives to the Credit-Reporting Agency

There are three basic ways to compensate for the restrictions on consumer credit reporting while staying completely within the law and adhering to journalistic ethics. First, the portions of the credit-reporting agency file on an individual obtained from public records (e.g., Uniform Commercial Code [UCC] filings and judgment docket listings) are available directly from state or county records or from database vendors who are not part of the credit-reporting industry. You can obtain this information in person or by mail from the county or state, or from an online vendor.

Second, the Fair Credit Reporting Act does not restrict the dissemination of business credit information. Thus, if you are backgrounding a business-person, you can run a comprehensive online credit check on his or her known business entities. For instance, you can search business filings in all 50 states via Dun & Bradstreet's Legal Search database. And you can obtain D&B credit reports on over 9.5 million business locations and TRW credit reports on nearly 12 million locations via NewsNet. These reports, including payment histories, may give you a better picture of subject's overall financial status than any individual credit check would provide: Mr. Jones may always pay his household bills on time, yet his business may be on the brink of bankruptcy. For more information on backgrounding a business, see Chapter 13.

The third way to compensate for consumer credit-reporting restrictions is simply to do some leg work—dig into real-estate mortgage records at the register of deeds office, search the plaintiff/defendant index and case files at your local courthouse, interview former associates of your subject, and so on. In doing this you may miss some things that are in the credit bureaus' files, but you will collect much information—especially from little-known public records the credit bureaus rarely consult—that may give you an excellent picture of subject's finances.

8.3 Uniform Commercial Code Filings

Whenever an individual or a business entity borrows money or leases property or equipment using personal (nonreal) property as collateral, the lender or lessor fills out a Uniform Commercial Code (UCC) financing statement and sends it to the state's department of state. A copy is also usually filed with the county clerk's office in the county where the transaction occurred.

Any quick search at the county level should be followed by a search of the statewide files. In some states you can get the information over the phone either for free or for fees ranging up to $25 (these states include: Colorado, Florida, Idaho, Iowa, Kansas, Michigan, Mississippi, Missouri, Montana, Nebraska, Ohio, South Dakota, Texas, Utah, West Virginia, Wisconsin, and Wyoming). In most other states (and in the above states as well, if you want a certified copy), you must request a search in writing using a UCC-11 form (Request for Search) and enclosing the required fee. Within a few days you will receive an abstract of all UCC financing statements statewide in which your subject is listed as a debtor. (If you need such searches often, you can purchase UCC-11 forms in bulk from Julius Blumberg, Inc., in New York City; the same form can be used for most states.) Note that in several states a search can be ordered only through a private title search company.

You can obtain UCC filings in 19 states via Prentice Hall OnLine, which also offers document retrieval from state and county UCC files that are not available online. For a list of other online vendors and document retrieval services that perform UCC searches—and the states covered by each—see *The Sourcebook of Public Record Providers.*

At the minimum, you should check the UCC files for subject's state of residence and for any state in which subject conducts business or has a vacation home. If subject resides in a multistate metropolitan area, check each state (e.g., New Jersey and Connecticut should be checked for any down-state New York resident).

If you are checking county-level files yourself, note that if a debt has been satisfied the UCC statement will be discarded after a fixed period. If the debt is not satisfied, the statement will remain in the file indefinitely. The statement will tell you the name(s) and address(es) of debtor(s) and creditor(s), the date on which the financing statement was filed, and whether or not the obligation has been satisfied (i.e., paid in full); it will also describe the asset offered as collateral. This collateral may be something tangible (a car, truck, or computer, or the debtor company's "inventory") or it may be intangible (a patent, a franchise, or the debtor company's accounts receivable).

The UCC statement will not tell the amount of the loan, but if the collateral is a car of a certain year and model or a computer of a certain model you can obtain an estimate of its value (and hence of the loan) by calling the manufacturer or a used-car or used-equipment dealer.

Not all of subject's debts and obligations will be reflected in the UCC filings; there must be collateral involved. You will not find information here regarding most credit card debts, retail installment purchases, noncollateral bank loans, etc. Although information regarding mortgages and other debts involving real property as collateral are mostly to be found in county real estate records (see section 8.7), you may find some information in the UCC files about subject's real estate holdings if fixtures in a building owned by subject have been accepted as loan collateral.

The UCC filings should be regarded as a guide to further investigation. For instance, if the collateral offered by the borrower is an airplane or yacht, this will lead you to Federal Aviation Administration, U.S. Coast Guard, and state registration records. If the collateral is a painting, this may lead you into an examination of subject's relationship to the world of art dealers, galleries, and museums. If the collateral is a racehorse, you will want to learn more about subject's involvement in the world of horse breeding and racing. (The racing world has specialized databases through which you can find out when subject bought the horse and from whom, the name of the horse's sire, the track records of both horses, and a list of other horses subject owns.)

If the creditor is a private individual rather than a bank or finance company, this may reflect a significant personal or business relationship that you might not otherwise have learned about. If more than one debtor is listed on the financing statement, this may be a business partner of subject or else a relative who acted as guarantor for subject's loan.

If the UCC filings reveal that subject obtained a recent loan from a particular bank, this may be the same bank at which subject has his or her main checking and savings accounts (see section 8.19). If the loan comes from a finance company rather than a bank, this may indicate that subject has a mediocre credit rating.

The most detailed information on UCC filings is contained in *The Uniform Commercial Code Filing Guide,* a five-volume work (also on CD-

ROM) with quarterly updates covering all UCC filing offices nationwide. This work is available in large research libraries and online from WESTLAW.

8.4 Judgment Books

Money judgments obtained against your subject in the local courts are usually on file at the county clerk's office. Recent judgments may be listed in a computer index; older judgments are listed in annual ledger books (with separate books for judgments against individuals and corporations). The ledger books are permanent records—you can access them going back as far as you like.

In New York City, each judgment book entry tells the amount of the judgment, the name and address of both creditor and debtor (and often of creditor's attorney), the date of filing of the judgment, the court in which the judgment was obtained, the docket number of the case, and the date of satisfaction (if any). If the judgment was also obtained against another individual or individuals, a partnership, or a corporation, this will be recorded in the entry for your subject.

The judgment books, which also include city and state tax liens, are a rich source of leads. For instance, the individuals listed along with subject as the targets of a judgment may be business partners you had not known about. A judgment obtained against subject by a hospital may be your first clue that he or she has a serious medical problem.

If the state attorney general is listed as the creditor, this may mean the state has obtained a judgment against subject because of nonpayment of a fine resulting from an enforcement action penalizing him or her for illegal activity.

Other judgments may provide the names of subject's former customers, clients, vendors, or spouses. In one recent investigation, I checked the Manhattan judgment books going back 10 years and found the name and address of a woman who had obtained a judgment for several thousand dollars against subject (a Manhattan restauranteur) in a dispute over an item of jewelry she had lost in his restaurant. As it turned out, she and the restaurant owner had many friends and business associates in common; I was regaled with extremely interesting gossip.

The judgment books in the county clerk's office will cover actions in state district court (often called superior court) and in the county or municipal courts; the books may also record judgments from other localities. Federal court judgments generally are recorded separately at the federal district court. Once you have the docket number, you can obtain the case file.

Note that a judgment may be obtained as part of a fraudulent conspiracy between creditor and debtor. Let's say that Mr. X has borrowed large sums with the intent to declare bankruptcy and thus evade payment. He gets a crony to obtain a large judgment against him. When bankruptcy is declared, the crony has a secured prior lien and gets paid first out of money that otherwise would go to legitimate creditors after tax debts are satisfied. Later the crony returns the money to Mr. X minus his or her own cut.

The LEXIS Liens Library offers searches of the judgment dockets in all New York counties, some Illinois counties (including Chicago's Cook County), and Philadelphia County in Pennsylvania. Prentice Hall OnLine offers searches of county judgment dockets in California, Illinois, Texas, and several other states. Both Prentice Hall and Mead Data Central's LEX-DOC service offer manual searches and retrieval of judgment files throughout the United States. Other databases and retrieval services (and the states and/or counties covered) are listed in *The Sourcebook of Public Record Providers*.

8.5 Tax Lien Files

A tax lien filing will give the amount owed, the date of perfecting (e.g., the date the lien was obtained), and the date of satisfaction (if any). Corporate and individual tax liens are generally filed separately. Like UCC statements, they are retained as long as the lien is unsatisfied. Once it is satisfied, the card will be removed from the file after a fixed period.

The size of the tax liens will give you some clues as to subject's annual income, business difficulties, and so on. If Mr. A is known by you to have a modest-paying civil service job, but the IRS is after him for $50,000 in back taxes, this indicates other sources of income that you will want to track down. If Ms. B has accumulated several liens over the last few years, it may indicate her catering business is barely keeping afloat. In addition, the addresses listed on the cards, as you trace the liens through the years, may provide you with previously unknown former residential or business addresses of subject.

The LEXIS Liens Library offers access to federal and state tax liens for California and New York and for several counties (including Cook County) in Illinois. Prentice Hall OnLine covers tax lien files in most Western and Midwestern states. For searches elsewhere, see various document retrieval services listed in *The Sourcebook of Public Record Providers*.

8.6 Wage Assignments (Wage Garnishments) Index

This index is usually located at the county clerk's office, with indexing by date and alphabetically by assignor (the person whose wages have been assigned). In New York City, the index gives the amount originally owed, the names of assignor and assignee, and a file number. This may lead you to a judgment obtained locally or to an out-of-town judgment. In some localities, assignor's place of employment at the time of the wage assignment will be part of the public record. If not, you can perhaps obtain this information from the assignee.

8.7 Recorder of Deeds Office

The telephone white pages lists subject as living at a suburban address; checking in the crisscross directory, you see this is a private house. You want to know: Is subject the owner or a renter? If an owner, how much did he or she pay for the property? What is the size of each mortgage and who is/are the mortgagee(s)? Is subject in default on his or her mortgage payments and facing a foreclosure action? If subject is a renter, who is his or her landlord?

The real estate files in the recorder of deeds office are your key to answering such questions. First, you must obtain the block and lot number of the property from the plat maps or from the CD-ROM terminal. Next, check the index of mortgages and conveyances either in the ledger books or on CD-ROM for a brief description of each transaction regarding the property; the index will tell you who the current owner is and when and from whom this owner purchased the property. Some localities do not record the sale price, but you can often estimate it from the recorded real estate transfer tax if your state has such a tax (note that prior to 1965 there was a federal transfer tax that allowed for estimates within about $1,000 of the sale price).

Recorded with each transaction will be a file number (reel number and/or liber and page numbers) so you can access the actual deeds, surveys, and certain other documents (depending on the locality, this may include copies of mortgages and leases) on microform. Examination of deeds and other documents may be necessary in order to figure out who the grantor and grantee really are if straw names are being used (this will be more common in real estate speculation than in ordinary transactions involving purchase or sale of a home). In addition, the file may reveal varied information for backgrounding purposes: the name of a parent (if subject inherited the property), the name of a spouse or ex-spouse (if he or she is listed on the deed or mortgage), the name of subject's attorney, the name of the lending institution (this may be the bank where subject has his or her main account), and a specimen of subject's (and possibly of subject's spouse's) signature.

In general, mortgage payments are the dominant financial obligation in the lives of moderate-income homeowners, and the size, position (e.g., first or second), and timing of a mortgage may provide clues to many aspects of your subject's life. For instance, if subject and subject's spouse took out a second or third mortgage on their home in 1992, this may reflect business difficulties they were experiencing at the time, a major uninsured medical expense, the need to pay for a child's college education, etc. (It also may suggest a negative equity in the property, especially if coupled with a decline in the appraisal price.)

If mortgage documents are available in the files at your local recorder of deeds office, they may help you gain a better understanding of subject's overall financial situation. For instance, a blanket mortgage document will inform you about other real estate subject owns; a package mortgage may tell you about subject's personal as well as real property; a reverse mortgage will reveal to you that subject and his or her spouse have received cash in a lump sum (or are receiving cash monthly) that they will not have to pay back until they sell or move; and a Veterans' Administration (VA) mortgage will alert you that subject or subject's spouse is a veteran, with all the government benefits that flow from that status and indirectly affect subject's net worth.

The recorder of deeds office will also have an index of liens against real property by block and lot number. These may include mechanics' liens (resulting from nonpayment for services, labor, or materials for which subject contracted during the construction or repair of a house or other structure on the lot) and also liens resulting from violation of city or county ordinances (e.g., pest control liens and sidewalk, lot, or fence liens).

Also at the recorder of deeds office you will find the *Lis Pendens*—public notices of pending litigation that inform prospective buyers of a given property that a lien may be placed on it in the future. Here you will learn about mortgage foreclosure, tax foreclosure, and property condemnation proceedings, and also about divorce and inheritance cases in which the opposing parties are contesting the division of real property.

If foreclosure proceedings on subject's home have been started, don't jump to the conclusion that subject is about to be evicted into the street: Only about one in seven of these proceedings results in a judgment (and, in turn, only about one in seven judgments result in eviction). However, such proceedings do suggest that subject is experiencing financial difficulties at the moment, perhaps because of a job layoff or a major medical problem.

The recorder of deeds office may have an alphabetical roster of owners with listings of all properties owned by each of them. The clerks who compile these lists may be aware of corporate names used by a local landlord or developer and hence will list the property under his or her personal name as well as the corporate name. If the recorder of deeds office does not have such a list, the local real estate directory, available at your public library or at a real estate broker's office, may include this information for commercial and apartment rental properties at least (you look under the address and get the owner's name, then look under the owner's name and get a list of all the other properties he or she owns).

If you need an out-of-town search of real estate records (for instance, to see if subject owns any properties elsewhere in your region or to find out about the mortgage on his or her vacation home), your best bet is an online database vendor. The big name in real estate databases is TRW REDI Property Data, which provides online data on almost every property in over 300 counties in 34 states. (It also publishes this information on CD-ROM and in print directories, which will be available at your public library.) TRW REDI's subscribers include appraisers, real estate brokers, mortgage lenders, law firms, title companies, government agencies, and private investigators. Its Property Data Research Center call-in service will accept database search requests from nonsubscribers.

An amazing feature of TRW REDI's databases is its collection of low-altitude aerial survey photos of neighborhoods and communities across the country. Do you want to know if subject has a swimming pool in his or her backyard, and if so how big it is? Want a peek inside the carefully guarded mansion of Swami Sam the cult leader? Want an overview of a particular block so you can better plan your surveillance of George the Bigamist? With these photos you can look at the homes of subject and his or her neighbors, almost as if you had rented a helicopter.

(To find aerial photo records of localities not covered by TRW REDI, check the U.S. Geological Survey's Aerial Photography Summary Record System, which is a master index to over 12 million aerial photos taken by over 500 federal, state, and local government agencies and private companies.)

8.8 Condominium and Cooperative Ownership Lists

TRW REDI Property Data publishes a number of local directories that contain information about condos and co-ops. For instance, *The Record and Guide Quarterly* reports on condo sales in Manhattan and includes both a buyer's and seller's index. TRW REDI's real estate directories covering New York City and other localities include a listing of all condo owners alphabetically by name; you can thus see quickly if subject's apartment falls into this category (and if he or she got stuck with a bad investment when the real estate market crashed). As to cooperatives, TRW REDI's directories for New York will tell if a building has gone co-op but will not provide information on individual co-op owners. Since a large percentage of the occupants of New York cooperative apartment houses are rental tenants left over from pre-cooperative days, or are tenants renting from nonresident co-op owners, you shouldn't jump to conclusions about subject's financial worth just because he or she happens to live in a co-op building. However, if an occupant lived in the building before the co-oping occurred (which you can determine via the crisscross directory), he or she may have bought at an insider price. Depending on the present market value of the apartment, he or she may have more equity than one would think from looking at other personal worth and income indicators.

Note: In a co-op, buyers have shares in a cooperative corporation; in a condo, they have a deed to their apartment and own it outright. Co-op boards have far more control over such matters as whether you can rent out the apartment, establish a bed and breakfast, and so forth. Information on a co-op's rules, insider prices, etc., can be found in the files of the state agency that regulates cooperatives.

8.9 City or County Property Tax Records

These records are usually listed by date and by block and lot numbers. Once you have a list of the properties your subject owns, you should check the assessment rolls (land value and the total value for each lot), the tax abatement books (amounts of abatements for each block and lot), the tax rolls (assessed valuation, quarterly tax, total tax, abatements, arrears), and the tax registers (balance due, charges, payments). Increasingly, county assessors are including in these records the market-value estimates from which the assessed values are derived. In most counties, the water-meter charges and the sewer rental charges are filed in the same office as the tax assessment rolls.

Do not judge the owner's equity by the amount of taxes paid, since property-tax rates vary widely and often irrationally. As of 1993, the owner of a house valued at $200,000 in New York City would pay $1,574 in property taxes, while the owner of a co-op valued at $200,000 would pay $3,273. Also, do not judge equity by the assessed value, since this often differs widely from market value: Some towns in New York State (which does not require periodic reassessments) have not updated their property valuations in 30 years or more. Even with periodic reassessments, wide differences are often found in assessed values and equalization rates between communities of comparable socioeconomic status.

Always check to see if subject has filed a challenge of his or her tax assessment with the county's Board of Assessment Review; this can generate a significant paper trail, especially if the property owner is dissatisfied with the board's decision and appeals to the county court or state district court. Also, if subject is in arrears on his or her property taxes, check if the city or county has instituted foreclosure proceedings.

Don't forget the property tax records on subject's weekend or summer home, which will probably be located in another county or state. (A recent trend is to buy a vacation home at a location hundreds of miles from the primary residence, e.g., New Yorkers with vacation homes or condos at Hilton Head, South Carolina, rather than in the Hamptons on Long Island.) Note that many prosperous urban residents choose to live in rental apartments; their vacation home may be the *only* home they own (indeed, they may end up living in it year-round while telecommuting to their "virtual office" in the city). Note also that some suburbanites will own a city apartment either as a pied-à-terre or for the use of an elderly parent, a child in college, etc.

Property tax records may be searchable via CD-ROM at the local tax assessor's office. In addition, tax assessment records from the most populous counties in most states are available from online database vendors such as TRW REDI or Prentice Hall OnLine.

8.10 Bankruptcy Court Records

If your subject has recently filed for relief under the bankruptcy laws, you're in luck. The case file, kept at the bankruptcy court while the case is open (and thereafter at the nearest Federal Records Center), will provide a quite detailed picture of subject's income, liabilities, and assets, including personal property such as automobiles, computers, and stamp collections. (In 1992, a recession year, there were about one million individual bankruptcy filings in the United States.)

There are two types of individual bankruptcy filings: Chapter 7, which involves immediate liquidation of most assets in return for exemption of such necessities as a person's equity in his or her home and car and cancellation of most of his or her debts (which may be much larger than the liquidated assets); and Chapter 13, which involves reorganization of the person's debts and payment of all or part of the debt in installments over three years. Generally, a Chapter 13 filing will provide an investigator with more useful information than will a Chapter 7 filing.

Be sure to inspect bankruptcy records for corporations with which subject has been connected. These records may reveal his or her corporate salary at the time of bankruptcy, how much stock he or she owned in the corporation, and so forth. Chapter 11 bankruptcy proceedings are often the result of a well-thought-out scheme to defraud a corporation's vendors and other creditors. If your subject is a principal in the corporation, you should examine his or her role carefully.

Note that bankruptcy records in some federal court districts are indexed by creditor as well as debtor. When this is the case, you should search to see if subject is listed as a creditor (and be sure to look under the names of companies he or she owns or controls as well as under his or her own name). In filing his or her claims, subject may reveal significant bits of information about his or her finances and business affairs (not the least being subject's relationship to other creditors as well as to the debtor). Also, if the creditor's relationship to the debtor is a complex one, the documents filed by the debtor may include many direct and indirect leads regarding the creditor's own business affairs. (You might just call up the debtor and see if you can induce him or her to discuss this.)

The majority of federal bankruptcy court indexes nationwide are covered by the Voice Case Information System (VCIS), an automated system that enables you to search the court index from any touch-tone phone. Many bankruptcy courts are also linked to PACER (see section 9.3); if you sign up for online access through this government network you can search both indexes and docket sheets together.

Prentice Hall OnLine offers searches of bankruptcy court databases covering 40 states; its document retrieval service can search older records not included in these databases as well as the records of courts that are not yet online.

8.11 Probate Court Records

The local probate court is also a vital source of financial information if subject has inherited any money or property. Wills offered for probate are kept on public file, as are other records pertaining to the protection and transfer of the estate. Important documents to look for include the estate appraisal and the reports filed by the administrator or executor regarding payments to the heirs. If the will is contested, much information will become part of the public record that otherwise would remain private. Probate court records are generally indexed by the name of the decedent; thus, to find all records that might shed important light on your subject's finances, you will need the names of any deceased grandparents, parents, in-laws, or other close relatives who might have left property to subject, as well as the locations of the probate courts that handled these cases. (The Social Security Death Benefits Index is useful for this purpose.) Note that if decedent owned real estate in a state other than the one he or she lived in at the time of death, a separate probate may be necessary in the nonresident state.

8.12 Court Records of Civil Suits

Frequently, court records of civil suits will be the richest single source of information about an individual. See Chapter Nine for a description of the different types of court records and how to search them.

8.13 Federal and State Income Tax Returns and Related Information

If the Internal Revenue Service (IRS) has settled a claim against subject for less than the amount originally owed, then IRS Form 7249-M will be filed at the regional IRS office for one year and thereafter in Washington. This form will contain rather detailed information about subject's salary and other income, assets, and liabilities.

If subject's dispute with the IRS has found its way into the U.S. Tax Court in Washington, the case file will contain a wealth of financial documentation, including income tax returns, affidavits, depositions, and court testimony concerning subject's financial affairs. The case file is publicly available, but you'll have to go to Washington to examine it (or else hire a Washington researcher). To interpret it, you may need an accountant's help.

If subject is involved in civil litigation and his or her personal finances become relevant, federal and state tax returns may be produced during pretrial discovery and possibly entered in the case file; they may also be entered as evidence at trial. Be on the lookout, especially, for divorce cases involving alimony, child support, child custody, or property division; tax returns are often key evidence in such cases.

If subject is indicted on white-collar criminal charges such as securities fraud or income tax fraud, the prosecution may enter federal and state tax returns and other personal financial documents as evidence.

8.14 Securities and Exchange Commission Filings; State Securities Filings

A publicly held corporation's registration statement, prospectuses, proxies, Form 10-Ks (annual reports), and other Securities and Exchange Commission (SEC) filings are a crucial source of financial data about the firm's top officers, directors, insider owners, and beneficial owners of 5 percent or more of the shares. The data disclosed will include salaries of top officers and payments to directors as well as any personal financial transactions, gifts of stock, and so forth that might create a conflict of interest for officers or directors. In addition, you will find out the number of shares they own (see section 8.15) as well as the number of shares they hold in trust for their spouses, children, or grandchildren.

In Form S-1 registration statements, look at the sections on Management and Executive Compensation. Especially note the Summary Compensation Table (salaries, bonuses, stock awards, and stock option exercises) and the subsections on Employment Contracts, Profit Sharing, Retirement Plans (this will include a Pension Table), and Security Ownership. Also note any details you find regarding top executives' medical benefits, life insurance, accidental death and dismemberment insurance, long-term disability plans, and so forth.

Pay careful attention to the information regarding executive stock options, which are pledges by a company to issue a fixed number of shares to an executive at a fixed price for a fixed period. Although most corporations issue stock options to their top executives, the options are not always clearly reported as compensation expenses in the company's annual reports to its stockholders. Stock options are the major device by which a chief executive officer can inflate his or her income far beyond his or her reported salary, even when the company is not doing well.

The SEC monitors and requires filings from 12,000 broker-dealers and 5,000 investment companies as well as from 11,000 publicly held corporations. Broker-dealers and investment company officers must provide detailed financial information in the periodic statements they file with the SEC.

Additional information on the finances of corporate insiders, broker-dealers, and investment company officers may become available via an SEC investigation of securities violations. To find out if your subject (or a company in which he or she is involved) has ever been the target of such an investigation, consult the *Securities Violations Bulletin*, an SEC quarterly publication that is consolidated into volumes. Look in the index (or search on LEXIS) for subject's name and the names of relevant companies. If you find anything, write to the SEC for copies of the opening and closing reports of the investigation. If you then want other documents referred to in these reports, you may need to make a Freedom of Information request.

Note that the SEC regulates only those companies that trade stocks across state lines. State securities offices, however, regulate companies trading stocks within individual states. Like the SEC, they require public filings that may reveal information about the finances of a company's officers and directors. Many companies that file reports on the state level will never be required to file with the SEC. The state securities offices thus offer, at least in part, access to financial data regarding a different layer of the business community.

8.15 Disclosure/Spectrum Ownership Database

An excellent investigative tool for tracing the financial affairs of people in the corporate world is the Disclosure/Spectrum database available from DIALOG. Disclosure/Spectrum provides detailed ownership information (based on SEC filings) on about 5,000 publicly held companies. You can search by subject's name and find every instance in which he or she has been reported as an insider owner or 5 percent beneficial owner (i.e., owner as custodian or trustee) of shares in any of the companies in the database. The database will tell you the number of shares held, rank of this holding among those of other reported insiders, filing date, and the type of insider (e.g., chairman of the board, officer, director, trustee, beneficial owner as trustee, and so on; there are 24 relationship codes for types of insiders). Especially interesting is the ownership summary of total shares held by corporate insiders and the total market value in millions of dollars.

Much of the information in the Disclosure/Spectrum database is also contained in *Who's Wealthy in America* and *Who Owns Corporate America*—annual reference volumes published by The Taft Group, a division of Gale Research Inc. Data on insider transactions can also be gained via the SEC's own Securities Reporting System database available at computer terminals at the SEC's Public Reference Rooms in Washington, D.C., New York City, and Chicago.

8.16 Financial Data on Civil Servants, Elected Officials, and Government Appointees

Salary information is available on millions of Americans working at city, county, state, school district, or federal jobs. On the local and state level, there may be a salary roster giving each employee's base pay, overtime pay, and total pay for the year. If not, the job title of a civil servant, and the salary range for that title, will surely be on the public record. In addition, the city or state's pension plans and health insurance plans will be a matter of public record, so you can find out, in general, what kind of benefits subject and his or her fellow employees are entitled to.

On the federal level, the Freedom of Information Act entitles you to be told the job title, grade, salary, and duty station of most civilian employees; contact the department or agency at which subject is employed. If subject is a former federal employee, write: NPRC, Civilian Personnel Records Correspondence Section, 111 Winnebago Street, St. Louis, Missouri, 63118.

All elected officials on the federal level and most elected officials on the state and local levels must file periodic financial disclosure statements. In addition, about 10,000 federal political appointees, ranking civil servants, and congressional aides must file disclosures. Laws regarding disclosure by state and local legislative aides and executive appointees vary from locality to locality (in New York City, disclosure statements from all city employees earning over $30,000 per year are filed with the city clerk's office), but in general the salaries of such people are a matter of public record.

For salary and expenses of members of the U.S. House of Representatives, their staff members, committee staffers, and other House employees, see the quarterly *Report of the Clerk of the House*. For similar information on U.S. senators and Senate staffers and employees, see the biannual *Report of the Secretary of the Senate*. For salary information on approximately 3,000 top federal appointees, see *U.S. Policy and Supporting Positions* (the so-called Plum Book).

8.17 Financial Data on Candidates for Public Office

Every candidate for federal office and most candidates for state or local office must file campaign financing reports with a designated agency. On the federal level, the statements are kept by the Federal Election Commission; on the state and local levels, they are kept by state and local boards of elections. This holds for candidates in party primaries as well as general election candidates. Over 1 million Americans have filed such reports while pursuing public office over the years. Campaign financing reports will frequently reveal the names of contributors (both individual and corporate) with whom subject has had or will later have a close and often secretive business relationship. Vendors used by subject's campaign committee and consultants hired to help out subject's campaign may also fit into the picture of subject's ongoing business relationships (such information from Lyndon LaRouche's FEC filings in 1979 helped to prove his secret control of a major computer software company and his close business and political ties with several known associates of organized crime.)

8.18 Government Statistics and Other Indirect Indicators

If you think your subject is living beyond his or her means, you might attempt a rough estimate of his or her income via government wage and salary data.

The U.S. Labor Department's Bureau of Labor Statistics issues reports that tell the average earnings in hundreds of occupations and trades broken down by area of the country and type of firm. The bureau's annual multi-volume *Area Wage Survey* and its monthly *Employment and Earning* are the standard guides to this type of data. Further statistical breakdowns are available from the bureau's databases (contact its public affairs office for advice on this).

For still more detailed information, contact your state's labor information office. State labor departments often track as many as 1,000 occupations on the county as well as the state level, using the quarterly unemployment contribution reports from every employer in every county as a basis for their statistics.

If subject belongs to a labor union, its contract with subject's employer will stipulate wages, linkage of wages to years of service, overtime rates, hours, and various benefits. Union contracts are often available from either the state or federal labor department. The Bureau of Labor Statistics has a file of over 5,000 of these contracts (including almost every agreement covering bargaining units of 1,000 or more workers) while the Federal Mediation and Conciliation Service maintains a database of collective bargaining agreements that is searchable by company name.

Data for estimating a person's earnings is also available from many other sources. For instance, the U.S. Education Department's annual Higher Education General Information Survey (HEGIS) compiles information on academic salaries by rank and contract length at individual colleges and universities. The reports provided by each school can be obtained from the National Center for Educational Statistics, the state board of higher education, or the school itself. Other excellent sources are the nation's professional and trade organizations, many of which publish detailed salary and benefit data according to job category, region, and other indices; for example, the American Payroll Association's biennial *Survey of Salaries and the Payroll Profession*.

A knowledge of the statistics on local wages, salaries, and fringe benefits may help you avoid hasty assumptions. For example, attorneys are generally regarded as a high-income group, especially by fans of the TV show "L.A. Law." Yet many attorneys in your region (especially those working as public defenders or assistant D.A.s) may earn less money than do unionized blue-collar workers in certain job categories.

Be aware, in using wage statistics, that most people have other sources of income besides their primary jobs, and wages from primary jobs often fluctuate. Millions of people work overtime at irregular, unpredictable intervals, thus boosting their annual income significantly. Millions more work at trades that involve seasonal layoffs. Others work two full-time jobs, often keeping this fact secret from one or both of their employers. Still others may do part-time moonlighting (e.g., police officers who double as private security guards). A person working at a moderate-income job may have sizeable investments as a result of savings through the years, an inheritance, or a dead spouse's life insurance. In addition, the homemaker in subject's family may be boosting the family income through a part-time job or office temp work, or the family may be benefitting from some special situation (e.g., a rent-controlled apartment in New York City that costs only 10 percent of the family's annual income). To make matters even more confusing, there's the problem of the underground cash economy: The subject you believe is living beyond his or her means may gain extra income from growing marijuana on the family farm. Or the extra income (exaggerated in your mind) may actually be the modest receipts from weekend yard sales. In speculating about someone's income, take nothing for granted; always assume that there's something you don't yet know.

8.19 Bank Account Records

A bank will not tell you how much money subject has in his or her accounts or any other details without subject's permission. However, someone with a clear need to know—such as a potential employer or landlord—may be told whether or not subject has an account at that branch and whether or not the account is "satisfactory" (i.e., is not overdrawn). In addition, someone who calls up the bank and claims that he or she has been given a check by subject (say, for $1,000) may be told whether or not subject's balance will cover it. (This might not work if the caller is unable to furnish subject's account number as listed on subject's checks.)

8.20 Loan, Job, and Apartment Applications; Résumés

In researching a subject's background assiduously, you may from time to time come across a copy of a loan, job, or apartment rental application—or a résumé—filled out by subject in the recent past. Such a document may provide some interesting details about subject's salary history and other financial matters, although applicant will probably have slanted the information to present himself or herself in the most favorable light.

Note that an unscrupulous investigator might pose on the phone as a personnel agency headhunter to persuade subject to send in a résumé to an agency that is really a mail drop. Likewise, such an investigator might call up subject in the guise of a loan officer or apartment rental agent to inform him or her about a seemingly miraculous low-interest loan or low-rent apartment that is available if and only if subject acts fast. In most cases, subject will then eagerly supply the investigator with application information over the phone.

8.21 Credit Card Records

Records of credit card transactions are confidential. If your subject is an elected official, political appointee, or civil servant, however, you can make a Freedom of Information request for access to the records of the city, state, or federal government credit card(s) he or she uses.

8.22 Financial Information from Subject's Garbage

This is really a word of warning to readers: If you throw out credit card receipts, monthly credit card statements, bank statements, or cancelled checks, a private investigator (or a thief) can sift through your garbage (see section 11.4) and obtain these documents.

Once investigators have your bank account and credit card account numbers (and if they also have basic identifying information such as your SSN, date of birth, residential zip code, telephone number, and mother's maiden name) they can call up the customer information number, pretend to be you, and find out your current bank account and credit card account balances, your total and available credit limits (including cash advance limits), information on your money market accounts, and so forth. Often they won't have to speak to anyone; they'll just use a touch-tone phone to get the information from an automated account information system.

If your garbage also contains old telephone or gas and electric bills with the account numbers on them, the unscrupulous snoop—if he or she is trying to gauge whether or not you are experiencing financial difficulties—will call up the telephone and gas and electric companies in your name to find out how much you owe, how many months behind you are in your payments, and whether or not you are or recently have been on a deferred payment plan.

Moral of the story: Don't throw out financial documents or, if you must throw them out, shred them first.

8.23 Financial Information on Nonprofit Employees and Consultants

Federal 990 forms filed with the IRS by charities and other tax-exempt organizations may contain salary and expense disbursement information regarding the organization's top officers and also the amounts paid to outside counsel and consultants. If the organization is the recipient of federal grants, it must file additional information about the finances of officers and consultants with the agency or agencies providing the grants.

You should also check the tax-exempt organization's annual filings with the state's department of state.

8.24 Financial Information on Labor Union Officials and Employees

Forms LM-2 and LM-3, filed by union locals and higher union bodies with the U.S. Department of Labor, will tell you the salaries and disbursements paid to each union officer regardless of amount and to each union employee who received more than $10,000 from the union in the given year. These reports will also list all direct or indirect loans of more than $250 made by the union to any union officer, employee, or member, or to any other person or business.

Form LM-30 is a detailed financial disclosure form that union officers and employees must submit if they or their spouses or children have business dealings with a firm whose employees are represented by the union in question. It may include important information about a union official's outside sources of income, his or her investments and debts, and so forth.

8.25 Financial Information on Philanthropists and Other Wealthy People

Numerous reference works have been published to help charities and charitable institutions identify potential donors. To gain background financial information on the wealthy, just go to the following Taft Group publications: *Who's Wealthy in America* (profiles of 103,000 individuals including data on their stock ownership); *Who Owns Corporate America* (comprehensive listings of over 75,000 insider stockholders); *Owners and Officers of Private Companies* (information on 105,000 individuals that you won't find in any SEC filings); *Major Donors* (data on over 16,000 philanthropists and their major gifts); *Guide to Private Fortunes* (a three-volume set profiling thousands of generous donors); and *New Fortunes* (profiles of prospective donors with a net worth of at least $2 million). All except the last two are published annually.

Information on ownership of yachts and summer estates may be found in *Social Register Summer* (for more on yacht ownership, see the *Register of American Yachts*). For information on art collectors, see *Who's Who in American Art*.

8.26 Ownership of Airplanes, Boats, Cars, and Other Valuable Personal Property

Nationwide files of FAA aircraft registrations and U.S. Coast Guard merchant and recreational vessel registrations are available from Prentice Hall OnLine and LEXIS. In addition, subject's ownership of an aircraft, boat, or other valuable personal property may be recorded in the "grand lists" at the county clerk's office. You should also check with the state agency, if any, that registers recreational vehicles (from snowmobiles to dune buggies), mobile homes, and motorized pleasure craft (note that LEXIS offers online searches of Florida boat registrations). And don't forget the department of motor vehicles (DMV) files: Family cars are an important element in the net worth of ordinary working families, while ownership of a late-model Mercedes or Cadillac may be a significant factor in the net worth of a well-to-do person. DMV databases can give you a list of all cars registered in the name of subject or any member of subject's household together with the liens on any of these vehicles.

8.27 Corporate, Partnership, and D/B/A Files

If you know of businesses that subject owns or is affiliated with (say, from a civil court case or a judgment docket entry) you may find much valuable information in the state or county business files (see section 13.1). For instance, if subject is a limited partner in a real estate investment, the partnership agreement may contain information as to how many shares he or she owns. It may also contain information about shares owned in the names of subject's spouse and children. And the list of limited partners may include the names of business associates of subject about whom you would not otherwise have learned. (If you do a little paper trailing of some of these associates you may learn about other ventures in which subject is involved.)

If you do not know the names of any of subject's business entities, try checking under his or her surname (e.g., the Richardson Organization) or under the wife's or daughter's first name (e.g., the Lucille Cab Company). You should also check out businesses which include subject's initials either in capital letters or in phonetic form. For instance, in searching for local real estate companies controlled by one Lawrence Cole, check the records for any entities with names such as "LC Enterprises," "Elcee Corporation," or "El Cee Incorporated."

To find nonprofit entities established by subject (either in the state corporate files or in the IRS's *Cumulative List of Organizations*) try combinations such as the following: the Johnson Foundation, the Johnson Family Foundation, the James and Sarah Johnson Foundation, the Sarah and James Johnson Foundation, the James T. and Sarah E. Johnson Foundation, and so forth. (Of course, if you are searching records online or on CD-ROM you can begin by getting a printout of all listings that contain the name "Johnson.")

9.

Court Records

9.1 Introducing the Court System

Researching court records is a complicated matter due to the wide variety of courts and records systems. If you are starting out as an investigative journalist, one of your first steps should be to familiarize yourself with each court located in or having jurisdiction over your city, county, and greater metropolitan area, and learn how to use the various court indexes to maximum effect.

The trial courts in any locality are divided into local courts and district state courts on the one hand and federal courts on the other. Each has civil and criminal divisions and a system of higher courts to which appeals are made.

The lowest level of a state court system is the village, town, city, or county court, which handles relatively minor matters—say, claims of up to $10,000, and misdemeanors like prostitution and driving while intoxicated. These local courts, which usually do not offer jury trials, go by many names: magistrate's court, district court, city court, or superior court. Some may have specialized jurisdictions, for example, small claims court (to handle claims of $1,000 or less), traffic court, or landlord–tenant court. These courts exist throughout every state, although their names and functions may vary from town to town within a single state according to local custom.

The next level is the state courts, which offer jury trials of larger monetary claims (say, claims of over $10,000) and the more serious criminal offenses. Anyone disputing a city court judge's decision will also come here for a trial de novo (new trial). These state courts, each of which may have jurisdiction over one or more counties, are referred to, variously, as the district court, superior court, county court, circuit court, or state supreme court (note the overlap in terminology with the municipal courts). Various specialized divisions are usually included in this level of the court system; for instance, the probate court (also known as surrogate's court), which handles the probate of wills, administration of estates, and appointment of guardians; and family court, which handles child custody cases and various other marital and family disputes (and, in some localities, juvenile criminal cases).

The federal court of original jurisdiction is the U.S. district court, which may cover an entire state or several counties within a state (e.g., the U.S. District Court for the Southern District of Iowa). Most federal district courts have more than one court location (or "division"); for instance, the Iowa southern district has a Council Bluffs division, a Davenport division, and a Des Moines (headquarters) division. Federal district courts handle suits brought by or against the federal government and other civil cases involving federal law. They are also the trial courts for all federal criminal violations.

The U.S. bankruptcy courts handle all bankruptcies of individuals and businesses. Generally they follow the same territorial lines as the U.S. district courts, but within these lines the bankruptcy court may have fewer court locations or divisions. For instance, the U.S. District Court for the Northern District of New York (NDNY) includes four divisions, while the U.S. Bankruptcy Court covering the same area has only two divisions. Federal district courts and bankruptcy courts will usually have their headquarters at the same court location (e.g., Albany for the NDNY).

9.2 Working with Court Indexes

Each court keeps indexes of all civil and criminal cases brought before it. In some courts, the indexes for the most recent years may be searchable at a computer terminal. In others, you may have to look through bound computer printout volumes. In still others, the indexes may be on microfiche, in an automatic rotating card file, or even (for older local records) entered in ledger books. Criminal court cases are listed by defendant; bankruptcy cases, by petitioner (either debtor or creditor); probate actions, by the decedent's name. Civil suits are listed alphabetically by either plaintiff or defendant, although some courts have both a plaintiff/defendant and a defendant/plaintiff index (or else one index that merges both in a single alphabetical listing in which each case appears at least twice—this is called a "party index"). In general, the plaintiff/defendant or defendant/plaintiff index will list only the first-listed plaintiff and first-listed defendant in multiparty cases.

Some computerized indexes and some microfiche indexes generated from the printouts of computerized indexes will list all parties (if a system combines index and docket information in a single database it almost certainly will be all-party searchable). Computerized systems are not available in every trial court, however, and where they do exist the coverage usually doesn't extend back very many years. If you want the names of those 10 other plaintiffs in the 1981 product liability suit *Barnett et al. v. Ace Toys*, you will have to go to the docket sheet or the case file.

To find all the local civil suits involving your subject in a nonelectronic index requires considerable ingenuity if there is no cross index and/or if indexing is restricted to the first-listed parties. Yet this type of search—not only for active cases but also for closed or dormant cases from past decades —is often of vital importance in investigative journalism. This is especially true in tracking a corrupt politician or an organized crime figure; the conspiracies in which such people are involved often go way back, and today's trickery may be understandable only in the light of courtroom revelations from a decade or more ago.

The following are some methods you might find useful in getting around the limitations of your local court indexing systems. These methods (which should be used in tandem with LEXIS searches and other techniques described in section 9.3) are intended for the most difficult type of search— to find cases involving your subject in an index in which the cases are listed alphabetically by first-named plaintiff only, with no cross indexing by defendants.

- Look up all cases in which the state or city is the plaintiff. Depending on local practice, these may be listed under "People of ———," "State of ———," or "City of ———," or possibly under the official designation of the state or city attorney (e.g., "Anystate Attorney General," "Anystate Department of Law"). Under the most commonly used of these government plaintiff headings, you may find hundreds of defendants listed in alphabetical order.

- Flip through the plaintiff indexes, looking for examples of plaintiffs who file massive numbers of cases. In the metropolitan and/or state district court indexes of any large city, hundreds of defendants may be listed alphabetically opposite the name of the city hospital corporation and other public and private entities that deal with consumer debt problems on a large scale.

- Go to the judgment books (see section 8.4). If a private or governmental plaintiff has obtained a judgment against your subject in the local courts, the case file number will be listed alongside subject's name.

- Whenever you find subject listed as one of several plaintiffs or defendants, check the names of the other parties separately in the index to find other cases that might include subject as a party.

- Whenever you find a case involving subject, look on the docket sheet and in the case file for references to other lawsuits. Especially look for countersuits or cross suits. Examine the transcript, if any, of subject's deposition or court testimony to see if he or she was asked about previous litigation. Also, check directly with the other parties (or their attorneys); they may be aware of cases you would otherwise miss.

- Look in newspaper and business periodical databases and clippings files for reports of any lawsuits involving subject.

- Check for "bad blood" suits. If you learn from the plaintiff index that your subject is suing Mr. X, check to see if Mr. X has independently sued your subject about another matter.

- Use the federal court party index to find possible leads to state court cases indexed only by plaintiff. A person who is suing your subject in federal court might have sued him or her on a related or entirely separate matter in state court.

- Follow clues that emerge from other aspects of your investigation. For instance, check in the plaintiff index under the names of subject's ex-spouses or ex-lovers, former business partners (especially in businesses that went bankrupt), political rivals, and others. They may be suing subject or current associates of subject. Any time you find an antagonist or associate of subject listed as a first-named plaintiff or first-named defendant, check the docket sheet or the case file to see if subject is one of the unindexed parties. (All this should apply to any businesses linked to subject as well as to individuals.)

- Check the bankruptcy court index to see if subject or his or her business has ever been involved in a bankruptcy proceeding, either as debtor or creditor. Debtors in bankruptcy cases must file with the court a list of all outstanding judgments against them and all pending litigation in which they are involved in any jurisdiction.

Note that when you are searching court indexes that are not online (e.g., microform, CD-ROM, or bound computer printout volumes), you should always search any supplements produced since the last cumulation.

9.3 Finding Cases in Other Jurisdictions

Your subject may have moved around a lot or may do business in many states simultaneously. How can you identify cases involving him or her in localities other than your own?

Begin by searching for subject's name in LEXIS. This giant collection of legal databases covers most of the decisions handed down by the nation's federal and state appeals courts since the last century. It also covers trial court decisions in New York and Ohio dating back many years, as well as decisions in the U.S. Tax Court and other specialized federal courts. You can search court decisions by state (e.g., the LEXIS Maryland Library) or by type of case (the LEXIS Family Law Library); you can also seek news articles about litigation involving subject in the LEXIS/NEXIS News and Business Library (over 2,300 full-text information sources).

Author Steve Weinberg used LEXIS and its competitor, WESTLAW, in researching his unauthorized Armand Hammer biography. He located about 300 cases involving Hammer and/or close associates and relatives of the oil tycoon. Reading over the judges' decisions, Weinberg selected certain cases that seemed to warrant further digging. He then went to the various courthouses or Federal Records Centers to examine the case files and photocopy selected portions.

The cases searched via LEXIS will represent only a tiny fraction of those filed nationally each year, most of which either don't go to trial or don't get appealed. A case that does get appealed is often a richly complicated one, however, and the case file may be full of juicy revelations.

As an alternative to using LEXIS, you can search the case law digests in your county bar association's law library. For federal court cases, see *West's Federal Practice Digest*. For state cases, see the various state digests. For New York State, one would go to *West's New York Digest 4d* (for cases since 1978), *West's New York Digest 3d* (for cases from 1961 to 1978), and *Abbott New York Digest 2d* (cases before 1961). Both *West's* and *Abbott* have plaintiff/defendant and defendant/plaintiff tables. Note that case law digests give comprehensive coverage only of appeals court decisions. Trial court rulings may be covered, however, if they involve significant points of law.

To find cases that never went to trial or were never appealed, you must go directly to the court index. Generally this must be done court by court, although online searches of multiple court indexes are available for some localities via LEXIS or other online public records providers (see below), and some federal district courts will have the indexes for several nearby district courts on microfiche.

Searchers can access court indexes in person, by mail, by telephone (in some localities), or via modem if the court has an online electronic index. The case file itself generally can be obtained only in person or by a mail request to the court clerk (the latter's staff will photocopy and certify the case file or individual documents therein for you). Often it is best to hire a document search service to handle index searching and document retrieval in person at a distant courthouse. This type of help is especially useful if you don't know the case number or year of filing, or if you need a thorough search of older noncomputerized indexes, or if you need the entire court file photocopied quickly.

Court indexes/dockets from over 50 U.S. district courts and bankruptcy courts are now searchable via the online PACER (acronym for Public Access to Court Electronic Records) system or via online systems that predate PACER. In most districts, PACER costs $1 per minute, but in a few districts it's free.

Note that cases closed before a particular district court's index was computerized will usually not be included in the electronic database.

The Sourcebook of Federal Courts (see bibliography) will give you the number to call to register on PACER for a particular court district, as well as information about mail and/or phone searches, search fees, turnaround time, and the length of time between a case being closed and the file being transferred to the nearest Federal Records Center.

Note that the indexes/dockets of the several divisions (court locations) within a single federal court district may not always be linked into a single electronic system. In addition, the microfiche and other nonelectronic indexes at a particular court division may not cover the other divisions within the given district. Always ask if separate searches are necessary for each division. Of course, even if the index/docket is an all-district one, you will still have to go to the division in which the case was filed to obtain the case file (unless the case was transferred to another division).

If a case has been assigned a number beginning with the letters "MDL," which stands for Multi District Litigation, you will know that the judicial panel on multi-district litigation in Washington, D.C., has consolidated this and other cases into a single action. Typically, such consolidation is effected to handle numerous product liability suits involving the same product and the same defendant manufacturer(s).

Federal court cases are only a tiny fraction of the total number of cases filed on all levels of the American court system. The real heart of court-records searching is at the county level (county and municipal courts plus state trial courts). For detailed information on how to obtain index and file searches of these courts in every county in the United States, consult *The Sourcebook of County Court Records*. It tells what is on computer and how far back the computer records go, as well as covering mail and telephone search requests. It also includes a city/county cross-reference index.

The LEXIS Docket Library covers court indexes and dockets for the state district courts in metropolitan-area counties of California, Illinois, New York, and Pennsylvania. It also covers, for some counties of these states, the county/municipal court indexes as well as the judgment dockets and lien files.

If electronic searches of the court index are not available for a particular county, you may nevertheless be able to search online the judgment docket for that county. Prentice Hall OnLine offers electronic searches of judgments in over 20 states. *The Sourcebook of Public Record Providers* (see bibliography) lists search services and information brokers in every state and region that handle judgment and lien searches.

If you find a judgment against subject in a certain county's judgment docket, it will include the docket number by which you can access the case file. You might not want to bother with the case file if the judgment was for only a trivial amount of money, but it may be that the person who obtained that small $500 judgment is subject's next-door neighbor who has long feuded with subject. He or she will know far more about subject than will the business creditor who may have obtained a $25,000 judgment but for whom subject is just a faceless name on a piece of paper.

Note that the judgment dockets will *not* help you find court cases that never went to judgment, including those settled out of court, or in which subject was adjudged not to owe any money. In other words, a search of judgments will miss the overwhelming majority of court cases.

Besides searching court indexes and judgment dockets, you can find court cases involving subject via newspaper and periodical databases. A case with general news interest will usually be reported in the daily press; cases with specialized news interest may be reported in regional or local business or trade publications. A search of these databases often will turn up several cases not found in LEXIS or WESTLAW. For instance, a divorce case involving a certain movie star may have zero interest as case law and thus not be reported in any legal database, but you may find a hundred references to it in DataTimes or NEXIS databases covering tabloid newspapers and popular general-interest magazines.

9.4 Obtaining the Civil Case File

In many courts, there will be separate civil indexes for individuals and corporations. The index will tell you the date the case was filed, the name of the first-listed plaintiff, the name of the first-listed defendant, and a docket number. It will also tell you if the case is still pending or if it is closed. You can then fill out a requisition form and give it to the clerk in the file room, who will bring you the file.

Always tell the clerk that you want *all* the folders in the case file, including any supplemental folders with depositions in them. If certain of the documents listed in the docket sheet of an open case are not in the case folder(s), they are probably in the judge's chambers. To make an appointment to examine them, call the judge's law clerk.

If the case is closed, the file may be on microfiche or stored in an archive at another location. The files of closed federal court cases are usually sent to the regional Federal Records Center. To access the files there, you must first get the case locator numbers of the file boxes from the originating court. Note that after a period of 20 to 30 years, records at the Federal Records Center are transferred to the National Archives and Records Administration's regional archives.

Don't expect to find too much beyond the original pleadings in the court file of your average closed case. Of all civil cases, about 97 percent nationwide are settled with very little court involvement. Often in an out-of-court settlement, the parties will agree to keep secret the conditions of the settlement, including the amount of money paid by defendant to plaintiff (this is especially important to defendants in product liability and medical malpractice cases). The agreement may also include a court order sealing all records of the discovery process and perhaps even the entire court file. (During the early 1990s, some states moved to reverse this widespread practice, barring secret settlements and the sealing of discovery records in cases involving potential threats to public safety and health. Of course, such legislation cannot unseal records sealed prior to the passage of the legislation.)

If a case is appealed, all or part of the trial court file is sent to the appeals court. Locating the portion you need can get rather complicated (especially if an appeal is on its way from a lower to higher appeals court). The portion of the file at a particular appeals court can usually be examined there by a news reporter. After the appeals court decision, the file is sent back to the trial court's file room (and from there to the court archives) unless there is a further appeal. The briefs filed with the appeals court (which sometimes bring out facts not found in the trial court case file) are usually sent to a depository library.

One might think from the above discussion that chasing down court papers can be extremely time consuming. Fortunately, there is often a shortcut. You call up one of subject's opposing parties in the case (or their attorney). The attorney may have the complete file in his or her office, if the case is still open. If the case is closed, the attorney may still have the file, or the client may have taken it home. Note that this file will frequently have deposition transcripts and documents produced under discovery that are missing from the courthouse file.

9.5 Studying the Case File

You may find that a case that began several years ago is still open, yet the folder contains almost nothing except the original affidavit of service, plaintiff's complaint, and defendant's reply. In such instances, the plaintiff may have simply decided not to pursue the case. Or there may have been a delay because of a crowded court calendar, the obstructionist tactics of defendant's attorney, or the dilatoriness of plaintiff's attorney (for these and other reasons, civil cases often don't go to trial until several years after the filing). If a case is being vigorously pursued, however, the folders may be filled to overflowing with motions, countermotions, and other legal documents. Some of these will contain useful facts; others will be (for your purposes) legal mumbo jumbo. The case docket sheet is your guide to the case file—it lists in chronological order all papers filed, appearances, process served, orders, etc. Although the docket can be confusing to a nonlawyer, a good rule of thumb is always to examine the original pleadings (the plaintiff's complaint against the defendant and the defendant's reply) and attached exhibits, any affidavits dealing with the substance of the complaint, and any pretrial discovery materials (especially depositions). Get these records while you can: Most such cases will be settled before trial (see section 9.4) and the settlement may include the sealing of the court file.

If the trial has already occurred, the transcript (if one was ever made) will probably not be included in the file unless the case was appealed. If you want the transcript, and can't get it from any of the parties, you will have to order it from the court reporter at a cost, possibly, of thousands of dollars. For this, if for no other reason, appeals cases are extremely important for an investigator: The party who is appealing must order a transcript and usually will file it (or significant portions of it) with the appeals court.

As of 1994, courts in about 20 states are using videotape (albeit to a limited extent) to replace or supplement the court reporter's transcript. The cost to the court for a videotape of the day's proceedings is minimal, and copies are often deposited in the case file.

9.6 Pretrial Discovery

Often, the most valuable material will surface during pretrial discovery—the process by which each side seeks information from the other to clarify issues and strengthen its own case. For an investigative reporter, this material may be more important than the trial transcript itself, because pretrial discovery is much more freewheeling than a trial in respect to the questions that can be asked and the evidence that can be collected. The reason for this is that pretrial discovery is not limited by the rules of admissibility at trial, the judge's rulings about specific evidence or testimony, or the plaintiff's and/or defendant's desire to avoid laying certain facts before the jury. During pretrial discovery, all sorts of things come out that a jury would never be allowed to hear.

Pretrial discovery involves the following procedures that are conducted according to federal or state court rules of civil procedure:

- Discovery and inspection of documents: A party to the action serves process on another party demanding the production of business correspondence and other documents relevant to the issues at law. In a corporate suit, thousands of pages of correspondence, internal memoranda, and financial records may be produced for inspection and copying. In a libel suit, the plaintiff may demand to inspect and copy the reporter's notes and article drafts and any documents on which the reporter's allegedly libelous statements were based. Documents produced under discovery will not be found in the court file unless filed in support of a motion or as deposition or trial exhibits (see below). If the documents produced are not covered under a permanent protective order, however, you may be able to examine them after the settlement or trial at the offices of the attorneys for the party that conducted the discovery and inspection.

- The posing and answering of interrogatories: A party to the action serves written questions on an opposing party which the latter must answer in writing under oath. Interrogatories are often used as a means to identify documents that will then be demanded under an order to produce.

- The taking of oral depositions (also known as Examinations Before Trial, or EBTs): In a deposition, a person answers questions under oath from the attorneys for one or more parties, and the proceedings are recorded by a court reporter. The person questioned (called the deponent) may be a party to the action or a nonparty with knowledge of relevant facts. In cases that are settled before trial, the deposition is the closest thing to actual court testimony you will find. Some of the questions posed in a deposition will be designed to gain broad background information (thus, the deponent's attorney may complain on the record that the attorney taking the deposition is on a "fishing expedition"). Depositions can go on for days, generating thousands of transcript pages. Unfortunately for journalists, these transcripts are not always filed with the court, although brief excerpts may be included in support of a motion or brief. The rules of procedure regarding public access to deposition transcripts vary widely in both state and federal jurisdictions. For instance, in some jurisdictions transcripts of depositions and exhibits marked for identification therein must be filed with the clerk of the court for public inspection unless there is a protective order. In other jurisdictions, they are not filed *except* by judicial order.

Note that court reporters in recent years have begun to provide attorneys with deposition transcripts on disk rather than on paper; you should get a copy of the disk if possible so you can search the deposition by key words and combine it into your larger database (see section 3.3). In addition, many depositions nowadays are being videotaped; the attorneys for both sides can thus replay a segment over and over to study the expression on the deponent's face and the tone of his or her voice as well as the verbal content of his or her statement.

If the court file does not contain much in the way of pretrial discovery facts, it at least may give you an idea of what types of documents were produced and what lines of questioning were pursued. (Indeed, a motion to compel production of documents may itemize exactly which documents are being demanded.) You can then try to get access from a friendly party. However, you may find that the party who is the target of a particular discovery process has obtained a court order stipulating that access to documents, deposition transcripts, and interrogatory answers will be limited to the parties in the case (or sometimes just to the parties' attorneys) and the judge. On occasion, however, this will only be a temporary order; the materials will show up in the court file or can be easily obtained from one of the parties after the case is settled.

9.7 Dealing with Subject's Opponents at Law

The attorneys for your subject's opponent may be your best source for copies of depositions and other pretrial discovery materials as well as the trial transcript. Often the attorneys will let you examine or copy documents if you have information to trade, or if they think you might write an article favorable to their client's viewpoint, or if they're simply curious to see what you might dig up.

Once the appeals are over and the case is closed, the attorney may give the case file to the client, who takes it home and tosses it in a closet. If you want to know about subject's divorce, and your state bars public access to divorce filings, you might approach the ex-spouse to see if he or she would be willing to dig the papers out of the closet. (The case file in a legal battle over division of property, child support, alimony, and so forth can be extremely revealing about the finances of one or both parties.)

Even if you don't need their help in obtaining deposition transcripts and other documents, it's still useful to talk with subject's opponents at law. They may give you much valuable information off the record. While backgrounding a certain businessman a few years ago, I found a single case in the court index in which he was being sued for fraud. Meeting with the plaintiff's attorney, I was treated to a fascinating lecture on subject's corporate veil and his ties to organized crime, based mostly on private investigators' reports and confidential internal documents of subject's business entities. I learned more about subject in that one session than during weeks of prior research.

9.8 Criminal Court Records

Arrest and Conviction Records

Criminal records are kept by county and municipal courts and state trial courts (which all send data regarding convictions to a central state repository) and by federal trial courts. Each criminal court will have an index listing the defendants alphabetically and telling the charge, the disposition (if any), and the case file number.

Public access to arrest and conviction records varies from county to county as well as from state to state. In general, if a person has been convicted of a felony or misdemeanor (or if the case is still pending), this information can be found in the criminal court index, although in some localities you will need a release to obtain a records search. If the person was acquitted or the case was dropped, the record usually will be expunged.

In attempting to find out if someone has a criminal record, there are two basic approaches: searching the records of the state repository, or searching at the county (trial court) level. If you search the state repository (assuming these records are available without a release), you will miss many cases—the trial courts at the county level are often negligent or tardy in forwarding data to the state repository, and some state repositories do not accept misdemeanor or lesser felony records. On the other hand, if you just search the records in subject's home county, you may get reliable results for that county, but you'll miss subject's felony conviction in a neighboring county.

Experts at backgrounding suggest that you always search both the state re-pository and the trial courts of those counties where subject is most likely to have gotten into trouble.

The Guide to Background Investigations describes the procedures for ob-taining a criminal records search from every county and every central state repository in the nation. It tells which jurisdictions will provide information only by mail and which will provide it by phone. The book also gives the separate procedures for obtaining misdemeanor and felony records and tells which jurisdictions require a release. Finally, it includes city/county cross-references so you can match any city with the county courthouse that con-trols its criminal records.

You can also find out from *The Guide to Background Investigations* how to obtain a criminal records search of federal district court files. Note that you can search criminal indexes/dockets in some districts via PACER, but not for cases prior to the early 1990s (for thorough backgrounding in a given district, you are thus advised to order a full search by mail or via a documents search service).

If you think your subject is or has been a federal prison inmate, you can call the Inmate Locator Line at (202) 307–3126. Give them subject's name, and they will tell you if this name is in the database, which covers inmates back to 1981. If the name is in the system, the locator service will provide you, over the phone, with conviction, sentencing, and parole information and will tell you where subject is or was incarcerated. (For records prior to 1981 you must make a special request.)

Another shortcut is to do a full-text search for subject's name on LEXIS. If subject ever appealed a conviction to a state or federal appeals court any-where in the country, LEXIS will probably have the appeals decision; you should search the LEXIS state libraries for any states in which subject has lived or worked. You should also check the LEXIS Federal Sentencing Li-brary; the Racketeer-Influenced and Corrupt Organizations (RICO) Act case law file within the LEXIS General Federal Library (this covers both criminal and civil RICO cases); and the Military Justice Library.

As noted above, an arrest and prosecution record may be expunged if the person was acquitted or the charges were dropped. In such cases, you will have to go beyond the ordinary criminal court records to find out anything. Here are a few suggestions:

First, try the police or sheriff's department arrest logs and jail books. These records, if available to reporters in your city or county, will tell you the offense the person was charged with and the date of arrest. In addition, the jail book will tell if subject made bail and how. These records are some-times not expunged along with the court record, either because there is no policy of doing so or because of inefficiency. The problem is that the records are only filed chronologically, so if you don't know the approximate date of the arrest it will often be difficult to find the entry.

(Note that the availability of police arrest information has been expanded to include campus police security reports, following a 1991 federal court ruling that federal laws protecting the privacy of student educational records do not extend to crime reports involving students.)

Second, consult local newspaper databases and "morgues." If all police and court records have been sealed or expunged, this may be your only practical way to find out about subject's arrest(s), but be aware that it's a hit-and-miss method—especially in cities with high crime rates where a majority of arrests are never mentioned in the press.

Third, test the memory of a longtime crime reporter or someone in law enforcement (or retired from law enforcement) who specializes or once specialized in tracking the type of criminal activity in which you believe subject has engaged.

Fourth, ask a friend in law enforcement to run a check on subject in the National Crime Information Center (NCIC) computer network, which contains data on felony arrests and convictions throughout the country. Be aware, however, that your friend could get into deep trouble for this— reporters are not supposed to have access to the NCIC.

Fifth, check with your state or city Crime Control Commission, if there is one. It may have clippings files on organized crime (such as the files maintained by the Chicago Crime Commission ever since the 1920s), and its research director may have a long memory.

Sixth, check other special clippings libraries when appropriate. The Anti-Defamation League of B'nai B'rith maintains a massive collection of newspaper clips on arrests and convictions for hate crimes and hate-related violence dating back decades. The library of the Drug Enforcement Administration (DEA) in Washington has extensive clippings on drug raids and drug arrests, including the DEA's daily "press book" compiled from newspaper clips sent to Washington by 19 field offices. The National Criminal Justice Reference System, the Justice Department's information clearinghouse, has a large collection of books, government reports, and newspaper and magazine articles on organized crime that it will search for you for a modest fee.

Seventh, look for evidence of subject's possible arrest record and/or subject's ongoing criminal activity while searching through indexes and files of civil cases and administrative proceedings. Some of the cases that may have relevant information are:

- Actions by the state attorney's office seeking an injunction or other civil remedy against subject's alleged illegal activity. Such an action may precede an indictment or follow an unsuccessful indictment.

- Civil RICO actions filed in federal court against subject and his or her associates either by the government or a private plaintiff. These also may precede or follow criminal indictment.

- Civil rights suits filed by criminal defendants against the police officers who made the arrest and/or the prosecutors.

- Suits filed by crime victims or their families seeking monetary damages from an alleged rapist, hit-and-run driver, etc. Such suits may be filed parallel to a criminal action or after the authorities have failed to obtain a criminal conviction. (Note that in cases of childhood sexual abuse, these suits may be launched many years after the cut-off point for criminal indictment under the statute of limitations.)

- Eviction proceedings filed by landlords (often with the encouragement of prosecutors) against tenants because of alleged drug dealing, prostitution, gambling, and other criminal activities in an apartment, store, or house rented by the tenant; often the case file in such a proceeding will include information about arrests made on the premises.

- Forfeiture proceedings in federal, state, or county courts. Federal law enforcement authorities are empowered to seize the cash, autos, planes, boats, and even the homes of suspected drug traffickers. In many states, the law also authorizes state and local police to seize the property of suspected drug dealers. (Some cities interpret these state laws as authorizing the police to seize the automobiles of prostitutes' customers.) In many instances—and this is true on all levels of law enforcement—the person whose property has been seized during or after an arrest is never brought to trial, much less convicted. Yet the forfeiture action filed by the authorities with the appropriate court, the challenge if any filed by the person from whom the property was seized, and the resulting civil forfeiture hearing may remain part of the open court record.

- Administrative proceedings and/or disciplinary hearings by various regulatory, licensing, and professional agencies or boards. The district attorney may have failed to win a conviction against Dr. X for sexual assault against a patient, but Dr. X's license may nevertheless have been lifted as a result of a proceeding before the state medical board. And the files of that proceeding, if you can get them, may contain most of what was in the sealed criminal file (and more). Administrative proceedings on every level are a goldmine in this respect. For instance, the federal Securities and Exchange Commission, the various state securities commissions, and the National Association of Securities Dealers (NASD) all maintain records on investigations of and disciplinary action against stockbrokers. (These records can be searched online via the LEXIS Federal Securities Library and the LEXIS State Securities Library; you can also obtain information on investigations/disciplinary actions regarding a broker by calling NASD at [800] 289–9999.)

- Civil lawsuits in general. A large percentage of civil cases essentially revolve around plaintiffs seeking civil remedies for what are alleged to be illegal activities, especially fraud. Often the complaint in such a case will present as clear a picture of defendant's criminal mind as any prosecutor could provide (the plaintiff's attorney becomes, in effect, the prosecutor). Thus, if you are unable to get the court file on the prosecution of George Roe for selling forgeries of Renaissance paintings, the civil case filed against him the previous year by the purchaser of one of his so-called Old Masters will give you a pretty good idea of why Roe decided to plead guilty to a misdemeanor rather than face a jury of his peers on felony charges.

The Official Case File

This is accessed via the index case file number. Generally it will contain the information sheet and complaint against defendant, arrest and search warrant applications, the indictment, the bail affidavit and receipt, subpoenas for witnesses, motions and answers, the exhibits list, the judge's instructions to the jury, and the verdict and sentence. The file may also include the trial transcript, the transcript of defendant's bail hearing (which may include detailed testimony from police officers as to why they think defendant is too dangerous to be set loose), and the transcripts of witness depositions taken before trial.

Public access to the case file will vary from locality to locality and according to the disposition of the case. Generally while a case is current the file can be examined by reporters, although you may have to go through the prosecutor's office to do so. If the case was dropped or the defendant was acquitted, the case file will usually be sealed. But even if the defendant was convicted, you may need a release to examine the case file.

Appeals Briefs

If a criminal case is appealed to a higher court, the briefs prepared by prosecution and defense will remain part of the public record no matter if the trial court case file is sealed. These briefs, often 50 pages or more in length, may be your best window on the indictment and the trial. Even if you have access to the trial court case file, you should look at the appeals briefs since they sometimes bring out facts or viewpoints not contained in the original trial record. Federal court appeals briefs usually end up in the Library of Congress or a local law library or archive designated as a depository, e.g., the library of the Association of the Bar of the City of New York. Likewise, briefs from state appeals court cases will often be found in a university law school or bar association library in the state in question.

Subpoena Records

The records of subpoenas issued to witnesses in a grand jury investigation or trial may be available depending on the locality. If so, contact the subpoenaed persons to ask whether they would be willing to discuss the testimony they gave.

Prosecutors' and Defense Attorneys' Files

Both sides will usually have extensive files that go beyond anything in the official court file, including much evidence inadmissible at trial. A prosecutor seeking publicity may allow reporters to see portions of this file (e.g., portions of wire-tap transcripts in an organized crime case) or will brief them on what's in it. Defense attorneys may also cooperate with a reporter, especially if defendant was the victim of egregious prosecutorial or police misconduct—the reporter is given inside information as a means of exonerating the defendant in the court of public opinion if nowhere else. Of special interest in the defense team's files will be the reports of private investigators hired to gather evidence for the defense.

Contacting the Victim

If you find an old newspaper article about subject's arrest but no article about the disposition of his or her case—and the court records are sealed—you can always try to obtain information from the victim. Often (except in cases of surviving rape victims) the article will give the victim's name. The victim or the victim's surviving relatives will probably recall many details about the case (they may even have portions of the court file), and they may have closely tracked the subsequent activities of the defendant. If your state has a victims' rights statute, subject's victim may have obtained copies of the sentencing reports and may also have gained access to ongoing information about subject's parole applications and hearings, the conditions of his or her parole, and so forth.

Don't restrict your inquiries to victims of violent crimes. I have found that the dupes of a white-collar scam can be unremitting in their thirst for revenge against the person who scammed them, even a decade or more afterward.

When Your Subject Is Not the Defendant

A criminal case file or trial transcript often becomes important in tracking someone other than the defendant. Generally your attention will be drawn to such a case by an old newspaper article rather than the court index. Your subject, according to the clips, may have been an unindicted co-conspirator, may have testified for the prosecution in exchange for immunity in this or another case, or may simply have been a witness who was questioned at length about his or her past during cross-examination. Indeed, your subject may even have been the purported victim of the crime. In 1981, one Richard Dupont, a former gay lover of attorney Roy Cohn, was prosecuted in New York for harassing Cohn. Dupont's attorney, John Klotz, turned the trial into a probe of Cohn's own criminal activities, providing future researchers and historians with a remarkably detailed portrait of New York's premier power broker. When I interviewed Klotz afterward, he told me about evidence he had not been allowed to present during the trial (and questions he had not been allowed to ask witnesses) about Cohn's criminal activities. I also spoke with Dupont, who gave me a wealth of accurate details about Cohn and also about Cohn's lovers, business partners, and clients.

9.9 Other Specialized Court Records

For housing court records, see section 4.22; for bankruptcy court records, see section 8.10; for U.S. Tax Court records, see section 8.13.

10 ·

Backgrounding the Individual—Miscellaneous Records and Resources

10.1 Vital Records

Vital records include the indexes and certificates for births, marriages, divorces, and deaths. Access to these records differs from state to state, and often county authorities will have a policy differing from the state's.

Issuance of birth and death certificates is handled by the state vital records bureau in most states. However, certificates are also issued by about 7,000 local registrars throughout the United States. As for marriage and divorce records, the state vital records bureau may keep a central index of marriages and divorces but usually will refer you to the county or city for a copy of the certificate.

The U.S. Department of Health and Human Services has prepared a pamphlet, *Where to Write for Vital Records: Births, Deaths, Marriages, and Divorces*, which gives the address of each state vital records bureau and tells how many years back the state records in each category date (earlier records are usually found on the county level only). This pamphlet is chiefly intended for people who want certified copies of their own records and already know the date of the given event and other identifying details. Journalists, however, are not usually interested in obtaining a certified copy of the certificate, only the information on it. The index alone may have what he or she needs (e.g., date of birth and mother's name). If the journalist needs more information, an abstract of the certificate rather than a certified copy would be sufficient.

The following steps are suggested for obtaining vital statistics about your subject and his or her family as easily as possible. First, if the recorded event(s) occurred in your own county, go directly to the county authorities. Marriage and divorce notices are often filed in ledger books in the county or city clerk's office. Birth or death records may be at the same office or at the county or city health department.

If your county no longer issues birth and death certificates, it still may have the old records (or at least the old indexes) available for public inspection. In addition, the old indexes may be available on microform at the local public library or the nearest Family History Center maintained by the Church of Jesus Christ of Latter-day Saints (the Mormons).

If the event occurred after the county stopped maintaining records in the given category, or if you don't know in which county the event occurred— or if it occurred in another state—you should call the vital records bureau at your state's (or the other state's) health department. Before requesting any specific record, inquire about the bureau's policy on that category of records: Are copies available to the general public? If not, can you at least get a search of the index?

In about 10 "open record" states, there are no restrictions on obtaining vital records at the state level. In some of these states you can get information over the phone, and if you want a copy or abstract you can order it over the phone and pay by credit card. (Elsewhere, you will have to write a letter, enclosing a check or money order.)

Sometimes there are restrictions at the state level on releasing certified copies of birth certificates because of concerns over ID fraud. This is why you should check if it's possible to get an abstract of the birth record (which could not be used as readily for fraudulent purposes) or simply an index search. If even the latter is not available from the state, ask the clerk at least to tell you what county the event occurred in, and then try the county office.

In some states, copies of birth and death certificates are not supposed to be provided to anyone except the person to whom the birth record pertains or the members of the deceased's immediate family. In many counties in these states, however, no proof of identity is required of anyone making a request in person, by mail, or over the phone. Indeed, persons requesting certificates by mail or telephone (as opposed to those appearing in person) often aren't even asked to fill out an application. Paper trippers (see section 7.5) of course fill out the application, if required, in the name of the person whose records are being requested. If ordering by mail, they pay with cash or a money order rather than a personal check or credit card that would reveal their real identity.

If the state vital records bureau won't help you at all, a county registrar often will. Although, as noted above, some states have taken control of vital records out of the county's hands, most of these same states have allowed local registration to continue in selected metropolitan areas.

If you find both local and state records closed to the public, it is possible that they were photocopied by the Mormons—or that a copy of the indexes was provided to the local public library or the state archives—prior to the passage of the law restricting access.

If you can't find subject's birth record in either the state or county files, this may mean you have been given a false lead about subject's place of birth. It may also mean that a record of the birth was never filed. In such cases, look for the birth information in local church baptismal and christening records, which are almost always open to the public.

The easiest way to find the date and place of death of subject's parents is to look in the Social Security Death Benefits Index (see section 4.2) or the version of the SSA death masterfile available at the local Family History Center or your public library's genealogy division. If the information is not there (which will usually be the case if they died prior to 1962 when reporting became mandatory), you might obtain it from a newspaper obituary or funeral notice, cemetery records, church funeral records, or the local coroner's office.

A new category of vital records is emerging in cities with ordinances allowing the registration of gay and lesbian domestic partnerships. Several newspapers, including the *Minneapolis Star Tribune*, are now publishing announcements of gay and lesbian partnerships in their wedding and engagement pages.

For more tips relating to vital records, see sections 4.12 and 7.2.

10.2 Department of Motor Vehicles Records

Motor vehicle and owner/driver records searches are available from the state Department of Motor Vehicles (DMV) in most states. Typically a search will cost you about $3 with a turnaround time of no more than two weeks. For quicker service you can go through a public records vendor.

Abstracts of driver's licenses are available from most states. Depending on the state, the abstract may tell you subject's date of birth, license number (in some states this is or includes the SSN), address, sex, physical characteristics, and driving restrictions (if any).

In many states you can also obtain subject's driving record, which will tell you about his or her license suspensions and revocations as well as his or her convictions for moving violations (including drunk driving). The driving record may also include information on accidents (date, location, and report file number).

Driving-record information is maintained on any individual found guilty of a moving violation in a given state, whether or not he or she is a resident. Hence, you should try states in which subject has traveled frequently for business or pleasure, as well as his or her home state. Once you obtain an abstract of subject's driving record, you can search the traffic court records on each violation as well as state police accident reports, records of insurance coverage at the time of the accident, and so forth.

The DMV also offers searches of license plate numbers (tags), vehicle identification numbers (VINs), and records of vehicle ownership and liens.

Public records search specialists can perform these searches on an all-state basis. Give them the license plate number, and they'll give you the owner's name and address. Give them the VIN, and they'll give you the year, make, and model of the vehicle and the names of any lien holders. Give them subject's name and address, and they'll come up with a list of all registered vehicles he or she owns.

Important note: In 1994, Congress passed the Driver's Privacy Protection Act which allows auto drivers or owners a measure of control over the dissemination of personal information about them contained in state DMV records. They can now opt out, if they wish, from their state's system for providing DMV records to direct-marketing firms and the general public. However, the records of the drivers and owners who exercise this privacy option will still be available to debt collectors, businesses seeking to verify the information on job or insurance applications, and so forth. And the privacy option does *not* cover information on vehicular accidents, driving violations, and driver's status.

For a description of the regulations and procedures governing access to DMV records in each state, see the latest annual editions of *The MVR Book* and *The MVR Decoder Digest* (bibliography).

10.3 Selective Service Records

Under the current selective service registration law, any male born in 1960 or later is required to register at his local post office upon reaching the age of 18. The completed registration form, including name, date of birth, SSN, address, and phone number, is sent to the Selective Service Board data center in Illinois, where a number is assigned to each registrant. This number, the first two digits of which are registrant's year of birth, may one day become an important identifier if the draft is reinstituted. At present, however, the registration forms and numbers have little significance, especially since the Selective Service Board does not reveal registrant's address (or any other personal information) except to law enforcement authorities. The only thing the board will tell you is whether or not subject is in compliance with the registration law. To get this information you must write to the board and include the registrant's full name, date of birth, and SSN.

The old registration system, in effect until 1975, produced quite useful records for investigators. The individual registered with his county draft board and was given a number and a draft classification. His classification records were kept at the local board and were open to the public. After the draft was abolished, these records were sent to regional Federal Records Centers around the country, where they are still available to the public. (To obtain them, you must supply the registrant's full name, date of birth, and home address at time of registration.)

The classification records include the individual's Selective Service number, birth date, every classification (1-A, 4-F, etc.) he ever held and the date the notice of classification was mailed to him, the date of his Armed Forces medical exam and the fact of whether he passed or failed, the date (if ever) that he entered the Armed Forces and whether he enlisted or was drafted, and the date he left the Armed Forces (assuming that he was discharged before the old registration system was abolished). There are gaps in these records, however: The date of leaving the Armed Forces is not always included in the records of World War II veterans; men who enlisted before they reached the age of 18 (the time at which draft registration was required) are not included at all, even if they became career soldiers; and Armed Forces women are not included.

In the days of the draft, personnel managers and bank loan officers often found the Selective Service number useful in checking the accuracy of an applicant's statements about his past. This was because the number contained (as does the SSN) coded information. Even today—if you come across the number in an old job or apartment rental application—it can be useful in finding out where a person grew up. It consists of four groups of digits connected by hyphens: The first group designates the state or territory of the United States where the individual first registered; the second group corresponds to the number of the county draft board within that state or territory; the third group corresponds to the last two digits of the year of registrant's birth; the fourth group is the registrant's local draft board registration number.

The following are the numbers that correspond to each state and territory:

1 Alabama	25 Nebraska
2 Arizona	26 Nevada
3 Arkansas	27 New Hampshire
4 California	28 New Jersey
5 Colorado	29 New Mexico
6 Connecticut	30 New York
7 Delaware	31 North Carolina
8 Florida	32 North Dakota
9 Georgia	33 Ohio
10 Idaho	34 Oklahoma
11 Illinois	35 Oregon
12 Indiana	36 Pennsylvania
13 Iowa	37 Rhode Island
14 Kansas	38 South Carolina
15 Kentucky	39 South Dakota
16 Louisiana	40 Tennessee
17 Maine	41 Texas
18 Maryland	42 Utah
19 Massachusetts	43 Vermont
20 Michigan	44 Virginia
21 Minnesota	45 Washington
22 Mississippi	46 West Virginia
23 Missouri	47 Wisconsin
24 Montana	48 Wyoming

49 District of Columbia	53 Puerto Rico
50 New York City	54 Virgin Islands
51 Alaska	55 Guam
52 Hawaii	56 Panama Canal Zone

10.4 Military Service Records and Discharge Papers

Anyone can obtain anyone else's service record by sending a copy of Standard Form 180 ("Request Pertaining to Military Records"), or a letter requesting this information, to the appropriate records center. Form 180 can be obtained from the National Personnel Records Center (NPRC) at 9700 Page Boulevard, St. Louis, Missouri, 63132. For records of discharged, deceased, and retired military personnel, send this form or your letter to the NPRC's Military Personnel Records division (same address as above). For the records of active-duty personnel as well as reservists and members of the National Guard, send your request to the appropriate address listed on the back of Form 180.

On Form 180 or in your letter, state that your request is being made pursuant to the Freedom of Information Act. Ignore the notice on Form 180 that you need to get the veteran's signature on a release authorization (in fact, such a release is necessary only if you are requesting health records or detailed personnel records that are not part of the service record usually released).

If possible, you should provide subject's full name correctly spelled, SSN, approximate dates of service, and branch of service. If you do not have all this information, the NPRC staff may still be able to find the records.

The NPRC currently holds over 50 million military personnel records. An estimated 18 million records were destroyed in a 1973 fire, including about 80 percent of the records on Army personnel discharged between 1912 and 1959. Although about 3.1 million of these records have been partly reassembled from other sources, no one knows exactly what is missing—there was no index.

The information available from the NPRC under a Freedom of Information request includes date of birth; dates of service; dates of rank/grade changes; awards and decorations; duty assignments; current duty status; civilian and military educational level; marital status; and the names, sex, and age of subject's dependents. Releasable records also include court-martial records if unclassified and a photograph if available. In your letter or in a statement appended to Form 180 you should request each of the above items specifically. Note that the NPRC will *not* provide you with subject's SSN, address, or telephone number. The NPRC also will not release disciplinary, discharge, or medical records without the veteran's written consent or the written consent of the next-of-kin of deceased veterans.

If subject's military records were destroyed in the 1973 fire, try to obtain his military discharge papers. These are available at the county clerk's office of the county in which subject filed them. The trick is to figure out which county that might be. Your best bet is subject's hometown or the town in which he ended up when discharged. Note that the Army sends copies of discharge papers to the Adjutant General of the veteran's home state.

The Sourcebook of Public Record Providers lists several firms that specialize in checking military records.

10.5 Telephone Company Records

To access records of a person's toll calls, you will need an inside source at the phone company. If you don't have such a source, you can go through a private investigator who does. Other ways of accessing these records include calling the billing office and pretending to be the telephone subscriber, or calling the special number for toll records and pretending to be a billing office employee. Such tactics, which require considerable knowledge of phone company procedures and terminology, are *not* recommended by this writer.

If your subject is a government official, you can make a Freedom of Information request to examine the toll records of all calls made from or charged to his/her office phone or official car phone, or all calls that were charged to his/her government-issued telephone credit card. You can then reverse the numbers and see if subject is calling his or her broker or engaging in other personal business to an unreasonable extent on the taxpayer's time and at the taxpayer's expense.

10.6 Medical Records

Prior authorization from a patient is required to get his or her medical records from a hospital or a physician's office. However, bits and pieces of subject's medical history can sometimes be gleaned from the public record. Subject's driving restrictions may be included in an abstract of subject's driver's license (see section 10.2). Subject's driving record (also see 10.2) may include multiple drunk-driving incidents, suggesting an alcohol addiction; it also may list accidents in which subject was involved (the accident report by the investigating officer, available from the state Department of Public Safety, may tell if subject was seriously injured). Registration records from the draft era may reveal if subject failed his Armed Forces medical exam and was given a 4-F status, although the specific medical reasons will not be provided. Income tax returns filed by subject as evidence in a local court case or in U.S. Tax Court litigation in Washington may reveal large deductions for medical expenses. Aircraft pilot licensing files may contain medical information, as may various licensing files for occupations such as cosmetician or optometrist.

In some states, worker's compensation claims records can be obtained without a signed release (if not, you may at least be able to determine if subject has filed a claim). These records, if available, will include the original injury report with date and type of injury, body part(s) affected, and the work-related disability resulting therefrom. If the claim is contested by the insurer and/or the board's determination is appealed by the claimant, more information might be available.

Typically, worker's compensation claims are filed at the state compensation board by name of claimant, but you must furnish claimant's SSN and/or date of birth. In a few states, the records are filed by name of company, in which case you must know where subject has worked in order to access them. *The Guide to Background Investigations* will tell you where to write for these records (and the restrictions on access, if any) in all 50 states. Note that several states sell their worker's compensation databases, with periodic updates, to database vendors. *The Sourcebook of Public Record Providers* includes a list of the database vendors and document retrieval services which specialize in worker's compensation claims records.

In searching state and federal court indexes, you should keep alert for any case in which subject's medical condition might have been an issue (for instance, a product liability suit, a suit against a health insurance company by a policy holder, a personal injury suit alleging negligence by an auto driver, or a medical malpractice suit). Frequently in such cases, plaintiff will have to undergo a pretrial physical and/or psychiatric examination. The results of this exam may be filed as an exhibit to a pretrial motion or reply; it also may be presented as evidence at trial. Plaintiff may be questioned at length about his or her medical condition in a pretrial deposition and in court testimony. Likewise, the physicians who have examined or treated plaintiff may be questioned in depositions and at trial.

Further information on medical problems can be gleaned from county judgment dockets. You may find that several judgments or liens against subject have been obtained by physicians or hospitals because of nonpayment of bills. The judgment docket entry will give you the case file number, and you can then retrieve the file from the county or state court file room. Such cases will possibly give you the dates of subject's visits to a doctor's office and/or of hospitalization, which may fit together with other information you have gleaned. Once you have the names of doctors subject has visited you can look in *The Official ABMS Directory of Board Certified Medical Specialists* and other medical directories (or just call the doctors' offices) to find out what types of ailments they treat.

Criminal cases involving aggravated assault, driving while intoxicated, and so on will include information about the injuries suffered by the victim and also possibly information about the psychiatric problems and/or other mitigating medical problems of the alleged perpetrator. In addition, information about the victim's medical condition may be revealed in a sentencing hearing, while information about either the victim's or the perpetrator's medical condition may come out in a parole hearing. Searches of newspaper databases and clippings morgues may turn up a story about an automobile accident, assault, or other incident resulting in serious injury to subject at some time in the past. Inhouse newsletters at subject's place of employment (or subject's spouse's place of employment) and church bulletins at subject's church may include information about a serious illness involving hospitalization of either subject or a member of subject's family, and may tell what hospital the patient was in. Garbological examination of subject's trash (see sections 11.4 and 12.3) may turn up empty prescription bottles as well as medical/hospital bills.

The Medical Information Bureau (MIB) provides insurance underwriters nationwide with medical information on insurance applicants. Its databases include information on over 15 million people. A recently published manual for private investigators stated apropos of the MIB: "We are getting into some networks of information that the insurance industry wishes no one but them knew about. . . ."

10.7 Welfare Records

These are not open to the public. However, your subject might file copies of welfare checks or various welfare documents in a court proceeding (for instance, a family court case regarding child support payments). Welfare records would definitely be entered as evidence in a welfare fraud prosecution.

10.8 Immigration and Naturalization Records

U.S. Immigration and Naturalization Service (INS) records on individual immigrants are usually unavailable to the public. They become part of the public record, however, if filed by either the government or the immigrant in a deportation trial or in a suit launched by the immigrant against the INS in federal district court.

When an immigrant becomes an American citizen, a notice is filed with the county clerk's office in the county where he or she was naturalized. This is public record information. It may include subject's age, address, and occupation when naturalized; date of naturalization; date of arrival in the United States; and former nationality.

10.9 Voter Registration Records

These are generally kept by the county or city Board of Elections a/k/a Election Commission a/k/a Registrar of Voters. You can check the enrollment books of registered voters, which list all registered voters in each state assembly district and their party affiliation or independent status. The lists are often arranged by street address, as in a crisscross directory. Even if subject is not listed, subject's spouse may be listed, as well as subject's children of voting age who still live at home. The enrollment books from years past, which may be available in the city archives or the county historical society if not at the board of elections, are an excellent way to trace changes in the composition of subject's household and gather the names of ex-spouses and of children no longer living at home.

Another key resource is the registration records for individual voters. At some boards of elections you can check both current and back records on microform or at a computer terminal. Depending on the particular records system, you may find out subject's current residential address (and the address where he or she first registered locally) as well as subject's telephone number, SSN, party affiliation, date of registration, occupation, and business address. The records may also reveal how many times subject failed to vote in recent elections. (This is especially interesting in backgrounding candidates for public office; you may find that your local "good government" liberal or superpatriotic conservative almost never bothers to vote.) Finally, the voter registration records may include a specimen of subject's signature.

Many localities will not take mail-in requests for information, requiring that inspection of the voter rolls be done in person. However, voter registration data is available from database vendors who have purchased it for resale; 26 states currently allow unrestricted commercial use of their voter registration rolls. Aristotle Industries, a Washington, D.C., public records vendor, offers the only nationwide voter registration database, which is accessible both online and on CD-ROM. It covers 3,400 counties and municipalities and includes enhanced features such as telephone numbers and national change-of-address data.

10.10 Federal Election Commission Records

If subject gave $500 or more to any single candidate for federal office or any single political action committee during any single election between 1981 and 1988, and if subject gave more than $200 under these conditions in any election from 1989 on (and if the contributions were lawfully reported), you can find a record of it via the Federal Election Commission's Contributor Search System. You can access the FEC's records of the three most recent election cycles online (see the appendix). For earlier records, you must order a search of the FEC's inhouse database or purchase it on magnetic tape.

In searching via the FEC database, you can try different variations of subject's name and also all other persons with subject's surname in his or her locality. You cannot do this by street address—the names are entered into the database only by town and zip code (to find the street addresses you have to search the microfiche records at FEC headquarters or order specific microfiche or photocopied records by mail). But if you see that local contributors with the same surname have given money to the same candidate, you can check the telephone white pages or a crisscross directory to see if they are from the same household.

The FEC database lists each contributor's place of work and/or occupation. You can thus use it as a kind of city directory to compile lists of people who worked for the same employer in the same city as subject at various points over the years. If subject is the boss of the company this might be a way to find employees he or she sacked (especially executive-level employees). For instance, you see that John Brown was listed as working at Ace Missile Components in Houston in 1992; Brown gave $1,000 to a certain candidate that year, but when the next donation from Brown was reported in 1994, he was described as an employee of an unrelated company in New Orleans. You can infer from his large 1992 donation that he probably had been a high-level executive at Ace and probably knows a lot about his former boss. If he was fired and is still angry about it, he might be willing to talk.

The Contributor Search System is also useful in finding out if subject has any hate-group affiliations. Often people with bigoted beliefs are very close-mouthed in the presence of outsiders—you find out about their ferocious inner life only from the FEC filings. For instance, you may discover that the mild-mannered Mr. Deeds who is always ever so polite to black and Hispanic customers in his store has donated thousands of dollars in the last three presidential elections to candidates of the super-rightist Thunderbolt party.

10.11 Permits and Licenses

A wide variety of professions, trades, vending operations, and service-type businesses require a license from the city or state government or from a quasi-public commission or agency. You can get a list of the licenses required in your locality from the state and municipal government handbooks, but let's take New York City as an example:

If subject operates a grocery or restaurant, he or she must have a permit from the City Department of Health. If subject operates a liquor store or bar or sells alcoholic beverages in his or her restaurant, a license from the State Liquor Authority is required. If subject is a teacher, he or she should have a certificate from the state Department of Education. If subject earns his or her living as a real estate salesperson or broker, barber, hairdresser, cosmetologist, billiard-room operator, private investigator, or apartment referral agent—or if subject is a notary public or sells hearing aids—he or she must have a license from the Division of Licensing Services of the state's Department of State. If subject is a taxi driver, he or she must have a chauffeur's license from the state Department of Motor Vehicles and a taxi driver's license from the City Taxi Commission. If subject owns a handgun, he or she must have a permit from the Police Department. If subject is a master plumber, he or she must have a license from the city's Master Plumber's License Board; if an electrician, from the city's Electrical License

Board. If he or she carries a press card, it will have been issued by the Police Department. If he or she is involved in any of 54 different trades or types of business—from auctioneer to weighmaster, from bowling-alley operator to street vendor of hotdogs—he or she should have a license from the City Department of Consumer Affairs.

The above list of licenses, permits, and certificates (similar to the requirements in other cities) is only the tip of the iceberg. *The City of New York Official Directory* lists no less than 1,600 licenses required within the city by various local, state, and federal agencies for the conducting of various trades or professions or for the sale of various products or services.

Violations of law by licensees in any regulated area may result in summonses issued by city or state inspectors, or civil or criminal actions initiated by state or city attorneys. In addition, complaints against a licensee may be filed by irate consumers with the City Consumer Affairs Department, the State Attorney General's office, a professional licensing board, or the Better Business Bureau.

Across the nation, new types of licenses are constantly being created by legislators to meet new social needs. For instance, in 1994, following several tragic boating accidents, Alabama became the first state to require motorboat operators to be licensed and to adhere to the same drinking rules as automobile drivers. Favorable public reaction nationwide to this model safety legislation (at a time when boats are zooming around lakes and other waterways at 50 to 70 miles per hour) makes it likely that many if not most states will adopt similar laws by the end of this decade.

License, permit, and registration records from several states are available online; see *The Sourcebook of Public Record Providers*.

10.12 Professional Licensing

Professional licensing laws are a confused patchwork from state to state. A recent congressional study found that although 700 professions require state-level licensing in one or more states, only 20 professions require licensing in all states. In addition, the examinations and other licensing requirements may vary widely in their rigor. Thus, a person whose license has been revoked in Vermont may either move to New Hampshire, which has no licensing requirements, or Connecticut, where the licensing body will overlook the prior revocation (so you should always check the prior state's records). Likewise, a person who cannot pass the licensing exam or meet other licensing requirements in his or her home state may move to a state with an easy exam or no exam at all, and/or with loopholes in the other requirements.

By submitting to the licensing procedure a person creates yet another paper trail to follow him or her through life. For instance, consulting *McKinney's Consolidated Laws* we find that a licensed cosmetician in New York State will have filed, at one time or another, an application for a trainee license, an application to take the licensing exam, an application for a permanent license, a physician's certificate stating that applicant is free of disease, a photograph to accompany the license application, a diploma from a licensed training center, a copy of any license received in another state or in a foreign country, and change-of-address notices.

Just how much of such paperwork is open to public inspection varies from state to state; you may have to use the state freedom of information law to get it. At a minimum you will want to know if complaints have been filed against subject and if subject has ever been the target of any disciplinary action such as license suspension or revocation, a reprimand, or a fine. Depending on the profession and the laws of the particular state, complaints may be filed with the State Attorney General's office, the professional licensing board, or the private association representing that profession or trade on the county or state level; occasionally you may find that complaints have been filed and investigations conducted on all three levels. A complaint to the State Attorney General may result in a civil suit by the state or a criminal prosecution. A complaint to the regulatory board may result in an administrative proceeding followed by various appeals (and perhaps a suit by the licensee against the board). A complaint to the local professional organization may result in a more informal investigation, perhaps leading to the licensee's suspension or expulsion from the organization.

11.

Backgrounding the Individual—Special Problems and Methods

11.1 Backgrounding Subject's Educational Past

You may spot a college bachelor's, master's, or doctoral degree on subject's wall. Or you may learn about the supposed degree from his or her acquaintances or a biographical sketch in a vanity directory. Verifying the degree is a twofold process: first, find out if the college is a legitimate one; second, find out if subject really graduated. This is an important step in backgrounding: A congressional study has estimated that upward of 500,000 Americans have obtained false academic and/or professional credentials from diploma mills, credentials brokers, and other suppliers of instant status.

Checking Out the College
Make sure you have the name right. Some diploma mills utilize a look-alike name so people will confuse them with legitimate schools; for instance, "Darthmouth College" instead of Dartmouth College, or "Boston City College" instead of Boston College.

Once you have the correct name, check out the school in one of the standard reference guides at your public library: *Lovejoy's College Guide*, *The Right College*, or *American Universities and Colleges*. If it's not in these books, you have good reason to be suspicious.

Next check with the regional accrediting association that covers the state in which the institution is located. In the United States only six regional groups, operating under the umbrella of the Commission on Recognition of Postsecondary Accreditation (CORPA), are accepted as having the authority to accredit an entire college or university. These are the Middle States Association of Colleges and Schools, New England Association of Colleges and Schools, North Central Association of Colleges and Schools, Northwest Association of Colleges and Schools, Southern Association of Colleges and Schools, and Western Association of Colleges and Schools.

The situation is different for professional training aimed at achieving certification or licensing in a particular profession. Here each profession has its own accrediting agency or agencies for schools or programs serving that discipline. These entities—about 50 in all—are approved by CORPA and/or the U.S. Department of Education; a list can be found in *Lovejoy's College Guide.*

Professional training programs may operate either as independent institutions (e.g., a college of optometry) or as departments or special schools within a regular college or university (e.g., a university engineering department). In the latter case, there may be differences between the standards of the regional and professional accrediting bodies. On the one hand, the professional accrediting body may fail to accredit the given college department even though the college as a whole is accredited by the regional body. (The student's bachelor's degree thus is legitimate for all general purposes, but if he or she majored in psychology and the college's psychology department is not accredited by the American Psychological Association, he or she may experience difficulty in getting into one of the better graduate schools.) On the other hand, the professional agency may accredit the relevant department even though the regional accrediting body has refused to accredit the college as a whole.

In checking the accreditation status of any college or professional program that is not well known, it is important that you focus on the years of subject's attendance. A school that is fully accredited today may not have been accredited when subject studied there in the early 1970s. Likewise, a small school that has lost its accreditation in recent years because of a loss of income (and hence a decline in the quality of its faculty, library services, etc.) may have offered an adequate education when subject attended it in the late 1950s.

Never accept an obscure school's own claim that it is accredited; diploma mills will lie. And beware of regional or professional accrediting bodies other than those approved by CORPA and/or the Department of Education. A number of unrecognized accrediting agencies have been set up to provide alternate accrediting for unaccredited schools. Although some may attempt sincerely to impose minimal standards, others are just mail drops for diploma mills.

Note that displaying a degree from an unaccredited school is not necessarily fraudulent, nor is an education received from an unaccredited school necessarily illegitimate in the larger sense. A smart student who works hard at his or her correspondence courses may end up with a better education than a student who cruises through an accredited school taking easy courses. As alternate forms of education continue to flourish, some currently unaccredited schools will doubtless gain accreditation in the years ahead or, at least, de facto acceptance in the working world. (The official accrediting system has itself come under fire from Congress in recent years and will probably be drastically reformed in the near future.)

For an evaluation of a particular unaccredited school, check the latest edition of *College Degrees by Mail* (formerly *Bear's Guide to Non-Traditional College Degrees*) which describes hundreds of accredited and unaccredited schools that offer degrees under unorthodox conditions: correspondence colleges, colleges with minimal residency requirements, colleges offering generous credits for life experience and/or for passing an equivalency exam, and colleges offering learning contracts in place of required courses. *College Degrees by Mail* also lists over 100 diploma mills that sell degrees (including medical and law degrees) through the mail with virtually no work required, and it has a "Goodbye" list of institutions that could not be located or had discontinued operations (many but not all of these are defunct diploma mills).

You can also contact the state board of higher education and the regional accrediting agency for the state and region in which the school's offices or mail drop are located. One or both may have received complaints about the school. Another option is to contact the school itself, pretend that you want to purchase a degree—and see how they respond.

Checking Out the Degree

Once you have determined that subject's college is legitimate, you will want to know if subject's relationship to the college—and his or her degree—are for real. For unofficial confirmation, you can look in the alumni directory; for official confirmation, contact the college's information office. No college will give you details on a former student's academic records without his or her written permission, but most schools will confirm if subject ever matriculated and what degree, if any, he or she received and in what year. (Some schools will tell you a bit more, such as subject's major field of study, participation in intercollegiate athletics, awards and honors, and so forth.) Note that people who falsely claim college degrees on résumés or job applications will often list a school they attended but from which they never graduated rather than pick a school at random.

The Guide to Background Investigations (see bibliography) will tell you what number to call at each college to obtain confirmation of a student's attendance and degree. It will also tell you what identifying information must be provided (some schools require that you provide the former student's SSN and graduation date) and whether information can be obtained over the phone without a written request.

Defining the Years of Attendance

To trace subject's college career, you first need to know which years he or she was really in attendance. If subject graduated in 1984, it does not necessarily follow that he or she matriculated in 1980 and went through the standard uninterrupted four-year grind. Although this was the typical pattern until the 1980s (except during the two world wars), there have always been students who dropped out temporarily for a variety of reasons. And today, it is financially almost impossible for most students to complete their studies in four years: the average student in the California State University system, for example, now takes five and a half years.

If the college will not give you subject's dates of attendance but only the date of graduation, look in the alumni directory. Occasionally, these books will list the years of actual attendance, but more often students will be listed as members of the class with which they entered; for example, "class of 1973" refers to the year subject would have graduated if he or she had matriculated in 1969 and taken an uninterrupted four-year course of study. Thus, you will know to search the school's yearbooks, student directories, and other publications for the years between class year minus four and the graduation year.

Most alumni directories will not tell you if a student transferred from another school, although if he or she was on campus overall for less than four years this was probably the case. (Note, however, that since the early 1990s some colleges have begun to offer accelerated three-year bachelor's degrees.) The college may release information regarding transfers, but if not, you might check the information number at all colleges within commuting distance of subject's hometown. Many students will spend their first two years at a commuter college while living at home for financial reasons (if they need to drastically improve their grade-point average, the school will probably be a two-year junior college) and then will transfer to a college or university in another locality. You might also check the national membership directory of any fraternity or sorority to which subject belonged, since most students who join these organizations do so during their freshman year.

Student Directories
Besides helping you pin down subject's years of attendance, student directories can be used like city directories to trace where subject lived each year, either on or off campus (sometimes this will help you find a former roommate). In the case of a university divided into separate schools or colleges, the back issues of the directory may tell in which division subject was enrolled at the beginning of each year, thus revealing any sudden shifts in career goals, such as from engineering one year to liberal arts the next.

Yearbooks
College yearbooks will often contain many details about subject's campus activities and friends. Backfiles of the yearbook will be available at the college library (usually in the campus archives) or at the yearbook editorial office.

A typical yearbook will include sections on sports teams, fraternities and sororities, campus publications (newspaper, yearbook, and humor and literary magazine staffs), honorary societies, student government, music and drama, and religious and political clubs. For each organization, team, club, and so on, there will be a group picture with a caption giving the name of each person.

Look first in the yearbook for subject's senior year. Here you will find his or her class picture together with information regarding degree, major, scholarships, fraternity or sorority membership, and possibly the name of subject's hometown and the high school he or she graduated from. There will also be a listing of subject's campus activities, honors, and affiliations with the year or years of each. You can then go to the appropriate yearbooks, look up each cited activity or organization, and get a list of the other students in each picture. In this way you can rapidly collect the names of those former classmates most likely to remember subject well, such as subject's sorority sisters, field hockey teammates, or co-workers on the campus newspaper.

Many yearbooks will have a name index listing each page in which subject's name or picture appears; this can make your search much easier, especially if there is no senior class picture of subject or only a picture with no summary of activities. (Some seniors will have nothing but the degree and major listed, not because they were inactive on campus but simply because they failed to fill out the form sent to them by the yearbook staff. In such cases, simply look in the name index for each yearbook during subject's years of attendance.)

In recent years, African-American and/or Hispanic students on some campuses have begun to publish their own separate yearbooks. In such cases, information on a minority student will be divided between the ethnic and the campus-wide yearbook, so consult both.

Note that professional schools (medicine, law, nursing, pharmacy, etc.) will have separate sections in most yearbooks; look in this section for the student's class portrait.

Faculty Directory

Back issues of the faculty directory will provide the names and departments of professors who were teaching at the school during subject's years of attendance. The teachers most likely to remember subject will be those in his or her departmental major. Also, if subject was on a sports team, the coach may remember him or her quite well. If a professor or coach you need to contact has retired or moved to another school, get his or her new address from his or her former department or look in the latest edition and supplements of the *National Faculty Directory*, the *Faculty White Pages*, or the *Faculty Directory of Higher Education*.

Campus Newspapers and Periodicals

The campus newspaper for the relevant years may have published articles regarding subject and/or articles, letters to the editor, or Op-Ed pieces by him or her. Larger colleges have daily newspapers that cover campus life quite thoroughly. In backgrounding several followers of Lyndon LaRouche,

I found much information in Columbia University's *Daily Spectator* on their activities as campus protest leaders in the 1960s.

Campus papers are usually available on microform in the college archives; the microform for the years you need can be borrowed via interlibrary loan.

The staff of the college archives may have compiled a newspaper index or clippings files. These are likely to be organized by subject only, but you can zero in on articles mentioning a particular person if you already know a bit about his or her college career from the yearbooks or conversations with former classmates. Even without a clippings file you might be able to find some things quickly on microform; for example, if you know the person was on the basketball team just look through the sports pages for the basketball season.

If I were backgrounding the college career of a celebrity, I would find out who the editors of the campus paper were during his or her years of attendance; they will be more likely to remember any newsworthy events regarding subject than most other students would. Also, some of these former editors will have become professional journalists and thus will be naturally sympathetic to a fellow journalist or a biographer.

Note that colleges and the surrounding cultural milieu give rise to a great variety of newspapers, periodicals, and newsletters that are dutifully cataloged by the staff of the campus archives. Subject's college may have two rival campus-wide dailies; it may also have Jewish, black, or gay/lesbian newspapers as well as newspapers for the law school, engineering school, evening students, and so forth. There may be a conservative organ (e.g., the *Dartmouth Review*) and an environmental newsletter. In the 1960s, there was often a campus Students for a Democratic Society (SDS) chapter newsletter and assorted other organs of protest. Usually there has been a succession of literary and humor magazines. In addition, most large college communities have one or more off-campus weeklies (offshoots of the former counterculture or "underground" press, in many cases) that report closely on campus happenings for a readership that includes many students and faculty.

Checking Out Subject's Thesis or Dissertation

All universities will have in their library stacks the master's theses and doctoral dissertations of graduate students who obtained degrees at that school. (Note: Not all master's degree programs require a thesis.) Some college libraries, especially those of the colleges that require a thesis from every senior, will also keep copies of senior honors papers and senior theses.

Many theses and dissertations have an acknowledgments page in which the author thanks his or her adviser, the members of the dissertation committee (and other professors), friends, parents, spouse and children, the department secretary, and so on. Often 20 or more names will be mentioned. The acknowledgments are especially valuable in finding out the names of ex-spouses and ex-lovers. Also look for any mention of grants or scholarships received by subject.

If you cannot visit subject's college library, you can still easily find out details about his or her dissertation. Look in *American Doctoral Dissertations* and the *Comprehensive Dissertation Index* at your local research library. These indexes will indicate if subject indeed has the doctorate he or she claims to have. You can then consult *Dissertation Abstracts International* and *Masters Abstracts International*, which contain abstracts (usually written by the authors themselves) of dissertations (dating from 1938) and theses (dating from 1962).

Via DIALOG or CompuServe, you can access Dissertation Abstracts Online, which provides an index to the subject, title, and author of almost every dissertation accepted at a U.S. university since 1861 and master's theses since 1962. It also provides dissertation abstracts (from 1980) and theses abstracts (from 1988). Many research libraries will have this database on CD-ROM.

If you need the entire dissertation, you can order the microform or a photocopy from University Microfilms International (UMI) in Ann Arbor, Michigan. If a particular dissertation or thesis is unavailable from UMI, you can get it via interlibrary loan from the library of the university that awarded the degree.

High School Background

Subject's high school years can be researched just like the college ones. The yearbooks can often be found at the local public library or the county historical society; if not, a serious researcher can sometimes gain access to the backfile at the high school itself. The same goes for the weekly high school newspaper and other student publications.

As with college students, the most important yearbook is the one for subject's senior year, which will contain a summary of his or her activities for all four years. If a student transferred from another high school during his or her junior or senior year, this will often be noted to explain the lack of listed activities.

11.2 Backgrounding an Individual via Archival Collections

Although mostly used by scholars, archival materials can be invaluable to an investigative reporter. Such materials may include unpublished manuscripts, scrapbooks, newspaper clippings, leaflets, court documents, self-published pamphlets, personal correspondence, official papers and correspondence of an elected official, internal documents of a political party, internal memoranda of a corporation, oral history tapes and transcripts, photographs, home movies, and video or audio cassettes of TV and radio appearances.

Subject may have donated his or her personal papers to a library either for the sake of posterity or as a tax write-off. A person doesn't have to be famous to do this. Some libraries actively seek the papers of ordinary people for their sociological value. They also seek the papers of people who, although not well known to the public, played an important behind-the-scenes role in (or were well-placed observers of) significant historical events.

Although the chances that your subject has donated his or her papers to an archive are relatively small, there is a much greater chance that papers concerning subject, or memos or letters by or to subject, are contained in the archival papers of a notable person with whom subject was once associated. If I were backgrounding a longtime business agent of an Ohio Teamster local, I would want to know where the papers of the late Ohio Teamster leader and international president Jackie Presser are kept. (Conversely, if I were Presser and still alive, I would be very interested to know that an investigative reporter who once dogged me had donated his files to the University of Missouri.) If I were backgrounding someone who once worked in a minor appointive post in the Carter White House, I would check the indexes of the Carter Presidential Library. If I were backgrounding a longtime local Democratic county chairman, I would go to the state university library and look at the papers of the late governor whose rise to power was engineered by that county chairman.

Let's say you are investigating Tim, the former radical who is now a neoconservative pundit. You know that Tim was once a disciple and top aide to Max Swift, the Trotskyist leader. You check the RLIN database (see below) and discover that Max, who died several years ago, had donated his personal papers and correspondence to the radical history collection at New York University. You also ascertain from the database that a finder's aid has been prepared for Max's papers describing each box and folder and itemizing the most important individual documents in each. You obtain a copy of the finder's aid through interlibrary loan and learn that Max's papers include two folders of correspondence between Max and Tim as well as a draft of a never-published article by Max denouncing Tim after their quarrel. You go to New York City and examine the collection, finding that Max's unpublished article is a bitter tirade that, among other things, accuses Tim of stealing money from the movement and compulsive philandering.

Archival Databases and Other Guides
To find archival material nationwide, there are two major databases: the Research Libraries Information Network (RLIN) and the Online Computer Library Center (OCLC). One or both can be accessed via computer terminals at any research library. You type in a person's or organization's name and see how many "hits" you get. Unfortunately, the databases include only relatively brief descriptions of any given archival collection (although individual documents or letters of special importance may be noted), and if subject's name is not in the description you will not get a hit even if the particular collection contains a large amount of information about subject. To

find material beyond what's listed under subject's name, search under the names of his or her better-known colleagues or under the relevant organizational titles. In the case of Tim, you would search for material under "Socialist Vanguard Party," "Max Swift," or "Olga Strong" (Max's wife). You would also search under topic key words such as "Trotskyism" or "U.S. Left." Next you would call each library listed as having significant collections on Swift, Trotskyism, and so forth and ask for the archivist who best knows the collection and/or who prepared the finder's aid; he or she will probably recall if the collection contains significant material on Tim. You might also contact the eccentric former "Swiftie" who donated his files to New York University: first, because he might have personal recollections of Tim; second, because he will know his own collection better than any librarian would; and third, because he might have boxloads of additional documents in his basement.

An alternative to RLIN and OCLC is to look in the Library of Congress' *National Union Catalog of Manuscript Collections* (NUCMC) and the *Index to Personal Names in the National Union Catalog of Manuscript Collections* (the latter includes about 200,000 personal and family names). Unfortunately it is often a decade or more before collections from local libraries get listed in NUCMC.

To find material that is not listed either in NUCMC or in the databases, look in the subject index in the *Directory of Archives and Manuscript Repositories in the United States* and also in *Subject Collections* and the *Directory of Special Libraries and Information Centers*. Make a list of the repositories most likely to have material pertaining to your subject and call the archivist at each.

Government Archives

For government archival collections, see the *Guide to the National Archives*, which describes records held by the various departments and agencies of the federal government. The microfiche "National Inventory of Documentary Sources in the United States: Federal Records" lists about 1,400 finding guides to National Archives and Smithsonian Institution collections as well as to the seven presidential libraries.

Staff members at the various National Archives collections and presidential libraries will search for what you need and send you photocopies for a modest fee.

Oral History

Well over a million Americans from all walks of life have been interviewed as part of oral history projects. There are thousands of these projects sponsored by universities; by county, city, or small-town historical societies; and by corporations, trade unions, or churches desiring a record of their organizational life. Participants in these projects include the most unlikely people: For instance, the late Jackie Presser (see above) taped his recollections for a University of Nevada project.

Oral history transcripts and/or tapes (usually audio tapes but also occasionally video) are available at the library of the institution sponsoring the project. Well-funded university projects usually have transcripts (of which about 30,000 are listed in the *Oral History Index*), but your local county historical society probably can't afford this—you'll have to listen to the tapes and take notes. The purposes of oral history projects vary widely. If a person is interviewed only about a certain peripheral aspect of his or her life, the transcript may run less than fifty pages. If a person is asked to give an account of his or her entire life, the transcript may fill several volumes.

Finding tapes on a particular person is not very different from finding other archival material. Let's return to the case of Tim. You can search RLIN and OCLC for any tapes by Tim or by any of his former comrades (including Max and Olga) or any of his later right-wing associates who might have reminisced about him. You can also search by key word for tapes regarding the history of the U.S. Left, Trotskyism, the Socialist Vanguard Party, and the protest movements of the college campus where Tim had his moment of glory in 1968.

Although such a search will tell you if material relevant to your research has been entered into RLIN or OCLC by archivists at libraries connected to the system, it will not help you find tapes at small-town historical societies that are outside the system. To find the most promising of the latter collections, see the *Directory of Oral History Collections*.

11.3 Subject's Published Writings

The majority of books are written by part-time authors who make their living either in related writing fields such as journalism or who write to communicate their professional findings in science or scholarship or simply for the love of writing. At any moment, hundreds of thousands of Americans are churning out fiction, nonfiction, or verse manuscripts, and these hopefuls may come from any walk of life. Most of them will receive only rejection slips from America's major publishing houses. But many would-be authors, undaunted, will turn to the thousands of small publishers (including vanity publishers). Others will self-publish their own books and pamphlets using home computers and desktop publishing software. Meanwhile vast numbers of amateur and professional writers each year will publish articles, research studies, book reviews, short stories, poems, or letters to the editor in hundreds of thousands of publications ranging from nationally known newspapers and magazines through the most obscure and unindexed church newsletters, science-fiction fanzines, or high school literary magazines.

Never assume that your subject is not among the millions of Americans who have been published in one form or another at some time or another. As an experiment, I asked a friend to check with her family members. She came up with a list of over a dozen siblings, aunts, uncles, and cousins who had written for publication. Their output included bible lessons for a religious newspaper, a college textbook in education, a work on family genealogy, recipes for a cookbook, a self-published autobiography, and, in the case of one uncle, communist pamphlets in the 1940s.

Finding an Author's Books

How do you track down subject's books, including out-of-print, small press, vanity press, and self-published books? One quick way is to look in biographical dictionary entries about subject. A large proportion of book authors and other writers find their way into such dictionaries. This is true even of rank amateurs: The very energy that propels them to finish a book may also have propelled them into prominence in business or some other field. And however peripheral their writing is to their main career, they will proudly list (in the questionnaire they fill out for the dictionary editors) even that unreadable self-published autobiography distributed to only a few dozen friends and relatives.

Serious authors are just about the most exhaustively covered category in the biographical dictionary business. The chief publisher of biographical reference works on writers, with fairly comprehensive listings of each writer's published titles, is Gale Research Inc. Its *Dictionary of Literary Biography* (141 volumes so far) contains biographical-critical entries on even very obscure American writers in a wide range of categories: novelists, poets, dramatists, screenwriters, short-story writers, ethnic writers, magazine and newspaper journalists, children's writers, literary scholars and critics, humorists, science-fiction writers—the series even includes a volume on beatniks. Gale also publishes *Contemporary Authors* (142 volumes so far) and *Contemporary Authors New Revision Series* (43 volumes so far), both of which are available on CD-ROM. These and hundreds of other reference works are indexed in Gale's *Biography and Genealogy Master Index* (*BGMI*) (see section 5.2), which includes over 1 million citations to biographical entries on 400,000 authors (these figures do not include the hundreds of thousands of people in *BGMI* who have done occasional writing while following a career in some other field and whose writings may, as noted above, be mentioned in their entries).

Several other key reference works and databases will help you compile a full list of books and pamphlets written by subject:

- R.R. Bowker's *Books in Print* includes entries for over 1,120,000 books—virtually every English-language book in print from every press, in every genre, on every subject. This 10-volume set, available at most book stores and libraries, includes author and title indexes and a volume listing nearly 160,000 titles declared out of print or out of stock indefinitely during the previous year. It is kept up to date between editions by *Books in Print Supplement* and *Forthcoming Books*. Many public libraries and large bookstores have Books in Print Plus, a CD-ROM version of *Books in Print*.

- Books in Print Online includes complete records for almost 2 million in-print and forthcoming titles as well as over 600,000 titles declared out of print or out of stock since 1979.

- H.W. Wilson's *Cumulative Book Index* (*CBI*) has annual volumes dating back to 1969 and multiyear volumes dating back to 1928. *CBI* is available online and on CD-ROM for easy searching of any author's name.

- LC MARC, the commercial version of the Library of Congress's computerized catalog, contains bibliographic records for every book in English cataloged by the Library of Congress since 1968. (Books in other languages are covered beginning at various points in the 1970s.) Updated weekly and containing over 3 million records, LC MARC is fully searchable by author, title, subject, and so on. Library of Congress records prior to 1968 can be accessed via REMARC. Both databases are available through DIALOG.

- BRS's Books Information database, available via CompuServe, includes indexing of pamphlets, books from small publishers, books published in English overseas, and other hard-to-find publications.

Through these resources you will probably find the titles of any of subject's books if they were published under his or her name and if the copyright was registered with the U.S. Copyright Office. (Note that many self-published works bearing a copyright symbol are never formally registered.)

Perhaps the easiest way to find subject's obscure books or pamphlets is by simply calling up him or her and asking for a list. Ned the Nazi may be the most paranoid person in the state of Arkansas, but if you phone him at his rural bunker and say you're interested in his writings he'll probably react like any other proud amateur author—talk your ear off and then send you a complete collection of his out-of-print scurrilous pamphlets by Federal Express at his own expense.

If, however, Ned refuses to discuss his writings with you, run his name through RLIN or OCLC: Pamphlets bearing his name may have been cataloged by an archive of right-wing nativist publications.

What to Look for in Subject's Writings
Whatever their literary or scholarly merit, subject's writings may furnish personal background information unavailable from any other source and thus justify the often arduous search to find them. This is most clearly the case when subject has written his or her autobiography or memoirs. Once, after spending weeks collecting information on a New York businessman, I discovered to my chagrin that most of this information had been readily available all along in subject's self-published autobiography. Although most subjects of backgrounding have not written autobiographies, their books or articles on other topics may tangentially reveal many facts about themselves

and their close associates, and also may provide a window on their values and psychological makeup. In addition, that short story or poem they dashed off for a local newspaper contest may reveal secret desires and unresolved psychiatric traumas in disguised form.

To squeeze the maximum amount of personal information out of any book written by your subject, you must search systematically from cover to cover. The acknowledgments page may give you the names of relatives, friends, and colleagues of subject; his or her agent and editor; and foundations or government agencies that provided financial aid for his or her research. The page that faces the title page may include a list of subject's previous books. The dedication may provide you with the first name of subject's spouse or live-in lover. Indeed, the dedications of successive books may be the archeological strata of subject's relationships. (A famous science-fiction writer once dedicated a novel about a sexy android to 31 women, apparently his most fondly remembered sweethearts. Alas for any future biographer, he did not provide their last names.)

The preface or foreword may include autobiographical remarks (or, if written by someone else, appreciative comments on subject's work mixed with a few tidbits about subject's personal background). The bibliography may include several of subject's articles that you hadn't heard of before. The works by others that subject chooses to list in the bibliography or cite in the footnotes or endnotes may provide a window on subject's unspoken ideological biases.

Often the most important resource is the book's index, which may include numerous page references to the author and to organizations and individuals linked to the author, including those listed in the acknowledgments. Although the index of an autobiography or memoir by subject will be the most useful, the indexes of books in other categories may lead you to implicitly autobiographical passages both in the text and in the notes. This is especially true of works of journalism and contemporary history that include memoir-type material in passing. A good example is *The Rise of the Right*, William A. Rusher's excellent history of American conservatism from the 1950s through the 1980s. Rusher, publisher of *National Review*, was a key player in this history, and the index has hundreds of references to Rusher himself, his magazine, and his closest associates. Thus, although the book appears at first glance to be history rather than autobiography, it actually includes in scattered form a rich autobiographical profile of its author. The presence of such material cannot always be inferred from the title or library classification of a book.

Reviews and Criticism

To find reviews of your subject's books, use the *Book Review Index* (*BRI*). This standard reference work published by Gale includes a bimonthly index and annual cumulations. *BRI*'s 1993 Annual Cumulation includes over 146,000 review citations for about 75,000 works reviewed in over 500 periodicals and newspapers. There is a master cumulation for 1965–84 in 10 volumes, including 1.6 million citations; and a master cumulation for 1985–92. *BRI* from 1969 to the present is available online from DIALOG and on CD-ROM, offering 2.5 million citations to reviews of about 1.5 million titles.

Many scholarly and scientific periodicals that review books are not indexed in *BRI*. Such reviews, however, can be found in the specialized indexes covering these periodicals, which can be searched via DIALOG.

When you go to the cited magazine or newspaper issue to photocopy the review, look at the letters-to-the-editor section in the following issues: An unfavorable review of subject's book may have elicited an indignant reply either from subject or from a friend or admirer; a favorable review may have flushed out subject's detractors and enemies to express even fiercer indignation.

For quotes and summaries of critical opinion about an author—including material from books of criticism as well as periodicals—see the various biographical/critical dictionaries published by Gale. Also see H.W. Wilson's *Book Review Digest* (*BRD*), which provides excerpts from and citations to reviews of over 6,500 English-language books each year. *BRD*'s retrospective volumes date back to 1907 and can be easily searched via the cumulative author/title index. The contents of *BRD* since 1983 are available online and on CD-ROM. *BRD* is also easily searchable dating back to 1975 via the *Book Review Digest Author/Title Index 1975–1984* (print only).

Note that if you plan to interview your subject, familiarity with critical reviews of his or her writing is essential: first, because it shows that you take his or her work seriously; and second, because nothing will get a writer talking faster than an opportunity to criticize his or her critics.

Miscellaneous Writings by Subject

In backgrounding any professional or serious amateur writer, the following reference works from the H.W. Wilson Company should be checked: *Essay and General Literature Index* (over 250,000 essays published between 1900 and the present; print version from 1900 and online and CD-ROM versions from 1985); *Short Story Index* (over 150,000 short stories published between 1900 and the present; print only); and *Play Index* (over 30,000 plays published from 1949 to the present; print only).

Finding Subject's Newspaper and Periodical Articles

Your first step should be to search the relevant full-text, abstract, and index databases (see sections 6.4 and 6.5). For publications not included in any database—or for issues of a publication that predate its database coverage—your options will include print indexes (e.g., *Readers' Guide to Periodical Literature*); clippings files; article, book, and résumé bibliographies; and special bibliographical works. In the case of journalists who have written full time or as regular freelance contributors for an unindexed newspaper or magazine, just look for their byline in each issue on the microfilm or in the bound volumes.

If your subject is a journalist, a database search may turn up hundreds of articles; if a scientific researcher or scholar, scores of articles. This can compensate for the often paltry courthouse paper trail that intellectuals (as opposed to real estate developers and politicians) leave. The articles of a prolific writer comprise a rich chronological record of the topics in which he or she has been interested and the collaborators with whom he or she has worked. In the case of a journalist, one gains a fascinating record of the lives he or she has touched and the enemies he or she has made. This provides interesting options; for example, the Lyndon LaRouche organization, seeking negative information in 1984 about NBC investigative reporter Brian Ross, called up all the mobsters and Teamster hoodlums he had pilloried over the years.

Critics of Subject's Articles
While searching for subject's articles, also keep an eye out for replies, which may appear in a letter-to-the-editor format or as a full-blown article. Often such replies will be indexed under subject's name; if not, they can be found by looking through the next few issues of the publication following the appearance of his or her article. The essay or reportage you thought was so brilliant may have been subjected to devastating criticism. If the criticism is less than devastating, at least you've gained the name of someone who dislikes or envies the author.

Subject's Scientific and Scholarly Articles
In your public library you will find the various H.W. Wilson scientific, scholarly, and professional indexes, including *Applied Science & Technology Index*, *Art Index*, *Biological & Agricultural Index*, *Business Periodicals Index*, *Education Index*, *General Science Index*, *Humanities Index*, *Index to Legal Periodicals*, *Library Literature*, and *Social Sciences Index*. Most of these works provide coverage dating back to early in the century, often under a succession of different titles. Several of them lack a separate author index, but electronic versions enable you to search for an author's name for the years covered by the database (unfortunately none of the H.W. Wilson databases begin earlier than 1981). All are available at public libraries on CD-ROM; online access can be gained via CompuServe. To search all Wilson databases at once for any author's name, use the Wilson Name Authority File.

Through DIALOG, you can access indexes with somewhat broader coverage of recent years than the Wilson indexes provide (and often beginning much earlier than the online versions of the Wilson ones) in every major field of scholarship, science, and technology, and in every major profession. Some of the most important are:

- Arts & Humanities Search (indexes 1,300 of the world's arts and humanities journals, plus relevant material from 5,000 other journals; 1980 to present)

- ERIC (over 700 periodicals of interest to educators; 1966 to present)

- Legal Resource Index (over 750 law journals; 1980 to present)

- MEDLINE (over 7 million records from over 3,700 biomedical journals; 1966 to present)

- Scisearch (over 8 million records from 1974 to present, representing the vast majority of the world's significant scientific and technical literature)

- Social Scisearch (over 2.5 million records from 1,500 social science journals plus social science material from 3,000 journals in other fields; 1972 to present)

- Philosophy Index (indexing and abstracts from over 270 journals; 1940 to present)

- Religion Index (indexing and abstracts from over 500 journals and 450 multiple-author works; 1949 to present).

Several of these and other scientific and scholarly databases on DIALOG are also available in print form; for example, MEDLINE corresponds to three printed indexes: *Index Medicus, Index to Dental Literature,* and *International Nursing Index.* Some of the indexes cover not just journal articles but also monographs, multiple-author books, conference papers, conference panel discussions, book reviews, and other special modes of scholarly and scientific communication. Of special interest if you are backgrounding a scientist's work is the Conference Papers Index, which covers over 100,000 scientific and technical papers presented at over 1,000 conferences annually since 1973.

Note that a subject's entry in the *Directory of American Scholars* (over 39,000 entries) may include a bibliography of some of his or her articles. In addition, you can look in the bibliography of any of his or her scholarly or scientific books or articles. Scholars and scientists are usually careful to include all of their own prior articles, research studies, and books relating to the given topic. (Obviously to gain the biggest list, you would look at subject's books or articles in his or her main specialty rather than his or her forays into other fields.) For instance, research psychologist Theodore X. Barber's *Hypnosis: A Scientific Approach* contains in the bibliography a list of over 60 articles by Barber.

A search of subject's published writings through the years will provide several types of information to supplement what you find in biographical dictionaries or professional directories. For instance, an article will usually identify the university, think tank, or government or private-industry laboratory with which subject was affiliated at the time of writing; this may fill in gaps in what you know about his or her job history. By noting the names of subject's coauthors on various articles, you will learn who some of his or her closest colleagues and mentors have been at various career stages. You should also note the names of graduate students or junior scientists whose contributions to a paper were acknowledged in an apparently grudging manner (some of these may feel their work was ripped off or that subject otherwise took advantage of them, and they may be willing to talk about it).

An article or book may also include information about government or foundation grants subject has received. The preface to Dr. Barber's hypnosis book discloses that his research from 1956 to 1976 was supported by grants from the National Institute of Mental Health (MF-6343c, MY-3253, MY-4825, MH-7003, and MH-11521). Once you know the funding source, you can find details on a government grant via Freedom of Information requests, and you can find details on foundation grants via Federal 990 forms or foundation annual reports. Note that grants on federal research projects are preceded by a review of the application by a committee of government scientists. After the research study is completed, another committee of scientists will write a peer review summary report. This report is available from the grantor agency.

Also note that scholarly and scientific indexes usually cover letters to the editor and other communications disagreeing with an article or report. These polemical pieces can sometimes be scathing (as can attacks on subject's works found in the proceedings of scientific conferences). The indignant letter writer or outspoken panelist may become your best source in unmasking the pretensions of a pseudoscholar or pseudoscientist.

In searching scholarly and scientific literature (especially if you extend your search beyond the top journals with the highest standards), you will frequently find a large amount of flimflam. Scholars and scientists are under constant pressure to publish or perish (even if they are primarily teachers rather than researchers). The result of this pressure (and of the need to pad curriculum vitae bibliographies to qualify for a better post) is that professors often churn out research articles on trivial topics (or, in the humanities and social sciences, shallow opinion pieces requiring no research). A virtual industry of unrefereed scientific journals and obscure scholarly journals has arisen to abet this practice. In the sciences today, at least 40,000 journals produce a million articles a year, a vast percentage of which is of dubious value.

The various tricks involved include publishing a study in unnecessary installments (with each installment counting as a separate article), publishing two versions of the same findings in different journals, allowing colleagues to piggyback their names onto your articles as coauthors while you also piggyback onto theirs, and of course putting your name first on a study for which your graduate students did all the work. The most extreme padding occurs in the so-called team reports churned out by certain scientific laboratories. These labs will be working on many studies at once, and sometimes a dozen or more lab scientists will be listed among the coauthors of a given study even though the contributions of most of them were minimal. Department heads and research supervisors, in particular, get their names added to scores of articles—a kind of scientific "droit du seigneur."

Unpublished Academic Writings

Dissertations, theses, and senior honors papers from accredited universities and colleges are discussed in section 11.1. A frequently overlooked source, however, is the many dissertations and theses from *unaccredited* universities and colleges that are not indexed or abstracted in Dissertation Abstracts Online or in the print volumes on which it is based. Although it is unlikely that a diploma mill will keep such documents, your subject may have a degree from a legitimate unaccredited school (e.g., a bible college) that will be proud to give you access to its dissertation and thesis files. (See *College Degrees by Mail*.)

Anonymous and Pseudonymous Authors

Many books are published under pseudonyms, but the reason often doesn't involve any great desire for secrecy. A prolific author may decide that two books under one name in a single year won't sell as well as two books under separate names. A mainstream novelist may decide to write his or her trashy thrillers under a pseudonym in order not to undermine his or her "literary" reputation. Often you can find the truth simply by looking in *Cumulative Book Index* where the author's various pen names are cross-referenced with the real name. Library card catalogs usually have this information, taken from the Library of Congress catalog system. The Library of Congress card for Wall Street commentator Adam Smith's *Powers of Mind*, for instance, tells us that his real name is George J.W. Goodman.

Things are not so simple if an author is really determined to conceal his or her identity. The Library of Congress Copyright Office's Application Form TX does not require the copyright claimant to reveal the name of the work's author. In some cases, the claimant of an anonymous or pseudonymous work is in fact the unadmitted author of the work, but in other cases the claimant is an employer or other person for whom the work was "made for hire" or someone who simply purchased the contractual right to claim legal title.

Registration details on all active copyright and mask-work registrations on file at the U.S. Copyright Office (coverage from 1978 to the present) is available on DIALOG. (For earlier copyrights you must pay the Copyright Office a fee for a manual search.) The database includes monograph records and legal document records. The former provide information on the initial registration and renewal of a work; the latter, information on assignments and ownership status. If you are searching for the identity of an anonymous or pseudonymous author, you should check all successive Form TXs, supplementary registrations, and records of transfer of copyright ownership pertaining to the work in question. You should also examine the entire portfolio of works published under the given pseudonym: Clues to the author's identity may be found in the records for one of these works that are not found in the records of the work you first researched.

If an author is trying to conceal his or her name (for instance, on a self-published manual on how to grow marijuana) and also to retain control of the work, the copyright claimant may be the author's attorney or spouse (especially a wife under her maiden name), or a corporation or unincorporated business set up by the author or an associate. In such cases, the standard backgrounding techniques in this book may enable you eventually to discover the author's identity.

Some anonymous or pseudonymous authors will fail to register their self-published book or pamphlet with the Copyright Office (although they will probably put a copyright notice on the title page anyway). However, such works will usually have the name of a publisher on the cover or inside, and this publisher—even if it's just a one-book operation—will be a registered business. In addition, if the book is sold mail-order via a post office box, you can find out from the post office who rented the box (see section 13.1).

If you're still stumped, look for clues in the book itself: the printer and/or typesetter's name, the printers' union bug, the credits for a cover artist or other illustrator (or an artist's signature on one of the illustrations), and the photo credits. Any of these clues may lead you to someone who knows the author's identity.

11.4 Subject's Garbage

This resource has produced some interesting if smelly results through the years. A private investigator's examination of the trash of Skadden Arps Slate Meagher & Flom, a major Wall Street law firm, led to the arrest and conviction of two individuals for securities fraud. Freelance journalist A.J. Weberman's probe of the garbage of Bella Abzug during the Vietnam War led to the revelation that Abzug and her husband owned stock in two major defense contractors. Jack Anderson's snooping in J. Edgar Hoover's garbage turned up empty booze bottles that called into question Hoover's sanctimonious demand that all FBI agents be strict teetotallers. In the early 1980s I gained much information on Lyndon LaRouche's organization through my garbage rounds. (Landlords in Manhattan would call me at the newspaper *Our Town* when anything interesting turned up in the garbage of a LaRouche follower living in one of their buildings.) Once when a LaRouchian couple moved out of an apartment leaving behind heaps of papers and trash, I spent a happy afternoon crawling around in the dumpster on the street in front of the building collecting bank statements, phone bills (with lists of long-distance numbers called), and supposedly top-secret internal memos of the LaRouche organization.

The *National Enquirer* was criticized for going through Henry Kissinger's garbage. The tabloid's reply: How can Kissinger complain about privacy when he ordered the bugging of his own staff's phones at the National Security Council?

For tips on this unusual technique see A.J. Weberman's *My Life in Garbology*, published by Stonehill Publishing Company in 1980. You can obtain a copy of this out-of-print classic by writing to Weberman at 6 Bleecker Street, New York, New York, 10012.

Weberman cautions against trespassing on private property. Pick up garbage only from public sidewalks. With millions of homeless people sifting through garbage cans all over the United States today, it's unlikely anyone will challenge you, especially if you dress like a homeless person. Weberman's own specialty was to go to the Manhattan townhouses of the rich and famous where the garbage was either on the sidewalk or in an alley. To make sure he had the right can, he'd sift through a bag in search of a piece of junk mail with subject's name on it.

People generally put out their garbage the evening before (or early in the morning prior to) the scheduled pickup. If you want to snatch the garbage from in front of your local cult leader's mansion, call the sanitation department and ask on what days of the week (and at what hours) the garbage is picked up on that block. If you want to raid the office trash of a local business, note that the trash from commercial buildings is usually picked up by private carters. You can find out the pick-up schedule via a chat with one of the building maintenance employees or a pretext call to the building superintendent.

11.5 License Plate Surveillance of Subject's Visitors

Jeannie arrives at her boyfriend Tom's house earlier than expected. While parking her car down the block, she observes a seductively dressed blonde exit Tom's front door, get in a Toyota, and drive away. Jeannie would like to know who that woman is, but she doesn't want to ask Tom and thus tip him off that she knows he has extracurricular visitors.

Russ the anti-Klan activist has stationed himself on a hill above the cow pasture of Roy the grand dragon. Through his binoculars he observes several cars and pickup trucks pull up in the yard. Angry-looking men enter the house where they remain for several hours. A Klavern meeting? Naturally, Russ would like to know the identities of the visitors, but he is certainly not going to stroll down the hill and ask them.

If Jeannie and Russ manage to get the license plate numbers of the cars in question, they may get the answers to their questions (or at least clues to the answers) from the state Department of Motor Vehicles (DMV). Motor vehicle registration information is often publicly available. If you have the license plate number of a car, you can write to the DMV for the owner's name and address (for restrictions, see section 10.2).

In some states, an answer to a written request may take weeks, although you can sometimes get a speedier response by using the state's official request form. If you need the information immediately, go through an online public records vendor. If you need license plate searches on a frequent basis, open an account with an investigative gateway and learn how to do your own searching.

License plate searches involve two basic pitfalls. First, the license plates may have been switched so that you end up with information on the wrong car. To guard against this, note the car's make, year, and color so you can later check this against what you receive from the DMV.

Second, the driver of the car—the person you are trying to identify—may not be the owner of record. Jeannie, for instance, discovers that the owner of the Toyota is a man; she now must determine if the mysterious woman driver is his wife, girlfriend, sister, daughter, or whatever. Russ finds out that the owner of one of the cars at the Klavern meeting is a rental agency. He must now persuade someone at the agency to tell him who rented the car that day.

Depending on the circumstances, other sources of confusion might arise during Russ's ongoing license plate research regarding right-wing extremists. One of the cars he observes may turn out to be stolen. Another, apparently that of an out-of-state visitor to a Klan meeting, may actually belong to a local guy who's registered his car in another state to get lower insurance rates.

In spite of the above limitations, license plate checks can be quite useful. Essentially there are two types of surveillance involved: you can stake out a residence or business and see who visits, or you can do a drive-through or walk-through, e.g., go to the company parking lot and gather all the license plate numbers (especially of cars that have company parking stickers—see below). Do not use a pen and notebook; this might call unwanted attention to you if you're on foot—and it requires a partner if you're driving. I recommend a tiny microphone clipped to your shirt collar so you can dictate the numbers and vehicle descriptions into a tape recorder. Also, wear earphones so any observer will think you're just listening to music and that the movement of your lips is singing rather than dictation.

Both types of surveillance may help you find potential sources. A stake-out of visitors at subject's house (from a parked car down the street) may give you the name of a maid or relative. A walk-through of the parking lot of subject's small construction company may give you the license plate numbers of all workers in the front office. The uses of such information are only as limited as your imagination and initiative.

When examining parked cars up close, don't miss the information presented in the form of stickers and medallions on the windows, bumpers, and trunk. Registration and inspection stickers are only the tip of the iceberg here. The dealer's medallion will tell you who originally sold the car, and where. Parking-permit stickers may tell you where the car's current owner lives (e.g., a township or village parking sticker), where his or her vacation home is located (a private beach sticker), where he or she works (a company parking lot or university faculty sticker), and where he or she goes to school (a high school or college student parking sticker), as well as the fact that he or she has a bit of clout at city hall (a VIP parking sticker).

In addition, a car may have a trade union sticker, college sticker (if there's no campus parking sticker to go with it, this is probably a proud alumnus's car), ethnic celebration sticker (e.g., "Erin" or "Italia"), and an auto club membership sticker (this is usually an indication of middle-class status). Still other stickers (especially bumper stickers) may reveal which national parks the owner visited on his or her most recent vacation, what his or her favorite charity is, which candidates he or she voted for in the last presidential election, and his or her ideological beliefs (either right wing or left wing) regarding feminism, world peace, or street crime.

License Plate Codes

License plate letters and numbers—and also the plate colors and embossed captions and symbols—contain coded information. Thus, while observing license plates you can decide on the spot which vehicles to check out further. You can also learn information from the license plates that might not be contained in the abstract of registration. For instance, in several states the license plate letters reveal the county or congressional district in which the car was registered. Depending on the state, a plate may also reveal such information as the use or weight of the vehicle, the first letter of the owner's last name, the owner's occupation or professional status, his or her membership in a particular private organization or Native American tribe, and his or her status as a veteran, government official, handicapped person, or diplomat. Almost always, the plate will tell you if the car belongs to a rental or leasing agency.

New York State license plates are a fascinating example of the above. The dozens of codes include DCH (chiropractor), DAV (disabled veteran), TV (television industry), NYP (press), RX (pharmacist), and PBA (Patrolmen's Benevolent Association). If a New York plate has three numerals followed by a dash and a "Z" plus two other letters, the car is registered to a rental or leasing company.

License plates may also reveal if a car belongs to the state government and even may identify the particular government department. Who was using the car at a particular time—or who the car is assigned to on a regular basis—should be publicly available information, although you might have to make a formal request under the state's sunshine law.

Federal government license plates are coded for dozens of departments and agencies; for instance, "J" means Justice Department and "D" means Defense Department. But many government cars will simply have the letter "G" before the numbers, meaning Interagency Motor Pools System.

A detailed description of the coded information for all 50 states, the District of Columbia, and the federal government is contained in Thomson C. Murray's *The License Plate Book* (see bibliography).

11.6 Finding Your Subject in Books and Dissertations

Millions of living Americans are mentioned in books and dissertations, either in passing or as the subjects of small portions of the text. Finding these passages is important not just for the information they contain but also because the author and/or his or her sources often know much more than was printed. Begin by checking the *Biography Index*, which, among other things, indexes biographical information from otherwise nonbiographical works. Next, if your subject has a background in politics, big business, national security, or organized crime, check NameBase (see section 6.5), a cumulative index of over 400 books (mostly works of investigative journalism).

To go beyond these two works, you will need to apply the principles of parallel and indirect backgrounding (see sections 1.3 and 1.4). First, make a list of all notable persons, organizations, and events with which subject has been associated. Second, collect the titles of books that might have information regarding each name or topic; LC MARC and REMARC (both on DIALOG) will be helpful here. Third, go to the largest library and/or the library with the strongest relevant subject collection in your locality and search the name indexes of all the books on your list that are available; be sure also to examine any lists of interviewees in a book's acknowledgments or appendix to see if subject's name (or the names of any of subject's associates) crops up. Fourth, see if the library has copies of any other likely books mentioned in the bibliographies of the above books but that you missed in your earlier searching. (If you have direct access to the stacks, you might also do a little intuitive browsing in the relevant subject areas—I've often found crucial books this way.) Fifth, contact the authors of books that mention subject or subject's associates to see if they have any further information (including interview notes or tapes); also contact the authors of the most promising books not available in the library to see if they mentioned in print or have any background information on subject. If an author is dead or can't be located, call a library that has the book in question (the RLIN or OCLC databases can help you here) and try to talk a staffer into checking the name index for you; if the book contains citations that interest you, borrow it or get a photocopy of the relevant pages through interlibrary loan.

If you wish to extend your search to doctoral dissertations and master's theses, use Dissertation Abstracts Online to find the likeliest titles. Note that any dissertation or thesis accepted by a university in your locality will be available in that university's library, while photocopies of most dissertations and many theses nationwide are available from UMI (see section 11.1). Before ordering a photocopy, make sure the dissertation was not published at some point (the book, including revisions and updates not in the original dissertation, might be available in a local library). Once you get the dissertation or book, pay special attention to the lists of unpublished source documents and interviewees in the bibliography and appendix. If you feel any of the material in the dissertation requires further probing, contact its author (see section 11.1 for finding academics) with your questions and your requests for access to research notes, telephone numbers of people he or she interviewed, and so forth.

12 ∙

Self-Defense Backgrounding

12.1 Backgrounding a Physician

This section is intended for medical consumers who need to check a doctor's credentials and competence. The information given here could be a life-and-death matter for those who must choose a surgeon and an anesthesiologist or who would select a cardiologist or other specialist with the necessary skill to spot life-threatening illnesses at an early, treatable stage. The information could also be useful in choosing a primary healthcare provider for one's children, in preparing a malpractice suit, or in protesting an outrageously inflated medical bill.

Basic Background Information
The Physician Masterfile of the American Medical Association (AMA) is a computerized database that tracks every licensed physician in the United States from medical school through retirement. It includes both medical doctors (MDs) and doctors of osteopathy (DOs). It will tell you a doctor's address, date and place of birth, where he or she attended medical school (and year of graduation), dates/places of internship and residency, fellowships and board certifications (if any), disciplinary sanctions (if any), states in which the doctor is licensed, and the year each license was granted.

For information from the Masterfile, write the American Medical Association, 515 North State Street, Chicago, Illinois, 60610; or call (312) 464–5000. Much of the same information, although without the constant updating, is available at your public library in the AMA's *Directory of Physicians in the United States* (issued every two years). Brief professional data on both MDs and DOs can also be found in state medical rosters such as the *Medical Directory of New York State*, which includes 40,000 state-licensed doctors. Additional information on DOs can be found in the *Yearbook and Directory of Osteopathic Physicians*.

For information on specialists, consult *The Official ABMS Directory of Board Certified Medical Specialists*, a four-volume set (hereafter, *ABMS Directory*) published annually by Marquis Who's Who in cooperation with the American Board of Medical Specialties. This directory (also available on CD-ROM) includes biographical and professional data on most board-certified specialists in the United States (more than 428,000 doctors) and lists among other things the type/date of certification, postresidency fellowship training, and current academic and/or hospital appointments. Information on specialists certified only by DO specialty boards can be found in the *Yearbook and Directory of Osteopathic Physicians* (some DOs, however, are also certified by the ABMS board and hence are included in the *ABMS Directory*).

More detailed biographical information on doctors can be found in works such as the *Biographical Directory* of the American Psychiatric Association.

Is Your Doctor a Menace to Your Health?

According to Dr. Robert Derbyshire, past president of the Federation of State Medical Boards, 10 percent of America's doctors are less than competent. These are the doctors who are the targets of a majority of malpractice suits and state disciplinary proceedings. How do you spot them?

Consumer watchdog lists

Ask at your public library for *10,289 Questionable Doctors*, a two-volume directory published by Public Citizen. It includes physicians, dentists, chiropractors, and podiatrists nationwide who have been disciplined for providing substandard health care and for a variety of unethical and illegal activities. Covered are actions by state medical boards, Medicare, and the Drug Enforcement Administration.

Also check with consumer groups in your locality to see if they have published a guide to local doctors that includes information on disciplinary actions, malpractice awards, and so forth. Several of the state Public Interest Research Groups have published such guides.

State medical boards

Each year about 2,000 doctors nationwide are subjected to state medical board disciplinary action on such grounds as gross negligence, incompetence, sexual abuse, moral unfitness, fraud, professional misconduct, practicing while impaired with a psychiatric disorder, intoxication on the job, and failure to disclose a prior license revocation in another state. The most severe disciplinary action is license revocation. Lesser actions include license suspension, various license limitations (for instance, a temporary prohibition against prescribing addictive drugs), censure, or reprimand.

In a few states, all records of completed investigations are open to the public, even if no disciplinary action was taken. But in the majority of states, the public gets access to disciplinary records only when a public sanction is imposed. As most complaints are never seriously pursued (because of lack of staff), and of those seriously pursued most never result in any public sanction, the records of most state medical boards are clearly of limited use to the cautious medical consumer. Furthermore, even if disciplinary action is eventually taken, the administrative procedure may drag on for years, during which time the incompetent doctor continues to victimize unwitting consumers without hindrance.

If the physician you are checking out has no history of disciplinary action in his or her current state of residence, don't assume he or she is clean. Although safeguards are supposed to be in place to prevent physicians from skipping to a new state after losing their license, some state boards let dangerous doctors slip through the cracks. For instance, these boards will not tell the Federation of State Medical Boards about a license revocation if a doctor voluntarily surrenders his or her license. As a result of this administrative "plea bargaining," the physician is able to relocate to another state and establish a new practice.

A thorough background check on a doctor (as when you are contemplating a malpractice suit) should include requests for information regarding disciplinary actions from the state medical boards in every state in which you believe he or she might previously have been licensed as well as from states in which he or she currently holds a license. If the doctor you are checking out is a DO, be aware that in several states you must check with a separate osteopathic board.

The AMA's Physician Masterfile may be useful in your search at this point. This database includes an asterisk beside the name of each doctor against whom disciplinary action has been taken by a state medical board *if* the board reported that action. (Since the state boards are often negligent or tardy in their reporting, the lack of an asterisk beside a doctor's name should be regarded as meaningless.) The Physician Masterfile does not provide any details about the disciplinary action; for that, you must contact the state board.

Malpractice suits and other legal actions

The defendant/plaintiff index in the state district court in any locality where subject has practiced may list malpractice suits against him or her. Depending on how the court indexes are organized (see Chapter Nine), it may be difficult to find all the cases involving a particular doctor. If the index lists only first-named defendants in multiple defendant cases, you might compile a list of cases in which subject's clinic or one of the physicians who shares a private office with subject are the listed defendants—you could then check the docket sheet to see if subject's name is also included for any of these cases.

If you find any malpractice suits against subject, check with the plaintiff's attorney. And if you don't find any suits but wish to continue your search, check with local attorneys specializing in medical malpractice. They may know about horror stories that never reached the courts. They may also know of suits against your doctor that you didn't find in the court index or suits or disciplinary actions against him or her in other localities that you might not have located on your own.

You might also check the court indexes for any suits filed by a physician against a patient for failing to pay his or her bill. Although many of these patients may be deadbeats, some may have withheld payment because of sincere indignation over the poor treatment they received. This is a way to uncover medical victims who never sued the doctor. (Only a small percentage of malpractice atrocities ever result in a suit, since the patient is too intimidated and/or is unaware of his or her rights.)

An online search of the LEXIS Medical Malpractice Library, which includes malpractice case law from all 50 states as well as from the federal courts, might turn up a case involving your subject that was appealed to a higher court. However, over 90 percent of all malpractice cases never go to trial, much less to an appeals court, but are settled out of court.

County, state, and specialist medical societies

Peer review committees of these societies will sometimes investigate complaints against a doctor independently of the state board. However, their findings may not be publicly available.

Eyewitness informants

Former nurses or receptionists of a doctor may have horror stories to tell and may remember the names of victimized patients. (Whenever you visit a doctor's office, jot down the names of staff members just in case you have to contact them later if you file a malpractice suit.)

Indirect evidence

If a doctor's entry in the latest edition of a directory no longer lists him or her as having privileges at a certain local hospital, and yet the doctor is still in private practice in the same locality without any other hospital affiliation, this may mean his or her privileges at that hospital were revoked and other hospitals are avoiding him or her for some reason. Hospitals have access to the U.S. Department of Health and Human Services' National Practitioner Database, which tracks malpractice awards/settlements and disciplinary actions nationwide on a massive scale (but is not available to medical consumers due to pressure from the AMA). If a doctor lacks any hospital affiliation whatsoever (or has ended up with admitting privileges only at a single third-rate hospital), the hospital review committees may be exercising a justifiable caution. Until you know more, avoid this doctor.

How Competent Is Your Doctor?

The following are some of the elements to consider in selecting a doctor. If the doctor in question is a certified specialist, much of what you need to know on each of these items is available in the *ABMS Directory*. If you belong to an HMO, you can get background information on any affiliated doctor from the member services department. However, you should *also* raise directly with any doctor you visit your questions and concerns about his or her professional background and status. If the doctor expresses exasperation or anger, get another doctor.

Hospital affiliations

As well as being a warning flag (see above) regarding incompetent doctors, hospital affiliation can also be a pointer to the very best doctors. Look for a doctor who is affiliated with a prestigious hospital or medical center and who is on the attending staff rather than just having admitting privileges. Top hospitals seek the top doctors for their attending staffs, and applicants undergo rigorous screening. In addition, doctors affiliated with such institutions undergo periodic peer review by doctors who themselves are among the most highly qualified. Be aware, however, that the reputations of hospitals vary from specialty to specialty. The less-well-known hospital with which your specialist is affiliated may actually have the best reputation in that specialty.

For listings of the best hospitals and medical centers nationwide, see Dr. Robert Arnot's *The Best Medicine*, Herbert J. Dietrich and Virginia H. Biddle's *The Best in Medicine*, and local or regional guides. If your doctor is affiliated with a small hospital with which you are unfamiliar, you can obtain information on its accreditation status from the Joint Commission on the Accreditation of Health Care Organizations, which is located in Oak Brook, Illinois.

Academic appointments

An appointment to a medical school faculty is further evidence that a doctor's career is one that can withstand close scrutiny. But is he or she a clinical teacher involved on a daily basis in direct patient care? And is the medical school in the top tier? (See discussion below of medical school rankings.)

Specialty certification

The American Board of Medical Specialties (ABMS) is composed of 24 boards offering certification in 25 specialties (neurology and psychiatry share a single board). A board-certified doctor is referred to as a "diplomate" of the board. This title is evidence that he or she has undergone rigorous supervision and testing in that specialty. About 30 percent of the doctors who call themselves specialists in a given field are not certified by the specialty board, and their use of the specialty designation (e.g., "dermatologist" or "pediatrician") is somewhat misleading although not illegal. To see if your doctor is board certified, call the ABMS hotline at (800) 776–2378 or check the latest edition of the *ABMS Directory*. As noted above, MDs and DOs have separate specialty boards, although some DOs are also board certified under the ABMS system. To check a DO's status with the osteopathic boards, call the American Osteopathic Association at (800) 621-1773 or look in the *Yearbook and Directory of Osteopathic Physicians*.

Your physician may have a certificate hanging on the wall from a self-designated medical specialty board or society that is not recognized by the ABMS. Some of these groups do offer specialized training on their own. Others, however, exist chiefly to promote research in a particular field and do not offer any kind of training. It speaks well for your physician that he or she belongs to such societies (most ABMS board-certified specialists also belong to one or more), but his or her membership should not be confused with ABMS-approved certification. (Note that there are also a number of fraudulent boards—contact the ABMS for a list.)

Some physicians refer to themselves as "board eligible." This simply means they have completed their residency and are qualified to sit for the board exams in their specialty.

Board-certified physicians are organized into "colleges," such as the American College of Radiology. In each college, there are two levels of membership, that of "Member" and that of "Fellow." The status of "Fellow" signifies a higher level of peer recognition and experience. Note that this term should not be confused with a "fellowship" in the sense of a post-residency training program in a subspecialty (see below).

Subspecialty certification
Specialties in today's medicine cover a wide range of subspecialties. You will thus want to know if the specialist you are consulting has adequate training and experience in the subspecialty category that includes your own medical condition. Subspecialty certificates (e.g., the American Board of Pediatrics' certificate in Pediatric Endocrinology) are usually granted by the specialty board only to physicians who have completed a board-approved fellowship in the given subspecialty. There are also unapproved fellowships that may provide training in the same subspecialty but without leading to a certificate. Sometimes the unapproved status of the fellowship reflects the inferior quality of the training offered by the program (although an unapproved fellowship is better than none); other times the unapproved status may mean simply that the subspecialty is a new one in which approval from the board has not yet been obtained. Note that in some new subspecialties that do not yet have an adequate number of approved fellowship programs, physicians who have gone through not-yet-approved programs are accepted as candidates for the subspecialty certificate.

Recertification and Continuing Medical Education credits
Board certification used to be a one-time thing; once you were certified you remained so forever. Today most boards require their specialists to undergo reexamination and recertification every 6 to 10 years. Even if a board does not have this requirement, a responsible doctor will undergo voluntary recertification at least once every 10 years. Unfortunately, there is a grandfather provision in the rules of many boards; doctors who were certified prior to the adoption of recertification requirements are exempt from those requirements; only the newer doctors have to comply.

As well as requiring recertification exams, some specialty boards require a doctor to earn a certain number of Continuing Medical Education (CME) credits to maintain certification. In addition, the state medical boards in some states require CME credits as a precondition for medical license renewal, and the AMA encourages voluntary CME by presenting Physician Recognition Awards to doctors who complete 50 hours of CME each year (look for this award on your doctor's office wall).

Whether or not CME credits are required in a particular state or by a particular board, you should select a doctor who is on the cutting edge of his or her specialty and is well acquainted with any and all new findings or procedures that might save your life. This means a doctor who reads the refereed medical journals in his or her specialty, conducts clinical research, attends medical conferences and seminars, and participates in the work of medical societies related to the specialty.

Before you visit a doctor for the first time, read over some of the latest important research articles concerning your condition (you can obtain these by calling the research foundation/information clearinghouse for your particular illness, e.g., the Lupus Foundation of America). Ask the doctor about these research studies and see whether you get a knowledgeable and thoughtful response—or a blank stare.

Subject's published articles

Another index of a physician's competence is whether or not he or she has published articles or research studies in his or her specialty in recent years. This question can be checked in the *Index Medicus* or via MEDLARS, the National Library of Medicine's online system, or MEDLINE, a commercial version of MEDLARS available on DIALOG or LEXIS (see section 11.3). If you see an article by your doctor in the waiting room, don't be impressed unless it's from a refereed journal (i.e., a journal whose editors submit each article to a panel of leading researchers or clinicians before deciding to publish it). There are many "throwaway" medical journals that print substandard work and that are the medical equivalent of vanity publishers.

Never judge a physician's competence by the fact that he or she has written books for laypersons on diet, plastic surgery, holistic medicine, and other trendy topics, or has a column in a tabloid newspaper, or appears frequently on talk shows. Some of the worst quacks use these methods to attract victims.

Peer ratings

Consult *The Best Doctors in America*, by Steven Naifeh and Gregory White Smith, which lists over 3,700 physicians nationwide by specialty, and Robert Arnot's *The Best Medicine* (see above). In addition, see if there is a guidebook for your own state or locality (e.g., the Castle Connolly Guide, *How to Find the Best Doctors for You and Your Family, New York Metro Area*, which includes a roster of "Doctors of Excellence" based on peer rating by nurses as well as by doctors).

You can also conduct your own informal survey. When you need treatment in a given specialty or subspecialty, call several board-certified practitioners and ask whom they would recommend. Then make an appointment with the doctor whose name is mentioned most frequently (of course, you should get a second opinion no matter how good this doctor's peers say he or she is). Depending on the seriousness and complexity of your problem, you might want to search for the best local specialist or the best national one. In either case, the *ABMS Directory*, which provides listings geographically for specialists and subspecialists, can help you identify doctors who can provide you with the names of their top colleagues. And in conducting your survey don't forget to ask the opinion of your primary-care physician as well as any specialists you are already seeing for related conditions.

Subject's medical school training

All U.S. and Canadian medical schools are accredited and the standards are generally high (this statement does not apply, of course, to diploma mills). Various guidebooks for applicants will give you a sense of which are better than others (although relative ranking may shift over the years). See especially U.S. News & World Report's *America's Best Graduate Schools*, which rates the top 40 medical schools according to reputation ranking by medical school deans, senior faculty, and directors of intern/residency programs as well as by objective scores. Elements that various guidebooks use in ranking include median scores of those admitted on the Medical College Admissions Test (MCAT), the median undergraduate Grade Point Average (GPA) of those admitted, and faculty/student ratios. When you first visit a doctor, you might ask, among other things, what was his or her class standing in medical school. If you think it's not tactful to ask this particular question (especially of a doctor who has been out of school for quite a few years), ask instead where he or she did his or her residency: The larger and more prestigious hospitals tend to get the top-of-the-class medical school graduates.

The American system of medical education includes 16 colleges of osteopathic medicine. The majority are independent colleges but several are affiliated with major universities (e.g., Michigan State University and Ohio University); all are fully accredited. Students attending these schools must, like students at "allopathic" (mainstream) medical schools, be graduates of four-year colleges and must pass the MCAT. The education provided at an osteopathic school parallels that given at allopathic schools in most respects. One advantage claimed by osteopathy is its strong philosophical emphasis on preventive and holistic approaches (the majority of osteopathic graduates become primary-care physicians).

Subject's residency training

In general the best facilities for training of residents are in major teaching hospitals (i.e., those closely linked to a medical school and where there is a strong overlap between the hospital medical staff and the medical school teaching staff). However, a smaller and/or less well-known hospital may offer better and more varied practice in some fields.

Residencies last at least three years, but some states will grant a license to a doctor after only one year of residency. If a doctor did not thereafter complete his or her residency, you should want to know why.

Foreign-trained doctors

According to the AMA, graduates of foreign medical schools comprise about 20 percent of all doctors practicing in the United States (note that Canadian medical schools are not regarded as foreign in these calculations). For many years, any graduate of a foreign medical school wishing to practice medicine in the United States had to pass the Foreign Medical Graduate Examination in the Medical Sciences (FMGEMS) before he or she could obtain a hospital residency and be licensed to practice medicine in a U.S. state. There were problems with FMGEMS, however. In 1984, 9,000 physicians who passed were ordered to retake it after officials discovered that almost half had obtained the questions in advance. Beginning in 1993, foreign doctors were required to take the United States Medical Licensing Exam (USMLE) along with U.S. medical school graduates. However, in the first year of this new exam the failure rate on the clinical portion was 61 percent for foreign graduates as opposed to only 7 percent for U.S. graduates.

The problem of evaluating foreign medical schools (except Canadian schools) is quite complicated. If the degree is from an accredited medical college in a developed country such as Great Britain or Israel, it may represent an education as good as if not better than one obtained at a comparable U.S. school. But in some parts of the world entrance to a medical school (and even the degree itself) can be purchased through bribes. And medical schools in some countries may, as a result of lack of financial resources, offer a substandard and outdated education even for the most sincere and hardworking students. However, residency training at a U.S. hospital and the rigorous study required to pass the USMLE do guarantee that most foreign medical graduates who obtain U.S. medical licenses have a fairly high level of competence.

A special problem is the many Americans who gain medical degrees overseas after failing to get into U.S. schools. Some foreign medical schools, especially in the Caribbean and Mexico, cater exclusively to Americans or have special programs for Americans. Less than 10 percent of American graduates of Caribbean and Mexican medical schools, however, end up qualifying to practice medicine in the United States. Several of these schools are so notorious that California and New York won't license their graduates even if they pass the licensing exam.

Whether one is looking at the diploma of an immigrant doctor or of an American who studied overseas, one measure of the diploma's worth is the annual passing rate of graduates of the given school on the USMLE. The rates range from nearly 100 percent for Israeli medical schools to below 20 percent for some of the Caribbean and Mexican schools. (To find out details on a particular foreign medical school, contact the Educational Commission for Foreign Medical Graduates in Philadelphia.)

Unlicensed doctors

Thousands of medical school graduates in the United States are practicing without a license for a variety of reasons. This includes many foreign doctors who have immigrated to this country but have been unable to get into residency programs and obtain licenses even though they have passed the USMLE. Some of these frustrated doctors enter the "medical underground" and practice in inner-city or rural clinics that can't attract anyone else. Although many prove to be quite competent doctors, the same cannot be said for individuals with degrees from substandard schools who have been unable to pass the USMLE and the many doctors with U.S. degrees who have been stripped of their licenses for incompetence or unethical conduct. A doctor's medical license should be displayed on the wall of his or her office. If you don't see it or have doubts as to its legitimacy, check with the state medical board.

If you have chosen a physician out of the phone book, without any referral, there is always the possibility that he or she is a totally untrained fraud. In 1980, the FBI's "Dipscam" probe found that bogus medical diplomas could be purchased in the mail for less than $50. In 1984 a congressional subcommittee estimated that upwards of 10,000 individuals, including many totally untrained imposters, were practicing medicine in the United States with fraudulent credentials. Thus, if you *must* visit a new doctor without a referral, ask what medical school he or she graduated from and/or check the diploma on the wall. If you have any suspicions (i.e., if the office seems grungy, the doctor behaves strangely, or he or she suggests weird therapies), look up the school he or she claims to have graduated from in the list of all accredited U.S. and Canadian medical schools included in the *ABMS Directory*—and also check out his or her name with the state medical board.

Quack cures

Beware of any doctor, no matter how legitimate his or her medical license, who promises miracle cures via unorthodox methods for which there is no substantiation in research studies published in refereed journals. Such doctors frequently cite only their own haphazard clinical results (often reported in some throwaway medical journal or an interview with a nonmedical newspaper or magazine) with no real scientific backup. They often complain that they are being persecuted by a medical establishment that refuses to recognize their brilliance; or that their findings are being suppressed by a conspiracy involving the American Cancer Society, the National Institutes of Health, and even the CIA. Usually a search of the public record will turn up malpractice suits and/or medical board disciplinary actions against such a doctor.

If your doctor suggests a New Age or homeopathic cure, insist on seeing medical data that proves through double-blind experiments that the treatment provides more than a placebo effect. Also, if the cure is being suggested for a serious or life-threatening ailment, seek a second opinion from a board-certified specialist in the given area of medicine. Of course, many New Age treatments are harmless, and some elements of New Age medicine may be integrated into mainstream medicine in the years ahead. (Certainly the use of traditional herbs and acupuncture may be *less* harmful and quackish than the practice of those mainstream doctors who routinely perform unnecessary hysterectomies and caesarean sections and who, until only a few years ago, were telling their patients it was okay to smoke cigarettes.) Nevertheless, unproven shamanistic or "quantum medicine" practices should not become your primary form of medical care for major illnesses.

A word on surgeons
If you are planning to have surgery, you will want to check out your surgeon and anesthesiologist—and the hospital—as thoroughly as possible. In addition to the various means of estimating a doctor's professional competence outlined above, a new tool specifically for rating surgeons and surgery units may soon be available. In 1990, a New York State court ruled that state health officials had to comply with a Freedom of Information request from a daily newspaper and release data revealing the variable surgery death rates for hospitals and among surgeons within each hospital. Although some health-care experts believe that statistical scorecards of this type are not very useful because of random variability, patients facing the knife will be unlikely to ignore such data.

Is Your Doctor Honest?
Financial honesty is not the same thing as professional competence, but it's a good bet that a physician who cheats either the government or clients via billing practices is also going to skimp on the quality of health care he or she offers. In addition, the greedy doctor will be more likely than others to recommend unnecessary and dangerous (but lucrative to the doctor) surgical procedures. If you have doubts about a doctor, there are many places you can look for evidence of unethical and fraudulent behavior:

- The Inspector General's Office of the U.S. Department of Health and Human Services (HHS) publishes a list of physicians and other health-care professionals suspended from the Medicare program. This list, revised every six months (but with monthly updates in between), gives the length of and reason for the suspension. You can obtain a copy of the current list or learn whether or not a particular doctor's name is included by calling (202) 619–1142. Note that if a doctor is reinstated to the Medicare program, his or her name is taken off the current list; however, the name will still be on the cumulative sanctions list. To check the latter, call (410) 965–9600. If you want details on a particular case you must file an FOIA request.

- Local social workers employed at senior centers, officials of the area agency on aging, or spokespersons for senior organizations may have tips from their constituents about doctors who abuse the Medicare program.

- The Drug Enforcement Administration can tell you if a physician's controlled-substances license to prescribe addictive drugs has ever been revoked and if there is an open case against the physician. You can then file a Freedom of Information request for further information.

- The Health Resources and Services Administration of HHS maintains a list of physicians and other health-care professionals who have defaulted on government-insured loans under the Health Education Assistance Loan Program. In 1993, HHS first published in the *Federal Register* a list of 4,973 former students, most of them now practicing healthcare professionals, who had defaulted on loans obtained since 1979. The list of defaulters will be published annually.

Medical billing scams

The clearest evidence of your doctor's larcenous tendencies might be right before your eyes—in the inflated bill you received last month. This bill (or the backup documentation, if you should request it from his or her office or from your insurance company) may contain clear evidence of the "creative" billing techniques that allow doctors to increase their fees fraudulently. (Both the government and private insurers have charged that these techniques add billions of dollars each year to healthcare costs.) Essentially, the billing codes are manipulated so as to break a single operation down into four or five suboperations (this is called "unbundling") for each of which the doctor bills separately. The *New York Times*, on December 20, 1991, gave examples from cases in Chicago in which hysterectomies ordinarily costing about $3,300 were broken down into four separate procedures (e.g., "pelvic examination under anesthesia" and "abdominal exploration") with the bill thus hiked by more than $2,000 dollars. Some doctors were even charging separately for removing fallopian tubes and ovaries on the left and for removing those on the right!

Another form of unbundling is when doctors break down a single visit into separate procedures such as drawing blood, writing a prescription, and talking to you on the phone afterwards about your test results. This also jacks up the bill at the expense of patient and insurer.

The self-referral game

Your doctor may be practicing self-referral, defined as sending patients for lab tests, an MRI scan, walk-in surgery, etc., to a facility in which the doctor has a financial stake. A recent Florida survey estimated that 40 percent of the state's doctors had an interest in one or more clinical laboratories or other referral facilities. Often this type of arrangement results in "churning"—the ordering of unnecessary tests and procedures from which the doctor will get a cut in addition to already excessive fees.

To check this out, you can simply ask the doctor if he or she is an investor in the clinical lab, or you can look in the state corporation and partnership files. Self-referral joint ventures usually offer a doctor a limited partnership; the key element is not the amount of money invested but the number of patients referred (for which the doctor gets what amounts to a kickback). Doctors often try to hide their investment, as by investing under a corporate name (one medical lab in Florida was owned by 200 corporations, each of which was a front for a different doctor). (Note: If a lab won't accept Medicare or Medicaid this should be a warning sign; laboratory self-referral is legally prohibited under Medicare and Medicaid.)

Other forms of self-referral include sending a patient to a private hospital in which the doctor is an investor, and sending a patient to a specialist across town with whom, unbeknownst to the patient, the referring doctor has a legal partnership, a sort of "group practice without walls" (the referring doctor then shares in the specialist's inflated fees). In addition, doctors are now investing in pharmacies, especially in the Medical Associates of America (MAA) chain, and sending patients there to get their prescriptions filled. (MAA sets up and manages the pharmacies; individual doctors each invest $10,000 in their local pharmacy and reap profits from the referrals.)

12.2 Backgrounding an Attorney

The wrong lawyer can screw up a client's life. Many heirs have lost their inheritance when their attorney embezzled the money from the escrow account. Many divorcing couples have ended up in an unnecessary legal war because of the mutual provocations of greedy lawyers. Thousands of innocent people are currently serving long prison sentences (and many are on death row) because their trial lawyer was too lazy to do his or her homework. The choice of a lawyer should be undertaken with the same care as the choice of a physician or surgeon.

Many people choose a lawyer on the recommendation of a friend, or they are referred by their family lawyer to a specialist in criminal or divorce law. In a few states, the bar association offers a referral service that uses a list of prescreened attorneys chosen by a committee of their peers based on intensive interviews. In general it is unwise to pick a lawyer at random out of the yellow pages or via a private referral service that advertises on billboards, or via bar association referrals that are not based on any prescreening process.

The following sources and techniques will help you make an informed decision on whether to hire (or fire) a particular lawyer or law firm.

Collecting Basic Biographical and Professional Data

The 27-volume *Martindale-Hubbell Law Directory* lists alphabetically by state and city over 800,000 attorneys and law firms; this includes almost every active attorney in the United States. It provides each attorney's year of birth, year of admission to the bar, college and law school education, and affiliation (if any) with a law firm; it also may include a peer rating of the attorney's competence. A biographical section in each volume provides expanded information on about 40,000 attorneys and law firms. The coverage of large law firms often includes biographical sketches of every partner, associate, and "of counsel" attorney. Sketches are also included of attorneys employed in the legal departments of many major corporations.

If your research library keeps back editions of *Martindale-Hubbell* in the stacks, you can use them like a city directory to fill in gaps in your knowledge of an attorney's job history. Also you can use them to find additional biographical sketches: An attorney now practicing alone and not covered by a biographical sketch in the current edition may have been an associate at a large corporate firm several years back—by going to the right edition you will find his or her sketch.

Yet more sketches will be found in *Who's Who in American Law*, the *Directory of Bankruptcy Attorneys*, the *Directory of Women Law Graduates and Attorneys in the U.S.A.*, and other works of legal biography. In addition, you should check the *BGMI* and, on CD-ROM, The Complete Marquis Who's Who Plus. Given the prestige of the legal profession, and the large percentage of attorneys who are also influential in business, government, and politics, you have an excellent chance of finding subject in one or more nonlegal who's whos.

Legal News Sources

You can also search newspaper and periodical databases and clippings files for subject's name. If you can afford it, the best place to begin is the LEXIS Legal News Library, which includes general legal news publications such as *American Lawyer*, *Legal Times*, *The National Law Journal*; state and local law newspapers and magazines such as *New York Law Journal* and *The Texas Lawyer*; and legal specialty publications such as *Computer Lawyer* and *The Business Lawyer*. You might also check the LEXIS American Bar Association Library, which includes the *ABA Journal* and other ABA publications.

For a less-expensive search, try DIALOG's Legal Resource Index, which provides cover-to-cover indexing of hundreds of law journals and six law newspapers as well as legal news citations from Magazine Index, National Newspaper Index, and Trade and Industry Index.

There are about 60 state or local legal newspapers in the United States, most of them not available online. You might check the backfiles of the one for your locality to see if you find any articles about subject. Another possibility is your state or county bar association newsletter.

Subject's Professional Standing

Evidence that subject is highly regarded within the local legal community may be found in the legal newspapers and newsletters and in the daily press. Such evidence might include his or her election as an officer of the state or county bar association, active participation in bar association committees, or service on a commission appointed by the mayor or governor to investigate corruption. It also might include various awards he or she has been given. None of these things is in itself proof of an attorney's competence and honesty (nor is the absence of them proof of the opposite). But the legal profession is generally quite concerned about its public image. County and state bar associations are not going to elect as their spokespersons or give awards to the dregs of the profession (and the active lawyers who make these decisions know very well who the dregs are, even though they may not talk about it with outsiders).

An attorney's professional standing will also be reflected in informal gossip within the local legal community. You, as a mere legal consumer, can't just call up an attorney's colleagues out of the blue and expect frank answers regarding his or her competence and honesty. You will have to get someone with ties to the legal profession (a local reporter or court clerk, if not a lawyer whom you know personally) to act as an intermediary and gather the gossip for you.

Formal Peer Ratings

As noted above, *Martindale-Hubbell* includes ratings of attorneys. In addition, the *Martindale-Hubbell Bar Register of Preeminent Lawyers* lists over 7,500 blue-chip lawyers and partnerships selected as preeminent by their peers. Every two years, Woodward/White of Aiken, South Carolina, publishes *The Best Lawyers in America*, which lists about 11,000 attorneys based on telephone and mail peer-review surveys.

An Attorney's Track Record

To rate the competence of a trial attorney, you will obviously want to know if he or she wins a large percentage of his or her cases. You can find this out by talking to attorneys who know subject's work, by checking courthouse records (a friendly court clerk may steer you to some of subject's present or former cases), or by talking to a local news reporter on the courthouse beat. When you find out about a particular case subject has handled, look under the client's name in the plaintiff/defendant index for other cases in which subject may have represented him or her and which may give a better idea of subject's skills. In addition, check articles in legal newspapers (see above) regarding trials in which subject was involved.

A search of the state LEXIS libraries for each state in which subject is actively practicing and also the LEXIS library for his or her specialty (e.g., the LEXIS Corporate Law Library) may reveal how some of his or her trial cases turned out and/or how successfully he or she handled the appeal process. If your local court has a computerized system that merges index and docket in one database, you may be able to search by name of attorney or law firm, thus gaining a large list of subject's recent cases.

Don't be overly impressed by trial wins or losses. Ninety-seven percent of cases are settled before trial (and in many of the remaining 3 percent the lack of such a settlement was because counsel for one or both parties had defective negotiating abilities). You may need a canny negotiator—a good poker player—more than you need a practitioner of courtroom theatrics. Thus it might be important to look at the outcome of some of subject's negotiated settlements. Unfortunately, such settlements, especially in product liability and medical malpractice suits, are often kept confidential.

Political and Courthouse Influence

There is also the issue of subject's political clout and his or her clout with the judges and court administrators. Can subject maneuver to get your case before the right judge? Does he or she have implicit pull with that judge based on their mutual involvement in clubhouse politics (and the fact that subject's law partner, say, was a big contributor to the judge's last campaign for reelection)? These questions can be crucial to you not so much because subject's clout guarantees favorable rulings from the bench when your case goes to trial but because the other side knows that subject *can* exercise such clout (i.e., call in a favor) *if he or she has to*. This makes the other side more amenable to settling the case on terms favorable to you. They know a trial would be risky even if your case is not the strongest.

How Good Is Subject's Legal Education?

Ask your prospective attorney where he or she attended law school (or note the diploma on his or her wall) and then check with the American Bar Association at (312) 988–5000 to see if the school is accredited. As well as the 176 accredited law schools in the United States, there are dozens of unaccredited ones, ranging from those with a full course of study but substandard facilities/faculty through correspondence schools through outright diploma mills. In most states, a person cannot sit for the bar exam unless he or she has graduated from an accredited school. A few states, however, will allow graduates of unaccredited schools to sit for the bar or will admit to their bar graduates of unaccredited schools who have already been admitted in another state. Only California allows graduates of correspondence law schools to sit for the bar, and this only under special circumstances.

In California and five other states individuals are allowed to take the bar exam without having gone to law school at all if they have instead taken the old-fashioned route of apprenticeship to a practicing attorney (what used to be called "reading law"). Officials of the ABA disapprove of this practice, although it was the route taken by a majority of lawyers in past generations. As of 1991, there were only a few hundred individuals working in legal apprenticeship programs nationwide.

The ABA does not rate law schools as better or worse; it only accredits them. U.S. News and World Report's *America's Best Graduate Schools* rates the top 50 law schools and then divides the rest into tiers of relative excellence, using among other things reputational ranking by law school professors, judges, and practicing attorneys.

Arco Books publishes *The Best Law Schools*, which selects the top 40 schools in the country using three criteria: (1) admissions selectivity as measured by the median Law School Admission Test (LSAT) scores and median undergraduate Grade Point Average (GPA) of those selected, and by the acceptances-to-applications ratio; (2) placement power (percentage of graduates placed at graduation and their median starting salary); and (3) education effectiveness (percentage of graduates accepting prestige clerkships with federal and state appeals court judges).

Other law school guides provide such statistics for lower-tier schools (although not for purposes of ranking), and you can thus compare them to the alleged top tier. Such guides also include, as does *The Best Law Schools*, information on a school's student/faculty ratio, computer services, number of volumes in the law library, annual tuition, and affiliation (or not) with a prestigious parent university. From these facts one can make certain judgments about the relative significance of a degree from the school in question as of the year in which the data for the guidebook was gathered. Although one should look at back-issue guidebooks published during the years in which subject was a student at that school in order to be completely fair, it is a fact that law schools affiliated with major universities tend to remain in the same "tier" or "cluster" of schools over the years in terms of the quality of students they admit and the quality of the education they provide.

Don't make too much of the school tie in judging the competence of an attorney who's been in practice for many years: That he or she won admission to Yale Law School shows that he or she is smart, but it does not follow that a student who entered Brooklyn Law School the same year is not just as smart—it may just mean the latter didn't have the money to attend Yale. Schools such as Yale and Harvard undoubtedly have the most intellectually stimulating professors and give a superior education, especially for a would-be corporate attorney; but if you were a defendant framed by cops on a drug rap in the inner city, would you rather have a soft-spoken corporate-type WASP representing you, or a scrappy up-from-the-streets graduate of Brooklyn Law?

Subject's Academic Performance in Law School

This is perhaps best measured by whether subject passed the bar on the first attempt, and whether he or she obtained upon graduation a prestigious clerkship or an associate's position at a major corporate firm (both these hirings would have been influenced by subject's class ranking). You can also easily check if subject served as an editor of his or her school's law review (these posts are generally chosen based on academic standing, i.e., the top 10 percent of the class, and/or on writing ability) and if he or she was inducted into the Order of the Coif (a national legal honor society for which students are selected on the basis of scholarship as well as character).

Subject's Continuing Education

Bar association newsletters, legal newspapers, and biographical dictionaries will all give you clues as to how well subject is keeping up to date with the ever-changing law in his or her area of expertise. Some of the things you will want to know are: Does subject participate in legal conferences and seminars in his or her field? Does subject participate in continuing legal education programs as recommended by the bar association? Does subject teach courses part-time at a local law school? Has subject published a textbook or any recent articles in his or her legal specialty?

Subject's Legal Scholarship

Success as a legal scholar is no special indicator of success as a trial lawyer, but a legal scholar definitely has an edge when it comes to figuring out new tax loopholes for corporations or filing appeals in criminal cases. You might check if subject has an advanced law degree (all law school graduates receive a J.D.; those who go for further study receive the Master of Law, LL.M., or a doctorate). To find articles subject has written for law reviews and other law journals, consult H.W. Wilson's *Index to Legal Periodicals*, which currently covers about 600 journals and is available in print from 1952 and online from CompuServe and on CD-ROM from 1981. Or you can check the Legal Resource Index on DIALOG (over 750 law journals, 1980 to present). Full-text searches of over 70 of the most prestigious law reviews can be done through LEXIS's Law Reviews Library (which also includes the Wilson index and the Legal Resource Index). Although this full-text coverage does not go back earlier than 1981 for most journals, a search may turn up a citation or footnote that mentions an earlier article by subject.

Subject's Pro Bono Work

If an attorney is willing to spend a substantial amount of time working for free on worthwhile causes or for indigenous clients, it *may* mean that he or she takes a caring and conscientious attitude toward clients in general. But the opposite may also be true: the crusading lawyer may give paying clients short shrift because of his or her obsession with social causes. Always distinguish between high-profile crusading before the television cameras (which can just be a way of drumming up customers) and the nitty gritty of carefully preparing a pro bono case, taking it into court, and winning without any cameras around.

Why Didn't They Make Partner?

After perusing biographical information on an attorney's career, you may wonder why that attorney failed to make partner at the corporate law firm he or she joined fresh out of law school. Do not jump to the conclusion that an attorney who failed to advance beyond associate at a large firm and then ended up in a small partnership elsewhere is necessarily inferior or a discard. Apart from the issue of sexism and other forms of prejudice in the selection of partners, many associates today are actually turning down offers of a partnership in order to avoid possible liability if the firm should go bankrupt or become the target of criminal prosecution by the government. (The partnership form of organization exposes a firm's partners to great legal risk—and state regulators in most states will not allow lawyers to form limited liability corporations.)

Disciplinary Actions and Malpractice Suits

The ABA maintains a Discipline Database—a computerized listing of all disciplinary actions against attorneys reported to it by the discipline authorities in all 50 states, the District of Columbia, and Puerto Rico. On request, the ABA will provide you with a list of the states, if any, in which disciplinary action has been taken against a particular attorney; you will then have to contact the state authorities for further details. Note that the list will probably not be complete, since the tracking system depends on voluntary compliance by state authorities; also, the list will not include private sanctions against an attorney that were not made public by the state authorities.

Depending on the state, complaints against an attorney may be investigated by the bar association, a state appeals court administrative unit, or an office of court administration. Check with your local bar association to find out the procedures in your locality. A finding of culpability in a disciplinary proceeding may result in disbarment, suspension, or a lesser sanction (e.g., a private or public reprimand). News of a public sanction generally will be published in a bar association journal and/or a legal newspaper. Typical reasons for such a sanction might include drug use, a conflict of interest, or the misuse of a client's funds held in escrow. In most states, complaints of a more general nature regarding incompetence or negligence are rarely acted on by the disciplinary authorities, who also tend to give short shrift to complaints about excessive fees.

The amount of information you can obtain about pending investigations, closed investigations, and sanctions will vary from state to state. In Florida and West Virginia, records are public from the day the investigation is launched; in Oregon, they are public from the day the complaint is received. In 28 states, information about disciplinary proceedings becomes publicly available once formal charges are filed (since 95 percent of complaints are dismissed before reaching this point, this is not really very useful). In several states, the public never learns about a proceeding until after the disciplinary body has made its decision to disbar or suspend (which happens only in the tiniest percentage of cases).

Given the fact that many attorneys have licenses in two or more states, it is relatively easy for an attorney who is disbarred in one state simply to move his or her practice to another (note that lawyers often fail to disclose to state authorities a full list of states in which they are or have been licensed). In 1992, the ABA came up with a plan to give each lawyer a single identification number that will follow him or her from state to state and will be included in *Martindale-Hubbell*; this system was not yet in place as of 1994.

Without fail, you should check to see if your prospective attorney has ever been sued for malpractice or fraud in any of the states where he or she has practiced (see sections 9.2 and 9.3). As well as being listed in court indexes, such suits are frequently reported in local or state legal newspapers or, if the attorney is well known or the alleged misdeeds are especially egregious, in one of the national law newspapers and/or in the general press. Note that WEST-LAW, a legal database vendor, offers a Professional Malpractice Library that includes legal as well as medical malpractice case law from all 50 states. However, since legal malpractice cases (like medical ones) are mostly settled out of court, you should not rely exclusively on WESTLAW.

If you are considering hiring a particular attorney, feel free to ask him or her about any malpractice suits or disciplinary problems. If the attorney gets angry with you or questions your right to ask about such matters, you will know that he or she is *not* the attorney for you.

Subject's Ethical Lapses

Only .5 percent of attorneys are responsible for the most egregious actions such as absconding with a client's escrow funds or insurance settlement money. In New York, these tend to be middle-aged men with a drug, alcohol, gambling, or other addiction problem. Especially tempted are those who control estates and trusts with little or no oversight from their clients.

In most cases, a client's concerns will relate to less-serious ethical lapses, many of them built into the "culture" of the legal profession. These include fraudulent overbilling, which is practiced by attorneys serving private individuals as well as by those representing giant corporate accounts. Several companies now specialize in checking legal bills for corporate clients. A spokesperson for Legalgard, the oldest of these companies, told the *New York Times* in 1992 that his firm's investigators were finding irregularities in four out of five legal bills. Some typical practices include:

- a brief phone conversation with an opposing attorney is inflated into an hour-long telephone "conference"

- paralegals and secretaries at the firm are instructed to charge their downtime (while waiting for a new job to come in) to the previous client–matter number

- an attorney spends five minutes on LEXIS gathering case citations, then another half-hour moving around paragraphs of legal boilerplate with the help of a standard legal form software program, but charges the client for 20 hours of legal research and drafting of papers.

Some of the worst abuses occur in the world of divorce law. For instance, a male attorney may take advantage of a female client's emotional vulnerability during the divorce trauma and engage in sex with her on his office couch. Not only does he bill her for this time but he also mishandles her case. She ends up with insufficient resources from the divorce settlement to pay his inflated bill and he then initiates proceedings to foreclose on her house and attach her IRA account.

Verifying That Subject Is a Member of the Bar

Unfortunately, there are many individuals practicing law in the United States who are not legally entitled to do so. Some have law degrees but never passed the bar exam (occasionally you will read in the papers that even a corporate law firm partner or an assistant district attorney has been unmasked as having practiced law for years or even decades without having passed the bar). Some passed the exam but were denied admittance to the bar because of a prior criminal record. A few are imposters with no legal training whatsoever.

An attorney listed in *Martindale-Hubbell* will almost always be a member of the bar in the state under which he or she is listed. If you don't find the attorney's name in *Martindale-Hubbell*, or if something about his or her demeanor arouses your suspicions, you should—at a minimum—check with the state bar association before putting your legal affairs in his or her hands.

In general this will be a problem only if you pick attorneys at random out of the yellow pages or go to them on the referral of someone who in turn picked them at random for some minor matter such as the drafting of a will. Fake lawyers usually operate on the fringes of the legal profession with offices in low-income neighborhoods, and they target uneducated people.

12.3 Checking Out Your Date, Lover, or Spouse

Millions of American women are beaten by their boyfriends or husbands on a routine basis. An estimated 1,400 of these victims are murdered each year; thousands more are disfigured or maimed. In many cases, their children also suffer direct physical and sexual abuse from the out-of-control husband or lover. And many other tragedies can result from getting involved with the wrong man: He may be (or become) HIV positive as a result of high-risk sexual behavior or needle sharing that he neglected to tell the woman about. He may be a compulsive philanderer who will sleep with all her friends and make her life miserable even if neither he nor she becomes infected with any disease as a result. Or he may turn out to be a con man or professional bigamist whose ultimate aim is to loot her bank account and abscond with the cash.

If you have entered or are about to enter into a new sexual and/or marital relationship, you need to check out your partner. Some of the tips that follow are applicable to any and all new relationships, but others relate only to situations in which you harbor the strongest of doubts. In such cases, a thorough background check on your partner may be psychologically necessary for you to convince yourself to do what you already know deep down inside that you should do—split.

These techniques are presented in an order that reflects the dynamics of an average new relationship rife with conflicting emotions and ambiguous signals. We begin with simple things you can do to learn about your partner's background without actually snooping. We then examine various methods for learning about the things he may be attempting to hide from you. Certain methods involve a definite risk of embarrassment for you if he should find out; you will have to decide if you want to run that risk. Given the extreme dangers that women face in relationships not only with relative strangers but also with the sweet-tempered spouse they *think* they know, I believe it is better to risk a little embarrassment now rather than face major trauma in the years ahead.

Your First Steps in Protecting Yourself

You lessen your chances of getting involved with the lover or spouse from Hell by being extremely choosy about how and where you meet potential partners. The best situation is one in which a certain amount of prescreening is involved: Friends or relatives invite you to dinner to meet a man they know fairly well. Some dating services claim to prescreen applicants, but any screening they might actually perform will be extremely superficial.

If you meet a man who is entirely unvetted (as via a classified ad or at a bar or museum), always get his phone number rather than simply leaving him yours. Insist on getting his home number and address as well as his business number. If he won't give you his home number and address and refuses to say why, you'll know you don't need him in your life. If, on the other hand, he explains that he's already married or living with someone and doesn't want you calling his home, at least you're forewarned.

If a man gives you his home number and address, take a few seconds to look in the telephone white pages and/or consult Directory Assistance, just to make sure the name, address, and telephone number all fit. Also, its a good idea to spend an hour or so chatting with him on the phone before the first date; if you begin to pick up bad vibes you can always cancel.

In your early dates and phone conversations with subject, you should find out certain basic and easily verifiable facts such as where he grew up, where he went to school, what type of work he does, who his current employer is, his marital status, whether or not he has any kids by a prior marriage, and so forth. These are things that will usually come out spontaneously in conversation. If not, you can easily ask about them without seeming intrusive. (This means staggering the questions over the course of several conversations. If you ask all at once you'll sound like a cop.) If you're talking with him on the phone, write down any important names or other details on the spot. If he reveals a key name while you're on a date, jot it down as soon as you're alone (you might want to excuse yourself to the powder room to do so).

If subject was a complete stranger to you (and to your close friends) when you first met him, you should without fail check out some of what he says about himself. For instance: Call up his previous job (you can pretend to be from a personnel agency) and verify that he was in fact employed there. Call up his present job to make sure there's an extension listed in his name. Call up the registrar's office or the alumni association at the college he claims to have attended and verify that he's in their records. Call up his hometown to verify that his parents are listed in the phone directory (if not, call the telephone reference line at his hometown public library and get them to check a current or past city directory).

One easy thing to find out is his date and place of birth. Simply steer the subject to astrology or offer to read his palm as a pretext for asking this. Also at some point find out his full name and his mother's maiden name. If a thorough background check should become necessary, these facts will be important (see Chapter Seven).

Take your time getting to know this man before making any commitment, and get him to talk about himself as much as possible. Fortunately this is something most men love to do. With a little encouragement from you, he may tell you all about his past and present sexual conquests. If he's a narcissitic personality he will be quite vain about this and will talk in great detail if he gets a subtle cue that this turns you on (what you hear may be enough to decide you against pursuing this relationship).

Whether he's talking about former girlfriends or anything else, listen carefully and interject tactful little questions that can lay the basis for further investigation if necessary. When he talks about "this girl I was once involved with," ask what her name was; when he tells about the trip he took with her to Martinique, ask what year the trip occurred. Encourage him to elaborate with as much detail as possible and be alert for contradictory statements and improbable stories.

The telephone rather than a candle-lit dinner is the best medium for such conversations, because you can take detailed notes as he talks. But if for some reason he rambles best over drinks at a bar, write down afterward as much as you can remember—the whos, whats, whens, and wheres.

Encourage him above all to talk about his childhood and family. Most men who abuse their wives or girlfriends come from dysfunctional families in which abuse was a way of life. If Joe comes from such a family, you have a high probability of trouble unless he's gone through intensive therapy. Of course, Joe will not open up about the traumas of his childhood during the first or second date (and why should he? he doesn't want you to think he's emotionally disturbed), but eventually you should steer him into this area. Make things easy for him by first revealing a few of your own childhood traumas (if you can't remember any, invent a few).

If you jot down notes during each telephone conversation and after each date, you will soon have a considerable reservoir of information for potential checking. (Warning: don't leave the notes where he can find them if he decides to snoop on *you*.)

Don't expect that what he tells you will be 100 percent truthful. Most people have very imperfect and selective memories; they exaggerate things to put themselves in a better light (or to heighten the humor in a story); they smooth over their failures; they concoct all kinds of rationalizations for things that went wrong. However, you should be alert for any claims or stories that appear to go beyond the normal kind of fibbing that we all engage in. If Joe tells you he majored in psychology (because he knows you're interested in psychology) when he really majored in business but *wishes* he majored in psychology (and in fact took courses in psych), that's one thing. When Joe tells you he has a degree from Harvard when he really only briefly attended and then flunked out of a local community college, that's more serious. When Joe tells you he spent a year traveling around the world in the late 1980s when he really spent that year (as you learn later from a mutual friend) in prison for burglary, that should be the final straw.

You can never know for sure at first whether or not your new lover is hiding something from his past. One way to induce him to disclose it (if it in fact exists) is by casually remarking that your best friend's husband is a private investigator and that he checked out a boyfriend of yours a couple of years ago. Your new lover may then, upon reflection, start volunteering information so he can put a spin on it and thus minimize the damage or even make himself look like a martyr (ex-cons are often geniuses at this). For instance, he may tell you that a girlfriend once filed assault charges against him but it was really just a "misunderstanding" and besides she withdrew the charges. Although his story may sound plausible, you should remember that the woman in question isn't present to give her side of the story (nor are the cops who answered her 911 call or the emergency-room doctor who treated her injuries).

If Joe fails to talk about his past much on the first date or two, this might just be a natural reticence. But if he continues to be closemouthed about himself, try to discuss with him the reasons for his reticence. If he flatly refuses to recognize it as a problem, be aware that he'll probably take the same attitude to other problems in your relationship later on. This, as well as the possibility that he's hiding something, should be considered if you're trying to decide whether or not to continue to see him.

If you decide to get romantically involved with Joe, don't let it become a relationship that revolves exclusively around your own house or apartment. Insist on spending much of the time at his place, and while you're there keep your eyes open. I'm not talking about overt snooping, just the kinds of things you might normally notice. For instance, are there any prescription medications in his bathroom medicine cabinet? Don't ask him about this (he will regard it as a highly intrusive question, and even if he doesn't display any anger he'll hide future prescriptions that you might have an even greater interest in). If a medication arouses your suspicion, go to the public library and look in the *Physicians' Desk Reference*. This book, which is cross-indexed by brand name, generic name, and picture (color/shape of pill), will tell you exactly what a given medication is used for. If it has multiple uses, you can sometimes figure out which condition your friend is taking it for by the physician's name on the prescription label. This physician's specialty (if he or she is board certified) can be learned in *The Official ABMS Directory of Board Certified Medical Specialists*. If the physician is not listed there, you can learn his or her specialty via the guide to physicians (divided by practice) in the telephone yellow pages or via a call to his or her office.

If you notice women's clothing in plain view in one of Joe's closets or cosmetics on a dresser, this is something you should feel free to ask him about. It may be that another girlfriend spends enough time with Joe to keep some of her belongings there, although this is a matter you and Joe should have already resolved (you should have asked about other women, and he should have answered frankly before you ever set foot in his apartment). Of course, the presence of the clothing and makeup may simply mean that Joe engages from time to time in a harmless bit of crossdressing.

You may notice other things that are not *quite* as obvious; for instance, the sudden appearance of packages of herbal tea in his kitchen when you know he drinks only coffee and has zero interest in holistic medicine and health foods. Whether to ask him about such things is a tricky question. On the one hand, you're dying to know. On the other hand, if you ask him he may give you an extremely plausible (but totally dishonest) answer—and the only result will be that you've alerted him (as in the case of the prescription bottles) to the necessity of being more careful (i.e., more systematically deceptive). In general, you should *not* ask him about something you observed unless it was something in plain view and that you could have plausibly spotted without overt snooping.

Keep an eye out for pornographic magazines or videotapes that indicate kinky sexual interests he has failed to tell you about (for you to look at any magazine that's lying around or to examine his collection of videotapes is not regarded as snooping, even if it is, kind of).

If you really must do aggressive snooping, offer to cook dinner at his place—and then send him out with a list of things to purchase that should keep him occupied for a half-hour or more (i.e., things that require going to more than one store). Make sure he's well down the street before you start your search. The main things you should look for are his address book and/or his Rolodex, his appointment calendar, and his checkbook register. These will quickly give you a sense of the basic pattern of his life. Are there a large number of women's names in his address book? Does he have notations in his Rolodex about who's the best lay? (The latter information may be in a personal code of some kind.) What about doctor's appointments in his appointment book? And appointments with lawyers and/or court appearances? Checkbook registers are not as important in this era of plastic credit, but you might find a record of child support payments or payments to a psychotherapist.

If you see a phone bill on his desk, you might look quickly at the toll records. If you see any "900" numbers or audiotex numbers listed, write them down. If you call one of these numbers later, you might find that it's a phone-sex line specializing in practices or proclivities that you weren't aware your partner had an interest in.

Observe Him in Action

You can often learn more from observing how he interacts with his ex-wife, children, parents, and siblings (both in person and on the phone) than by any snooping. Does he see his kids frequently? Does he talk with them on the phone in a caring manner? (Also, does he pay child support regularly?) Before committing to this guy, you're well advised to spend some time with him and the kids and see how he interacts with them in person, not just on the phone. Does he lose his temper easily? Is he over-critical? Do the kids seem afraid of him or excessively withdrawn in his presence?

If possible, you should go with him to pick them up and observe how he interacts with his ex-wife. Does she seem afraid of him? Or do the two of them still seem to be pals? Some women get jealous if their new lover is still on friendly terms with an ex-wife or ex-girlfriend, but you should view this as a golden opportunity to observe his behavior in situations that offer vital insights into his personality and character.

Also, note how he deals with his parents and siblings. We have already discussed how you should encourage him to talk about them. But talk is cheap: The man who says his mother is the world's greatest mom may demonstrate the most grotesque loathing for her when you go with him to visit her. Before committing to a long-term relationship, insist on meeting any of your partner's parents or siblings who live within practical traveling distance. (Among other things, this is a good way of checking that he's really who he says he is and not a con artist using false ID.)

When you have dinner with his family it is important to observe not only his behavior toward the others (with you there, he may be artificially on his best behavior) but also their behavior toward one another. Do they appear to be warm and affectionate as a family group? Or is there tension in the air? The interaction at the dinner table may provide your first clue that he comes from a dysfunctional family (he himself may be blithely unaware of this on a conscious level and therefore may have given no indication of it when talking to you about his childhood). Of course, if you are not a mental health professional you can't really make a final determination on family dysfunction (in some families, yelling and screaming serves a healthy purpose). But you do have two eyes and two ears: If subject's father rules subject's mother through verbal intimidation and put-downs, you have grounds for concern that subject might try the same tactics on you at some point unless he has been through years of therapy.

Cultivating Informants

Always try to make friends with your lover's best buddies' girlfriends or wives. At least one of these women may have learned many of your lover's secrets during pillow talk with her own partner. If she likes and trusts you, she will pass on much of the gossip (unless, of course, she's the one secretly involved with your lover on the side).

Checking Out His Paper Trail

How deeply you want to look into your lover's past depends on many circumstances: If he's someone from out of town who was unknown to any of your friends and acquaintances prior to your meeting him, or if some of his stories don't quite add up, or if you just have an instinctive feeling that something's wrong, then you would be well advised to do some checking in public records.

First, see if he has a criminal record. To check this you must know where he has lived in past years, his date of birth, his SSN, and his full name. For tips on how to conduct such a search, see section 9.8; but be aware of the pitfalls: (1) county and state court records often are inaccurate and/or less than current; (2) a sloppy search can conjure up false links between an innocent person and crimes that in fact were committed by someone else with the same name; (3) records accessible to the public include only *convictions* (if Joe's ex-wife chose to drop the assault charges against him before trial you will not learn about it through a routine public-records check, nor will you learn about his rape trial if he was found innocent on a technicality); (4) a criminal records check will be worthless if Joe is living under a carefully crafted false identity and has not revealed to you his real identity.

If Joe has lived in many different places and you are becoming increasingly suspicious of his past, you might consider hiring a private investigator to verify his identity and do a *thorough* check for a criminal record. This advice is not just for new relationships but also for situations in which the guy you've been with for a couple of years suddenly starts to act verbally abusive or strangely secretive. Hiring a private investigator can be expensive, but if you're afraid subject might turn violent (and if you have kids in the house), do it.

If your lover is someone who's lived in your metropolitan area for a number of years, it's feasible for you to check out his financial stability on your own. You may already have questions on this score because of letters from credit collection agencies you've seen lying around in his apartment or because of dunning phone calls he's received while you were in the apartment. You can search at the county courthouse for tax liens, wage garnishments (the latter may be for child support), and listings in the judgment docket of money judgments obtained against him in court cases. You can search in the bankruptcy files at the federal courthouse to see if he (or any businesses he owns or used to own) has ever filed for bankruptcy. You can search the UCC filings to see if he has a heavy debt load. You can search at the register of deeds office for any foreclosure actions against his home. You can search at the parking violations bureau to see if he has a pathologically excessive number of unpaid parking tickets. What you uncover may suggest a pattern of disordered behavior that will inevitably spill over into his relationship with you. (It also may suggest that he has, or has had, a gambling or cocaine problem.)

Also check the local court indexes and those for any jurisdictions in which he lived previously to find any cases in which he is listed as either plaintiff or defendant. (Chapter Nine will tell you how to search the local court indexes on your own and how to obtain searches elsewhere.) You may find that he's been sued for fraudulent activity or for harassing a former girlfriend (be sure to get the full court record on *any* case in which a woman is the plaintiff and he's the defendant).

This brings us to the question of his divorce. If you've listened carefully while he talked (and talked and talked) about it, you'll already know where it was obtained and the approximate date. If court records in divorce cases are open to the public in the given jurisdiction, check to see if there's any allegations of spousal abuse (either physical or emotional) or of child abuse, any restraining order against your lover, and whether or not he has to pay child support or alimony under the terms of the divorce. If the court records are sealed, you can at least get the name of the ex-wife's attorney. It is probably not wise, however, to contact an embittered ex-wife directly while you're still involved with her former husband, but you might ask your best friend to call her on a pretext of concern for your well-being.

Just because there are no divorce records involving your lover does not mean he doesn't have an ex–common-law wife or has not otherwise fathered children. Indeed, a man who has never been formally married may still have a string of paternity suits, restraining orders, palimony judgments, etc., in his past. Always check for such cases in the relevant court indexes, and also check with the state office of child support (or whatever state agency serves the same function) in every state in which he has lived to see if he is wanted for failing to pay child support. If he has not told you about any children, you may still find pictures of them in his wallet or in his bedroom chest of drawers.

If You Think He's Not Who He Says He Is
Let's say you've checked out his paper trail and don't find anything dating back more than a few months. You might search his wallet while he's in the shower, or look in any desk drawers where he's likely to keep other I.D. while he's gone to the store. If you find I.D. under another name or multiple names, don't bother to confront him about it. He'd probably just tell you he's a government secret agent (the time-worn excuse of con men and other users of false I.D.). Simply walk out the door and never return.

Is There Another Woman?
Whether you're married to him or unmarried, all bets are off in this Age of AIDS if you have strong reason to believe that he's fooling around behind your back. You have the right to know for sure so you can make your decision either to leave him or to give him one final chance.

In this war of the sexes, the advantage is all with you. Most men who cheat want to get caught subconsciously and will provide you with little clues. Those who are psychopaths (i.e., lack more than a rudimentary conscience) may not want to get caught but they lack impulse control and thus also provide inadvertent clues. Likewise, men in both these categories have a certain contempt for women; they underrate their girlfriend or wife's ability to detect their deceptions.

Before you launch your investigation of your husband or live-in lover, make sure you're not on a paranoid jealousy trip. What seems strong evidence to you might not seem that way to an objective observer. Sure, he's taking showers twice as often, but maybe it's just because he's playing more racketball. Discuss things with your therapist or your mother (but not with your best friend—she might be the reason for those extra showers and that new brand of cologne).

You may suspect, among other things, that he's smuggling women into the house when you're not home. This may be a problem, especially, if you're working and he's not (he entertains the woman from down the block while you're slaving away to pay the rent) or if the two of you work different hours. You can check for hairs on the bed that are neither yours nor his by wrapping scotch tape around your finger and then rubbing it over the pillows and the area of the sheet near the headboard. (You could also hide a long-playing tape recorder under the bed before you leave for work, but this might be illegal in your state.)

If you and Joe still maintain separate residences, be more observant than ever when you visit his place—not only for the above clues but also for subtle evidence such as the remains of a Chinese take-out dinner for two in the kitchen garbage.

In your effort to collect evidence on Joe you may find that the other woman is your ally of sorts: She *wants* you to know and thus will accidentally leave cosmetics, shampoo, bobby pins, tubes of diaphragm jelly, or other traces of her presence in the bedroom or bathroom. Whether she's trying to drive you out of Joe's life or just being catty is immaterial. She's giving you the clues you need—use them!

More often than not, Joe will be cheating at motels, hotels, or at his secret lover's apartment rather than at home. Start keeping a record by date and time of every evening when he claims he has to work late or every weekend when he cancels on you because of alleged work emergencies or every night when you call him late but he's not yet home. You may need these records to crosscheck against his credit card charges at restaurants or motels (see below) or the toll calls on his phone bill. Also look for such telltale signs as matchbooks from a hotel or motel in his coat pocket or the smell of perfume on items of clothing he throws in the laundry hamper. Check his wallet for scraps of paper with women's first names and telephone numbers scrawled on them, suspicious credit card receipts, and so forth. But don't jump to conclusions—the woman's business card in his wallet *may* be that of the Xerox service representative and nothing more.

If you and Joe are living in the same household, you might decide to do a thorough search of the house. Arrange to stay home some day while he's at work or at a ballgame. Systematically search his closet, his drawers, his home office desk and filing cabinet, and especially the cabinet drawer (or shoebox) in which he keeps his financial and other personal papers. Look at the monthly statements, receipts, and cancelled checks on any credit card or bank accounts he has independent of you. Especially look for receipts from bars, restaurants, hotels or motels, or escort services (some of the latter will have names that are disguised to sound like something else). Look also for purchases that might be gifts for another woman (such as items from a florist or a jewelry or lingerie shop). Check especially the records of any periods when he was out of town on business—you may find that his week last winter at a business conference in Denver was really more like a week for two at an Aspen ski resort. (Note that some of his credit card charges may be made on a corporate rather than a personal card. The only way you can know about these charges is by peeking at the receipt in his wallet before he turns it in.)

To search the apartment systematically if you're not living with Joe is a drastic invasion of his privacy. I don't advise doing this, but if you feel you must then do it only when you are on the premises with his express consent. *Never* enter the apartment without his invitation—you could face criminal charges. One approach would be to arrange to stay in the apartment when he leaves for work some morning. Tell him the place is getting grungy and you want to clean it for him. If he accepts your offer, you will have gained the perfect cover for your search. You really *will* clean the apartment for him, until it's absolutely spotless. But in the process you'll keep your eyes open and let your fingers do the walking through the kitchen garbage bag, the bedroom and bathroom trash baskets, the outdoor trash can, and the medicine cabinet.

You'll also peek at his bills and private papers (just as a wife or live-in lover would do), especially if these papers are cluttered all over his desk and need straightening. In looking through them you might strike paydirt—a love letter or "Love You Forever" birthday card from his other girlfriend. If not, you might find suspicious credit card receipts and/or telephone toll records showing that he has been making lengthy late-night long-distance calls to a single number in another city or suburb (by reversing this number in a CD-ROM crisscross directory at the public library, you may find the other woman at last).

Whether you are a live-in or live-out lover, you can use this systematic house cleaning as a means to satisfy your curiosity about a wide variety of things that Joe may or may not have been hiding from you and that you never had the time or motivation to search for thoroughly—his medical bills, the little black book he once joked about, the pornography hidden in the locked drawer (if you can find the key) of his desk, and so forth.

You also might look at selected files on his personal computer. Many PC users today have special software programs to keep track of addresses, appointments, their checking account, and other aspects of their personal and business affairs; you might search these if you know enough about computers to access them (hopefully you will have induced him to explain the various directories and software programs early on in your relationship). You might also look for file names such as "Barbara" or "Judy" (or "Bar" or "Ju"), "XXX" (as in X-rated), and so on.

Note: Searching your lover's computer is something that could possibly be construed as illegal if the two of you are not living together. You will be on safest legal grounds if you have already used the computer with his consent and if other people have previously witnessed you working on your own files on that computer. Under no circumstances should you remove any printouts of his files and/or any backup disks from the apartment without his permission.

If you don't find evidence of his cheating anywhere in the house, it might be in his office desk at work. Here, if you're his wife, you have a definite advantage: You can show up unannounced a few minutes before he's to return from lunch and tell the secretary you'll wait for him in the office (with the door closed of course). When he comes in you'll tell him you just happened to be shopping in the neighborhood and decided to surprise him.

Don't forget to search his car; here the evidence again might be cigarettes in the ash tray, matchbooks or receipts of various kinds in the glove compartment, a used condom under the seat, and also the mileage on the speedometer—you may find he traveled a couple of hundred miles last weekend even though he *claims* he spent the entire weekend locked away in his office finishing an audit report.

You can also go down to the municipal building and check the parking violations bureau index. Get the index number for each of his unpaid parking fines and then pull the original ticket to see the location of the violation. It may have been a residential block in a neighborhood where you've never known him to go. Get the crisscross directory at the public library and copy down all the names and phone numbers on that block. Crosscheck it against all the names and phone numbers of women in his address book and/or in his company's internal phone directory.

If you're pretty sure he's seeing a certain woman and you have her street address, you can stake out her house during hours when he's likely to visit her. (You should only conduct this or any other form of surveillance described here if you are confident that you can stay cool and calm; if you are emotionally distraught, get a friend or a licensed private investigator to do it for you.) The traditional procedure is to borrow or rent a car he won't recognize, put on a wig and sunglasses, park down the street, and see if he enters or leaves; if he does, snap his picture using a telephoto lens.

If you think he's bringing women home to his own house, you can adopt a method from Sherlock Holmes. The great fictional detective watched the comings and goings at the evil Professor Moriarty's residence by disguising himself as a tramp. Well, you can disguise yourself as a homeless woman, complete with wig and sunglasses (as above), ragged old clothes, heavy makeup, and pillows to add the appearance of an extra forty pounds to your weight. (You can even change the shape of your face by stuffing your mouth with surgical cotton.) You can then ensconce yourself with a shopping bag full of old blankets (to conceal your camera, not a machine gun) down the block from your lover's house. If his new girlfriend arrives in her own car and you don't recognize her, jot down her license plate number (see section 11.5). If she later leaves the house alone and passes you on the way to her car or the bus stop, you can shout wild imprecations at her (if it makes you feel any better) without her having the slightest suspicion of who you really are.

You also might try shadowing your wayward lover. Again with the borrowed or rented car and the sunglasses, stake out his place of work in the afternoon and follow him when he leaves (or park near his house in the morning and follow him on his sales route). If you have only the evenings available, park near his home and wait for him to come out after supper for his tomcat prowl. A camera is essential if you want to confront him with your evidence, but you should also take along a tape recorder with a microphone clipped to your blouse so that, without taking your hands off the wheel, you can dictate a record of the addresses he visits. Also essential are binoculars so you can read off the license plate numbers of other people who arrive at those addresses (like the woman who arrives in her own car and goes into the motel room with him) as well as the names on the mailboxes of any houses he visits.

In tailing your lover, stay a couple of cars behind him and don't do anything to draw attention to yourself (like running a red light to keep up with him), even if it means losing the tail. You always can try again another day *unless* he realizes he's being followed.

If he goes into a bar, you can inquire later about this establishment to determine if it's a gay bar, a pick-up spot for heterosexual singles, or simply a friendly neighborhood watering hole like in "Cheers."

Note: If you have *any* reason to believe your lover at this stage in your relationship could turn violent if he knew you were following him or if you find that he's traveling into dangerous neighborhoods (after drugs or prostitutes, perhaps), do not attempt to tail him; hire a private investigator or, better yet, just get out of the relationship.

Finding the Women in His Past

In general it's not a good idea to seek out the women from his past while you're still involved with him. But if you've made a decision to leave him (or are strongly considering doing so), a chat with one or two of these women might strengthen your resolve. Perhaps this might be the time finally to have that heart-to-heart chat with the ex-wife he's always raving against. If you don't know where she lives, you may be able to locate her through her divorce attorney (see section 4.12 for other methods of locating ex-spouses).

If you had the foresight early in your relationship to encourage Joe to talk about his ex-girlfriends, you will already have a string of names to contact. But if you didn't, or if you suspect that he withheld certain names, you can look in his little black book and his regular address books from years back. You can also get the names from his best friend on a pretext (or from his best friend's girlfriend or wife without a pretext) or by looking in back-issue phone books, city directories, or crisscross directories (and campus student directories from his college years), or voter registration street listings, to see with whom he previously shared households. Also, his shoebox files may contain old letters or birthday or Christmas cards from ex-girlfriends, or he may have a book that one of them gave him with her signature and expressions of undying love on the flyleaf, or there may be pictures of ex-girlfriends in a photo album (if a picture doesn't have a name on the back you may be able to match it against the picture and name of a girl in his college yearbook).

As noted above, an ex-girlfriend or common-law wife may have sued him and possibly obtained a judgment against him. Or he and she may have jointly owned real estate or a business—or a pet—at some point (look in the register of deeds office, the property tax rolls, and the county pet license records). In general, the more carefully you have listened to his ramblings about previous romances, the more pointed the questions you have asked, and the better the notes you have taken, then the easier it will be for you to find his previous victims.

13 ·

Businesses and Nonprofit Organizations

By learning how to background an individual, you have picked up much of what you need to know in backgrounding businesses and nonprofit organizations. Many of the records that apply to individuals, such as UCC filings and tax liens, also apply to corporate entities. An experienced researcher will jump back and forth from corporate to individual files, using the clues found in one to search out information in the other.

13.1 Tracking Down Small Businesses and Fly-by-Night Enterprises

Directory Listings
As with hard-to-find individuals, the best place to begin is the telephone directory and city or crisscross directory. If you don't know what city the business is in, consult Dun's Electronic Business Directory, the online directory for over 8.9 million businesses and professionals nationwide. Available on DIALOG, it gives address, phone number, Standard Industrial Classification (SIC) codes and descriptions, and employee size ranges. As an alternative, check Dun's Business Identification Service, a microfiche register covering 10.2 million businesses, which is available in most research libraries. Both resources are compiled from Dun & Bradstreet (D&B) credit reports. If a business is listed in either resource, D&B will usually have additional information on it (see D&B credit reports, section 13.2). Another excellent source for business directory information is PhoneDisc, a CD-ROM crisscross directory with 9.4 million business listings (see section 4.2).

If you have an address for the business but cannot find a phone number listed in its name, look in the city or crisscross directory to see what other businesses or individuals are listed at that address. You may discover that your target business is a subsidiary of, or a registered business name for, another business with offices in the same suite. Or you may find that the address is a private residence, suggesting that the business is a small one that is operated via the residential phone line of one of the household members. In other cases, the address may turn out to be that of a corporate registration service (see below) or simply a mail receiving and/or mail forwarding service (a "mail drop"). To match the address of the business you are investigating against the addresses of known mail drops, check the yellow pages or PhoneDisc. The *Directory of U.S. Mail Drops* (see bibliography) may also be helpful because it is sold by mail-order booksellers who cater to tax evaders, scam artists, and criminal fugitives: A business that chooses one of the listed mail drops will sometimes warrant close scrutiny.

Some companies that serve as mail drops also offer a full range of related services: mail forwarding, telephone answering (with the person answering the phone pretending to be the full-time receptionist for a bustling business), and the part-time or occasional use of a well-appointed office (or even a suite of offices) to impress a client. In New York City, such services can provide the "prestige" of a Park Avenue or Madison Avenue address, thereby giving an entirely false impression of a company's financial solidity.

Be aware that many fly-by-night (as well as legitimate) businesses have an RCF (Remote Call Forwarding) number. In selling this service, the *NYNEX White Pages* for Manhattan describes it as a way of making customers think you have a branch office in a particular city when you really don't—the calls are forwarded without the caller's knowledge to an office in another city. A firm can meanwhile list as its local address the office of a mail drop or mail forwarding service that has instructions not to give out the real location. Note that NYNEX operators will not tell you if a number is on RCF.

Post Office Box Renters

If a post office box is used for business purposes—for instance, the sale of printed material or the solicitation of funds—the postmaster of the station is required by postal regulations to give you the name and address of the person or corporation renting the box. This is how you can find the identity of, say, an advertiser in your local newspaper's classified section if the ad provides no name. If the ad does include a business name, the postal records may give you a more recent street address than can be found in the business name or corporate registration files (see below) at your county courthouse.

Postal Mailing Permits

Businesses can obtain several types of mailing permits. If the permit is identified by a number on the envelope (as in the franking of metered mail or the use of envelopes with postage-paid imprints), you can obtain the name and address of the permit holder simply by calling the nearest U.S. Post Office mail classification center (there are 37 throughout the United States). If you want a copy of the permit holder's permit application, you must make a request under the Freedom of Information Act (FOIA) to the central post office of the city in which the business is located.

The types of permits include metered mail, precanceled stamp, imprint permit, first-class presort, and second-class mailing (the latter is used by newspapers and periodicals). Sometimes the different permit applications for a particular business will be filled out by different individuals; this may give you the name of a silent partner whom you otherwise would not have learned about.

Business Name, Corporation, and Limited Partnership Indexes

Even the shadiest of businesses needs a bank account for depositing its checks. To open an account (and to comply with state registration laws), a entity might file either as (1) a partnership or limited partnership, (2) a corporation incorporated within the state, (3) a corporation doing business in the state but incorporated in another state, (4) a not-for-profit corporation, (5) an unincorporated association, or (6) an individual, corporation, or partnership operating under an assumed business name (the assumed name is often called the d/b/a, which means "doing business as").

Corporations and partnerships generally file their registration papers with the corporations division of the state's department of state. In most states you can get the files searched over the phone. You can also get a search done by mail or on a walk-in basis. About 30 states sell their files on magnetic tape, while over a dozen states offer direct online access. Through Prentice Hall OnLine and/or LEXIS, you can search the state corporation and partnership files of the most populous states.

Business name or d/b/a certificates are usually filed at the county level in the county in which the entity has its office. Copies of incorporation or partnership papers may also be sent to the county files from the state office if the corporation or partnership has offices in the county.

The indexes to the business name, partnership, and corporation registrations may be merged into a single alphabetical listing that is searchable at a computer terminal (or in computer-printout index books) in the file room. The business name file will usually contain a copy of the business name certificate telling who obtained it and providing an address for service of process. If the business was subsequently incorporated, the business name file may include a notation to that effect and the file number of the corporation file.

The corporation registration file will include the articles of incorporation (and amendments thereto) as well as certificates of incorporation, merger, or discontinuance and change-of-name certificates. If required, the incorporation papers will reveal the names and addresses of the corporation's principals; if not, you may find only the name and address of an agent authorized to receive legal papers (this may be either the company's attorney or a company specializing in corporate registrations). You should look on the jacket of the registration papers for the address, if any, of a law firm. (If you see the name "Julius Blumberg," that is not the attorney but simply the company that prints the legal forms most widely used in many states.) If you don't find an attorney's name anywhere, the owners may have done the filing without an attorney's help—in which case the registering party is probably one of the principals.

Always take down the name and registration number of the notary public who witnessed the signature of the registering party: The notary may be the principals' attorney, a secretary for the attorney, or a secretary for the principals. A notary's address, and sometimes his or her license application, will be public record information that is filed with the county clerk and the state's department of state.

The limited partnership files are often more detailed than the corporate files, including names and addresses of general and limited partners, the percent ownership of each, agreements for how decisions will be made and profits shared, amendments to the rules, and all changes in the identities of limited and general partners and in the classes (e.g., Class A, Class B) of limited partners.

In searching the indexes, you should have the complete name of the business accurately spelled. The alphabetical listings in a large city will contain many very similar names (e.g., "Masada Associates, Inc.," "Masada Company," "Masada Corporation," "Massada Florists," "Masada Printing Company," "Masseda Enterprises," etc.). Before you begin to search the index books, familiarize yourself with the alphabetizing system. For instance, are acronyms listed at the beginning of each letter listing, or are they listed throughout in strict alphabetical order? Are names that begin with numbers, as in 301 West 13 Street Corporation, listed separately, or are they in alphabetical order as if spelled out?

Inexperienced researchers often waste time chasing down the names of apparent company officers who really are only employees of a corporate registration firm. One of the best known of these firms is CT Corporation System, which can register a business in all 50 states. Such firms are used by businesses that wish to operate in many or all states without opening an office in each. A corporation incorporates in one state only—either its home state or else a state with minimal regulation, such as Delaware—and then acquires certificates to do business in other states. CT Corporation System maintains offices in all states and can guarantee that state and local law is being complied with in each case; it can also provide an address within the state for service of process on the corporation.

Sometimes the registration company's name will be on the registration papers; in other instances, individual employees of the registration company will be listed without the registration company's name appearing. In still other cases, the names of one or more of the actual principals will be listed as an incorporator or officer, but the registration company still will be designated as the agent for service of process. The registration company usually will not give you any information about a principal unless authorized to do so; however, they will forward your request to speak with one of the principals.

The corporation file will usually include any name-change certificates. However, you will not necessarily learn from the file whether the corporation previously existed as a d/b/a business or a limited partnership (LP). When you request the file, therefore, you should also request the files on previously registered d/b/a's or LPs with similar names. For instance, if the Markco Corporation, Inc., was registered in 1983 and you see that a Markco Company or Markco Associates was registered as a d/b/a the previous year, the latter may be the predecessor entity. If you search the file for this entity you may uncover the name of a previous principal and/or previous attorney. And while you're at it, look for a Markco Foundation or Markco Fund set up for tax purposes.

If you are trying to chase down the various dummy names used in a sensitive real estate deal or a white-collar scam of some kind, the above indexes can be very useful. Often a complicated deal will involve a multiplicity of entities, each of which will be used only for a single transaction in a chain of transactions. You can sometimes spot the connection if all of the registrations of these entities were filed during the same narrow time span by the same attorney. The key to this is the file numbers, which generally designate the order in which registrations were filed during each year. If the index books are a cumulative alphabetical listing without any reverse listing by file number, this order of filing may be difficult to trace. However, you may be able to find the file numbers closest to your target company's by looking in the supplementary monthly indexes. For instance, if the company's file shows that it was incorporated in March 1989, you can ask the file room clerk if the supplementary volume for that month is still available. Also, there may be a separate record of the filings in a daily ledger book that will reveal this information (as will any electronic index at the courthouse, provided that the index is searchable by file number or date as well as name of company).

Corporations that fail to file their tax returns within a set period may lose their registration status. A notice to this effect will be placed in the corporate registration file, and the firm may also be listed on a roster of delinquent tax filers.

Annual State Corporate Filings

All states require domestic corporations (i.e., those incorporated in the particular state) to file an annual report with the secretary of state. These reports are more or less revealing, depending on the state's laws and regulations. Generally, if you study a corporation's annual reports going back to the first year of its incorporation, you can get some idea of its history: changes in address, changes in attorneys, and changes in officers and directors. If the corporation has changed its name, the name-change papers will usually be in the file. If the annual reports filed by the corporation under its old name prior to the change are not in the file, be sure to ask for them.

The paper trail of annual reports will sometimes turn up lively informants. A former officer may have quarreled with the principals and thus be willing to tell all. The office building manager at the corporation's former address may have information on its financial problems. In addition, the names of the firm's past and present attorneys may be a tip-off to secret corporate or organized crime links. If the business is controlled by a political or religious cult, the disappearance of a name from the list of officers and directors may indicate that the individual has defected.

Sales Brochures

A business may be extremely secretive around everyone *except* potential customers. In the late 1970s a computer software company controlled by Lyndon LaRouche published a glossy sales brochure that listed dozens of its supposedly satisfied clients. A foray into the waiting area of the computer company's midtown Manhattan office produced a copy of the indiscreet brochure. Likewise, a trip to the office of another business—a Miami export/import firm—produced a copy of a brochure intended for distribution almost exclusively in the Middle East. The brochure included a mail drawer address in the Bahamas that turned out to be the same mail drawer used by a Mafia drug bank.

Signs on the Door; Lobby and Floor Directories

A friend of mine was trying to trace the business affairs of a Ku Klux Klan-linked toy distributor who for many years had been running several small businesses out of a suite of offices in a Manhattan office building. My friend went to the building and copied from the lobby directory all the business names for that suite. Then he went up to the floor the suite was on and copied the names from the floor directory. Then he went to the door of the suite and copied the names listed on the frosted glass. The listings were somewhat different in each case, and he ended up with nine names. He then headed for the business names index at the county courthouse.

This was admirable attention to detail: My friend recognized that each of the three sets of signs had been put up at a different time (it was an old building), and he was able to read them off like geological strata.

Clues in the Office or Waiting Area

If you visit a company's offices on a pretext, note any business permits or licenses, diplomas, or testimonials framed on the walls—this will give you a fresh paper trail to follow. Note the receptionist's or secretary's name tag or the name plate on his or her desk—this person may become a source later. If there is a calendar on the wall, note the name of the company that gave it as a gift—this may be the business's printer, typesetter, or insurance underwriter. If there are magazines in the waiting area, note the names and addresses on the subscription labels—these may give you the home address of a company employee and/or they may be addressed to a company officer whose name you would not otherwise find. You may also discover in the waiting area various company promotional brochures (see above), an annual report, a copy of the company's internal newsletter, and other useful materials. The company's inhouse phone list or directory may be on the receptionist's desk or beside the waiting area phone provided for the convenience of visitors. In some offices, a copy of the latest internal newsletter or phone list will be tacked to a bulletin board above a water fountain or beside the coffee machine or in the snack room; look here also for state and federal Labor Department notices and Occupational Safety and Health Administration (OSHA) injury and illness notices. Sometimes employees will tack up personal notices offering cars or condominiums for sale or announcing that they need a roommate or that their cat just gave birth to three kittens who each need a loving home. Such notices (often found also in the company newsletter) will give you the names, the phone extensions, and sometimes the home phone numbers of potential sources.

Sleazy Small Businesses

These fall into two basic categories: the fly-by-night business, which rips off consumers fast and then disappears only to open under a new name at a new location; and the year-in-year-out sleazy business that stays put at the same location and just brazens things out (e.g., dishonest auto repair shops). Businesses of both types leave behind irate consumers who often will lodge complaints with public and private agencies. Check first with your city and state consumer protection agencies, both of which may give you information regarding a company's (or a fly-by-night artist's) complaint file over the phone. For further information, call your local Better Business Bureau.

If the business operates under either a city or state license (auto repair shops, for instance, are licensed by the Department of Motor Vehicles in some states) or is subject to a professional or trade licensing board or other oversight agency, see if there have been any complaints or disciplinary actions. Also check if summonses have been issued (e.g., a summons for health violations in the case of a restaurant) and if the business has ever been closed temporarily for violations.

Also check if the business and/or its principals have been the target of a civil suit or criminal prosecution by the state attorney general's office, which in most states is the consumers' legal watchdog. And search the court indexes for suits filed against your target business by consumers themselves, including actions in small claims court (usually claims up to $1,000) and civil court (usually claims from $1,000 to $10,000).

13.2 Backgrounding an Established Corporation

For established businesses in the United States there is a vast wealth of research sources. What follows is a capsule description; for full treatment of the subject, consult (1) Lorna M. Daniell's *Business Information Sources* and other business reference works listed in the bibliography; (2) the three-volume, 2,000-page *How to Find Information About Companies* (a non-current edition may be available in the reference department of your public library); and (3) the latest DIALOG and LEXIS/NEXIS catalogs. Note that for any sizeable corporation in our tightly interrelated economy, all good research work includes parallel, indirect, and operative backgrounding (see sections 1.3, 1.4, and 1.5). At the outset you should define a company's relationship to the company that controls it and/or the company or companies that are controlled by it or are under common control with it.

Business Directories and Databases

Sketches of the financial status and types of activities conducted by a business, as well as the names of directors and officers and other information, are available online and in various published directories. Check as many of these sources as possible. If you are using the print directories, do not neglect the weekly, monthly, or quarterly supplements that keep them up to date.

The following list includes databases available through DIALOG (some are available from other vendors as well) and either the print equivalent of the database or the most closely related print directory from the compiling publisher if such exists. Note that with DIALOG and other online vendors, you can do global searches of multiple files grouped by region, topic, and so forth.

- D&B—Dun's Market Identifiers: Information on over 7.3 million businesses with five or more employees or at least $1 million in sales.

- D&B—Dun's Financial Records Plus: Up to three years of comprehensive financial statements for more than 650,000 businesses, including balance sheet, income statement, and various business ratios for determining profitability, solvency, and efficiency; also includes capsule descriptions of the history and operations of an additional 1.2 million businesses.

- D&B—Million Dollar Directory: Current business information on over 161,000 companies with net worth of $500,000 or more. This information is also available in the *Dun & Bradstreet Million Dollar Directory*.

- PTS F&S Index: Covers company and industry information from 1972 to present (almost 3.5 million records). It corresponds to the print volumes of the *Predicasts F&S Index*.

- Thomas Register Online: A directory of providers of more than 53,000 classes of products and services; includes profiles on over 180,000 companies and an index of over 115,000 brand names. This database corresponds to the 27-volume *Thomas Register of American Manufacturers* plus the *Thomas Food Industry Register*.

- Company Intelligence: This database includes financial and marketing information on about 150,000 U.S. companies, with up to 10 of the most recent news items on each company from more than 3,000 newspapers and periodicals. Included are companies in *Ward's Business Directory* (companies with a gross annual sales volume of over $500,000) and also newsworthy smaller companies.

- Standard & Poor's Register—Corporate and Standard & Poor's Register—Biographical: The first is a directory of over 55,000 public and private companies with sales in most cases of over $1 million; the second includes brief sketches of executives and directors of firms listed in the first (over 68,000 records). The print version is the three-volume *Standard & Poor's Register of Corporations, Directors and Executives*. Using the online or the print version, you can trace the overlapping directorates of various firms.

- Standard & Poor's Corporate Descriptions Plus News and Standard & Poor's Daily News: The first file contains in-depth sketches of over 11,000 publicly held corporations; the second contains general news and financial information (including annual reports and interim earnings reports) on most of these from 1985 to the present. The print equivalents are, respectively, *Standard & Poor's Corporation Records* and *Standard & Poor's Corporation Records Daily News and Cumulative News*.

- Moody's Corporate News—U.S. and Moody's Corporate Profiles: The first of these two files contains summaries of news on about 13,000 publicly held companies from 1983 to the present; the second has detailed information on companies listed on the New York and American Stock Exchanges and about 1,300 other important companies (almost 4,000 records in all). The print equivalents are *Moody's Industrial Manual, Moody's Bank and Finance Manual, Moody's Public Utility Manual,* and *Moody's Transportation Manual*.

- Corporate Affiliations: A corporate family linkage directory for searching out the subsidiaries of a parent company or the parent of a subsidiary. Also contains summary information on each firm (about 100,000 companies). Corresponds to *Directory of Corporate Affiliations, International Directory of Corporate Affiliations,* and *Directory of Leading Private Companies*.

Company Credit Reports

Dun & Bradstreet's company credit reports on over 9 million business locations are available online to direct subscribers; other D&B credit information is available through CompuServe or NewsNet. TRW business credit profiles are available through CompuServe and NewsNet; the latter offers trade payment histories on about 12 million business locations.

Securities and Exchange Commission Filings

If the business you are investigating is a publicly held corporation registered with the Securities and Exchange Commission (SEC), then detailed information is available on the public record. Filings required by the SEC include stock offering prospectuses, proxy statements, the annual 10-K and quarterly 10-Q reports to the SEC, copies of annual reports to shareholders, and many other documents. In these, you will find out who the major stockholders are, who the officers and directors are (with biographical data on each), and who the attorneys and outside accountants are, as well as gaining information on the firm's lines of credit. You will also find audit reports detailing the firm's current financial status and capital structure, brief assessments of all legal suits in which the firm is involved, and information on the firm's subsidiaries, both domestic and international. The 10-Ks and annual reports to shareholders may include valuable information about the firm's major clients and the government contracts it has received. The proxy statements will reveal the holdings of officers and directors, institutional investors, and beneficial owners of 5 percent or more of the company's stock and also the details of any in-house loans or other financial transactions between the firm and any of its officers or directors. Always examine Form S-1, the registration statement filed by a company when it first comes under SEC jurisdiction; it contains details about the firm's finances and about the personal and business backgrounds of its officers that may not be repeated in subsequent filings.

By tracing SEC filings by a company over the years you can gather the names of officers, directors, and beneficial owners who are no longer associated with the company—these may be potential sources. You can also find out about persons who have made unsuccessful bids for control and those who have been squeezed out by hostile takeovers; see Schedule 13-D (Report of Securities Purchase), Schedule 14-D1 (Tender Offer Statement), and Schedule 14-D9 (Solicitation Recommendation).

The annual *Directory of Companies Required to File Annual Reports with the Securities and Exchange Commission* will tell you if your target company is required to file. SEC filings going back to the beginning of a company's filing history may be available on microfiche at the SEC's Public Reference Rooms and may also be available at university business school libraries or the business division of any major public library.

For online searches of SEC filings LEXIS's Federal Securities Library offers the full text of 10-Q and 10-K filings, proxy statements, and annual reports to shareholders since January 1987; the full text of 20-F filings since March 1988; and abstracts of other filings. The Disclosure Database, available on DIALOG, provides extracts from 10-Ks, 10-Qs, and 20-F financial reports, as well as registration reports of new registrants. The Disclosure/Spectrum Ownership database (also on DIALOG) reveals insider, institutional, and beneficial ownership data on about 5,000 publicly held companies. Summary information on past and current SEC filings of thousands of companies can be obtained from the Standard & Poor's and Moody's databases described above.

As of January 1994, the SEC began a two-year experiment to grant the public free access, via the Internet, to documents filed electronically with the SEC (of course, the user must pay the cost of his or her access to the Internet). Commercial suppliers of this data, such as Mead Data Central (LEXIS/NEXIS), currently provide search software that makes it much easier to find the document you need—and can get it to you 24 hours earlier than you can get it via the Internet. However, one objective of the SEC experiment is to develop search and retrieval mechanisms that will be comparable in efficiency to those of the commercial providers.

For help in interpreting the financial data in SEC filings, see works cited under "Business Research" in the bibliography.

State Securities Filings
Note that corporations selling securities within a given state must file a variety of disclosure statements with the state securities regulator. These disclosures can be almost as revealing as SEC filings and should always be checked when backgrounding a local corporation.

Newspaper and Periodical Business News
Start with LEXIS/NEXIS. It offers full-text searches for key words (the names of your target business, its subsidiaries or parent, and its officers and directors) in hundreds of city, state, regional, and national business newspapers and periodicals, newswires and newsletters, and the business and general news sections of hundreds of metropolitan dailies and popular magazines. Is your target firm in the Seattle area? The LEXIS/NEXIS News and Business Library includes several locally and regionally oriented business periodicals such as the *Puget Sound Business Journal* (from 1985) and the *Pacific Northwest Executive* (from 1986), and also the daily newspapers—the *Seattle Times* (from 1988) and the *Seattle Post-Intelligencer* (from 1992). Does the company manufacture aircraft components? You can search *Aerospace Daily* and *Aviation Daily* (from 1989), *Aerospace America* (from 1984), and *Aviation Week & Space Technology* (from 1975). Is the firm designing high-tech components for Navy jets? You can consult *Defense Electronics* (from 1983) and *Defense and Aerospace Electronics* (from 1990).

If you don't have access to NEXIS, try DIALOG, which offers Trade & Industry Index and Trade & Industry ASAP. The former provides complete indexing and selective abstracting of over 300 trade journals and industry-related periodicals as well as selective coverage of nearly 1,200 others (from 1981). It also includes the complete text (displayable but nonsearchable) of over 200 of these publications. Its companion database, Trade & Industry ASAP, provides the complete text (searchable) of selected articles from over 200 of the journals and periodicals covered by Trade & Industry Index (from 1983).

Rather than searching databases, you can check the published indexes in your local library. Most important are the *Business Periodicals Index*, which covers 344 business magazines and has retrospective volumes dating back to 1959, the Predicasts F&S domestic and international indexes, the *Wall Street Journal Index*, and the *New York Times Index*. Although all of these are available online, a relatively efficient search can be done in the print volumes because the latter include indexing by company name. Even obscure local businesses will be found if they were ever the subject of a news item relating to development of a new product, Chapter 11 reorganization, a liability suit, and so on.

There are thousands of trade journals covering every type of business, most of which are not indexed in the *Business Periodicals Index* or the Predicasts F&S indexes. Some you will find on LEXIS, but often for the most recent years only. To find the names of relatively obscure publications, look in *Standard Periodical Directory*. If the periodical you want is not in a local business library, check the local branch of the trade association in question; they may have it on file. Or you can contact the editors of the publication directly; they may agree to search their own files and send you clippings in return for access to your findings. They might also provide you with a bit of unpublished gossip about your target company.

Brokerage House Reports

Such reports are based on interviews with corporate officials and the individual judgment of the analyst preparing the report. They contain facts and analysis focusing on a firm's clients, management difficulties, government contracts, and future plans. These reports are available in business libraries or online via the LEXIS Company Library, which includes reports from over 110 international, national, and regional brokerage firms. For further information on a given company, call the analyst who wrote the report.

LEXIS Law Libraries

Specialized LEXIS law libraries enable you to search online a vast wealth of court decisions, administrative rulings, regulatory commission decisions, and government filings (as well as newsletters and bulletins reporting thereon) in over 30 subject areas. You can either do a global search of an entire library or look through various special file combinations. Some of the libraries are specific to a particular group of industries, such as the Communications Library and the Transportation Library. Others deal with specific problems that face industries across the board; for instance, the Federal Tax Library, the State Tax Library (files for each state), the Labor Library, and the Bankruptcy Library. In studying any company that does business with the government, you will want to consult the Federal Public Contracts Library. Note that the LEXIS law libraries offer broad coverage beyond the law itself; for example, the Patent Law Library includes full-text coverage, dating back more than a decade, of scores of business and technology journals in such fields as telecommunications, computers, and aerospace.

Government Regulation: Audits, Inspection Reports, Etc.

As you gather government data on a corporation step by step, keep asking yourself what other government departments or regulatory agencies might require it to file or might be investigating it. Information may be available from dozens of government sources. Is your target business a limited partnership constructing federally subsidized housing? There will be reports and audits available from the Department of Housing and Urban Development (HUD), which can be obtained either via a Freedom of Information request or via your local congressional representative. Is an office supply firm doing extensive business with civilian federal agencies? General Accounting Office (GAO) reports may be available. Is a computer software company doing business with the Pentagon? The public affairs office of the Department of Defense (DOD) can provide you with a printout—unless the data is classified—of all the firm's current and past contracts, broken down as to general purpose, location, and amount of money involved. You can then request the DOD's reports on how well the firm has fulfilled its contracts. (Note: Always check if a firm has been listed in the government's monthly *Lists of Parties Excluded from Federal Procurement or Nonprocurement Programs*.)

Environmental, Consumer, and Social Policy

Federal law requires every manufacturer with 10 or more employees to report to the Environmental Protection Agency (EPA) and state agencies the total amount of each of about 330 toxic chemicals it has released into the environment. The data is listed in the EPA's annually published Toxics Release Inventory, available on microfiche at federal depository libraries. Also see your target company's SEC filings: In 1989, the SEC ordered companies to begin disclosing on their 10-Ks any potential liabilities they might face under the federal environmental cleanup laws. The issue of such liability has helped to spark a number of national and regional commercial databases specializing in the environmental practices of companies as reflected not just in their 10-Ks but also in the huge number of documents filed with state and federal environmental agencies each year. Note that the LEXIS Environmental Law Library includes not only environment-related court decisions and administrative rulings but also the full text of newsletters that carefully monitor the public record, such as *Pesticide & Toxic Chemical News*.

Both federal and state levels of government are a gold mine of information about consumer complaints and product safety. An excellent guide to these sources is *Lesko's Info-Power II*, which describes, for instance, the various databases maintained by the Consumer Product Safety Commission. Many state consumer protection offices will give you information about a company's complaint record over the phone (a list of the offices for each state and their disclosure policies is in *Lesko's Info-Power II*).

Corporate misdeeds are monitored by numerous public-interest groups. The Manhattan-based Council on Economic Priorities collects data regarding such issues as corporate support for charities, job equality for women, and animal testing. New Foundations, a shareholder research group based at Harvard University, tracks corporate accountability to shareholders. The various state Public Interest Research Groups and Ralph Nader's Washington, D.C.–based Center for Study of Responsive Law are strong on consumer issues. Many other nonprofit agencies that monitor the corporate world can be found in the *Encyclopedia of Associations*—and don't forget state and national trade and industry associations, which sometimes keep files on the most egregious offenders in their ranks.

Bankruptcy Files

Whether a business is large or small, it may at some point have applied for reorganization under Chapter 11, under either its present name or a previous one. The bankruptcy files will contain a vast wealth of information about customers and clients, vendors and suppliers, claims by or against the firm, pending litigation in any jurisdiction, mismanagement, and possible fraudulent practices. The Chapter 11 status may continue for several years, during which period the firm must file extremely detailed reports on its business affairs.

Bankruptcy files in active cases are found at the federal bankruptcy courts (which generally cover the same jurisdictions as the U.S. district courts), indexed by debtor and sometimes also by creditor. Many of the bankruptcy court indexes and dockets are searchable online via PACER. For details on bankruptcy court records, see section 8.10.

Licenses and Permits

All legitimate businesses are subject to city, state, or federal licensing and permit provisions. Consult your local government handbook and/or call the city and state licensing agencies to find out which requirements apply to your target business.

Miscellaneous Public Records

Check the state and federal court indexes (both civil and criminal), the federal tax lien files, and the county judgment docket. Also check the statewide UCC filings to get a better picture of a company's liabilities.

Official Company Sources

Even relatively small companies publish sales brochures, annual reports, and other publications, and they issue press releases from time to time. Such literature can be obtained easily from the company's public affairs office. Press releases carried by Business Wire can be accessed via NEXIS (from 1983) and via DIALOG (from 1986). If the information in a press release is at all significant, it will usually have been included in a news article for some business or trade publication accessible online.

The slickly printed annual report that a firm circulates to stockholders and the general public should not be confused with the 10-K annual report sent to the SEC by publicly held corporations. Although the printed report may contain some hype, it will also include a financial statement, a list of directors and officers, information about major new contracts, and so forth.

Another good information source is the firm's house organ. See the *Magazines and Internal Publications Directory* (volume two of *Working Press of the Nation*). If your target firm is not listed there, call the firm's public affairs office. In general, they will cooperate with business students or freelance business writers. You might ask for an interview with the public affairs director and, in that context, ask for access to company publications of various types. Another possible route is through the firm's outside public relations consultants; under some circumstances these might be more cooperative than the inhouse public affairs office.

Former Officers, Directors, or Managers

Former officers or directors who resigned or were sacked may be willing to discuss the firm's past. To get their names, look in old SEC or state securities filings, old editions of *Standard & Poor's Register of Corporations, Directors and Executives*, or the firm's annual filings with the state department of state. If a person's name has disappeared from the list of a firm's top executives, it is almost certain that he or she would have left the firm rather than accept a demotion. (Note, however, that in some cases the disappearance of a name from the list may mean that the person was transferred to the firm's parent company or to another subsidiary of the parent company—see below).

The above method will help you to find only former top managers. For mid-level or lower-level former managers, try the following:

- Look in back editions of the local city directory for people once listed as employees who are no longer listed; if the old directory does not give their job title, you can estimate from the income level of their neighborhood whether or not they were likely to be on the management level.

- Get both an old edition and the latest edition of the firm's inhouse phone directory (from your source in the mail room), and compare them to see who's left the firm. If you have only an old edition obtained from the firm's garbage, call the extensions of people with management titles to find out which of them no longer work there.

- Request a search of the Federal Election Commission's Contributor Search System to get the names of all employees of the firm reported as having given substantial donations in past years to political candidates or political action committees (PACs), especially the corporation's own PAC. Most of these contributors will probably have been management-level employees at the time. Then search for more recent contributions from each of these contributors; this will provide you with the names of those who, at the time of the more recent contributions, no longer listed themselves as employees of your target corporation. (Note that the FEC databases cover elections back to 1977–78 and usually give a contributor's place of employment at the time of a given contribution.) For information on online access to FEC databases, see the appendix.

To find the current whereabouts of former executives, directors, and managers, look in the current edition of *Standard & Poor's Register* or the relevant professional or trade directories. Generally, former corporate officials will be easy to find.

Before calling a former executive of a given firm, check that his or her new employer is not affiliated as parent, subsidiary, or cosubsidiary with the old firm. This can be determined for over 114,000 companies by looking in the Corporate Affiliations database on DIALOG or in the print version of same, the six-volume *Directory of Corporate Affiliations Library*.

Labor Union and Shop Floor Sources

In their preparations for contract negotiations, unions have to keep well informed about the profit margins of the business—to know what the traffic will bear. If the union is locked in a bitter dispute with management, it may be willing to help you in the hopes that you will turn up something useful for its own purposes. The situation varies, however, from union to union and from local to local: Sometimes the workers are represented by a union whose leaders are so corrupt that it might as well be an old-fashioned company union. Sometimes the union will not want to rock the boat by cooperating with a journalistic probe (e.g., an article on the environmental effects of a certain company's logging operations) because the result might be a loss of jobs. In many unions, however, there are national and/or local rank-and-file groups at odds with the official leadership. Often it is best either to work exclusively with such a group or to work with both it and the official leadership simultaneously. For instance, if I were backgrounding a Midwest trucking firm I might or might not approach the official leadership of the Teamster local (depending on the recent history of reform efforts in that local), but I would surely talk to Teamsters for a Democratic Union, a rank-and-file group that is not only untainted by mob connections but happens also to be very well informed about the business woes of various trucking companies.

Even if the firm is not unionized, it is important to contact workers on the shop level. They will be familiar with who the firm's suppliers and customers are, whether orders are up or down in recent months, whether management is covering up shoddy production standards or violations of environmental laws, and so forth.

Contacting workers if the firm is nonunion or if the union leadership is uncooperative can be tricky. Obviously you can't just walk up to employees on the factory floor and start interviewing them. One way to find the names and home addresses of workers is through a city directory that lists each householder's occupation and place of work. Another method is to copy down license plate numbers of cars in the company parking lot and then get the owners' names and addresses from the Department of Motor Vehicles.

Of course, with the above approach you might inadvertently contact a supervisor who will inform his or her superiors. Dashiell Hammett's Continental Op in the classic detective novel *Red Harvest* had a way around this: When he arrived in town the first person he looked up was the local leader of the IWW (Industrial Workers of the World, or "Wobblies"). Today there are almost no Wobblies left, but there will often be a scattering of workers who have engaged in unsuccessful unionization drives or, if the plant is unionized, who belong to the national rank-and-file caucus. There will also sometimes be one or two radicals affiliated or formerly affiliated with left-wing parties. (These radicals will almost always be involved in the rank-and-file caucus, so if you find one you find the other.)

If you're doing an investigative journalism piece on, say, occupational hazards at a local plant (to illustrate, among other things, the greed of the corporate raiders who recently took over the parent company), you might contact local community activists who don't work in the plant—and thus don't have to look over their shoulders constantly—and get them to act as your go-between to workers at the plant whom they know personally.

Look for former shop-level employees with a reason to be angry at management: those who were fired on trumped-up charges after attempting to unionize, those who lost their jobs during the latest cutbacks, those who were forced into early retirement and now find their pensions almost worthless in the wake of that corporate takeover. Such people may be more willing to talk than workers still clinging to their jobs, although many will have left town for greener pastures.

Also try to find individual workers whose disputes with management are a matter of public record. The most obvious place to look is in the local court indexes—for lawsuits by employees or former employees against the company (sexual harassment suits and discrimination suits are a booming business all over the country). You might also search for the company's name in the LEXIS Labor Library, which includes labor-related case law and also National Labor Relations Board, Equal Employment Opportunity Commission, and Occupational Safety and Health Review Commission decisions dating back to the early 1970s.

Competitors, Suppliers, and Industrial Customers
To find companies that provide a particular product or service, look in the 16-volume Products and Services section of *Thomas Register of American Manufacturers*. There you will find producers and suppliers in over 53,000 industrial and service categories listed by state and city within each category. This will give you an idea of who your target company's competitors are. To figure out who its suppliers are (or the companies that it is supplying), you will have to learn something about the particular processes of the industry and then study carefully the relevant product or service listings and consult the eight-volume catalog section. In some cases, the supplier nearest your target company may be the most likely one if transportation cost is a significant factor. For some services, a nearby location will be likely because of the need for personal visits. (In figuring out who the smaller suppliers or customers might be, you may have to consult state manufacturing

directories and/or various online business directories and business profile databases, as well as the *Thomas Register*.)

As you gather lists of probable suppliers, competitors, or customers, look in LEXIS and also in your local court indexes for any litigation between any of these firms and your target company. Also look in the local corporate judgment books for any judgments obtained by your target company against a customer or supplier (or vice versa).

13.3 Investigating a Nonprofit Entity

Nonprofit corporations become plaintiffs or defendants in lawsuits, own real estate, experience cash flow problems, and engage in disputes with their unionized employees. Thus, in researching a nonprofit corporation you should proceed pretty much as if you were backgrounding any other type of corporation.

Not-for-Profit Corporate Registration Papers
Nonprofit entities must file their certificates of incorporation, amendment, change of name, or dissolution with the state's department of state. Copies may also be found at the county clerk's office.

State Charity Filings
Nonprofit organizations must file annual reports with the state division of charities under certain circumstances (in New York, if they solicit more than $10,000 in the given year).

State Attorney's Office
In most states, the state attorney general's office is responsible for investigating violations of the laws governing nonprofit organizations. If complaints have been lodged against a nonprofit, the charities bureau at the state attorney general's office may have an extensive file on it.

Federal 990 Forms
Tax-exempt nonprofit organizations must file an annual 990 Form with the Internal Revenue Service (IRS). To see if your target organization qualifies as tax exempt, check the IRS's two-volume *Cumulative List of Organizations*. All 990 filers must make their three most recent 990s available to the general public at their principal office during regular business hours. (The rules are somewhat different for the 990-PF filed by private foundations—see below.) Disclosure applies to all parts of the form except contributor lists.

An organization's earlier 990s can be obtained from the IRS via your district office, as can the latest 990s if you can't visit the organization's headquarters and it refuses to honor telephone or mail requests. The IRS can take as long as six months to send you the forms, however, and often it claims it simply can't find them. Fortunately, copies are often filed with the state division of charities along with the state-required annual report. In requests to various states I have usually received the 990s within a week or so. When you try the state division of charities, also try the state attorney's office; if it has a complaint file on your target organization, this file may also include copies of the 990s.

Note that if you request a nonprofit organization's 990s from the IRS, always make your request under IRS Code section 6104 rather than the Freedom of Information Act and be sure to include the organization's Employer Identification Number.

Contributor Lists
Although not required by law to reveal their contributor lists, most nonprofits will publish donors' names to enhance giving as well as to satisfy the vanity of the donors. These lists are found in everything from promotional pamphlets to annual reports and even in program publications of the local symphony orchestra. The contributor lists of cultural institutions as well as of universities or hospitals generally include many corporate donors.

You can find out about foundation grants to a particular nonprofit organization in the *Foundation Grants Index* (see below).

Court Cases
The LEXIS Corporate Law Library includes case law regarding nonprofit corporations from all 50 states. In addition, you should check the court indexes for the locality in which the nonprofit corporation has its headquarters (and other localities if appropriate).

Records on Private Foundations
A tax-exempt private foundation has a somewhat different legal status from a public charity or a nonprofit institution such as a church or university. To qualify as a tax-exempt private foundation, an entity must receive contributions from only a very limited number of contributors (a single family, for instance) and must make grants only to nonprofit organizations, not to individuals. If it chooses, it may operate its own charitable or public-service programs. There are currently over 30,000 private foundations in the United States.

All private foundations must file Form 990-PF with the IRS annually. This form provides a detailed picture of the finances of a foundation and how it spent its income during the previous year. The form also includes a list of officers and directors, the salaries of top officers, and information on any foundation political activities or any changes in control of the foundation.

The IRS requires private foundations to make their most recent 990-PFs available to the public for 180 days each year; during that period they must provide free copies upon request. If you need to examine previous forms or the current form after the 180-day period has passed, many foundations will gladly send you a copy. If not, you should check with the regional office of the Foundation Center, a private organization that collects past and current 990-PF forms as well as printed annual reports of many private foundations. If the center doesn't have the reports you need, you can order them from the state division of charities or the IRS.

Directories of Foundations and Charities
Brief descriptions of most U.S. private foundations are given in the Foundation Center's *National Data Book*. The center also produces the *Source Book* (which gives detailed profiles of the 1,000 largest foundations), the *Foundation Directory* (sketches of over 6,500 foundations with $1 million in assets or a minimum of $100,000 in annual grants), and the annual *Foundation Grants Index*, which describes grants to nonprofit groups (about 20,000 grants a year) from more than 800 large foundations.

Other directories in this field are published by Gale Research Inc., and its subsidiary, The Taft Group. These include *Charitable Organizations of the U.S.*, with sketches of almost 800 fundraising charities and a critical evaluation of each charity's expenses for administration and fundraising as opposed to program; *Foundation Reporter*, with information on the history and priorities of the top 1,000 private foundations in the United States; and *America's New Foundations*, with profiles of over 2,700 foundations established since 1988.

Foundation Databases
Via DIALOG you can access the Foundation Directory database, which describes over 32,500 grant makers. DIALOG also offers a cumulative version of the *Foundation Grants Index* with records from 1973 to the present (this file currently includes over 400,000 records with 20,000 new ones added each year).

Foundation Center Libraries
The Foundation Center operates four regional libraries—in New York City, Washington, D.C., San Francisco, and Cleveland—while affiliates of the center maintain smaller collections at about 175 public libraries and other locations around the country, focusing on the records of foundations in the given locality. Although the center's libraries are open to the public, the library staff will not answer complicated telephone or mail inquiries unless you are a representative of a member organization.

The center does not maintain systematic records on public charities, fundraising organizations, or tax-exempt institutions such as churches and private universities.

Watchdog Organizations
The National Charities Information Bureau in New York City monitors major national charities. It has information on conflicts of interest, fundraising tactics, budgets, and boards of directors.

The American Institute of Philanthropy in St. Louis, Missouri, grades charities by the percentage of their spending that actually goes for charitable purposes; the institute publishes the *Charities Watchdog Report & Rating Guide*.

The Council of Better Business Bureaus' Philanthropic Advisory Service in Arlington, Virginia, monitors nonprofits that raise funds from the public. It has records on about 7,000 entities.

14 ▪

Indirect Backgrounding

14.1 Finding the "Experts"

In looking into a topic on any but the most superficial level, you will develop questions that can't be answered easily from books. These will often be very detailed and subtle questions that require a chat with an expert. Indeed, you may need the expert to steer you to the books. An expert can rattle off the names of articles and books on the phone that you might find only by luck during your library research.

To locate experts and eventually to find *the* expert with the most relevant information, you can draw on a wide variety of sources:

- Public-interest advocacy groups, trade and professional associations, and other nonprofit organizations are almost always willing to help you. To find the most relevant groups, look in the subject and location guides of the *Encyclopedia of Associations* and the *National Trade and Professional Associations of the U.S.* Contact the research director or newsletter editor of the group. He or she may have the information you need or may steer you to another staff member or an outside expert.

- The *Directory of Experts, Authorities & Spokespersons* is the annual publication used by radio and TV talk-show hosts to find people to appear on their shows. It contains a number of offbeat specialties, such as UFO research, not easily found in other directories. As appearing on talk shows doesn't pay any money, the presence of a person's name on this list suggests that he or she is not stingy with his or her time but is an enthusiast eager to share knowledge.

- Many veteran journalists swear by the Heritage Foundation's *Annual Guide to Public Policy Experts* (supposedly, a large percentage of the experts listed therein are unusually generous with their time in tele-phone interviews). A similar work is *The Reporter's Source Book*, pub-lished by the Center for National Independence in Politics.

▪ *Newsletters in Print* provides detailed entries, arranged by subject, on over 12,000 specialty newsletters. Although the editors of nonprofit newsletters are usually helpful, some editors of commercially produced newsletters (which sell for high prices to very small subscriber lists) are reluctant to share information. Nevertheless, the high quality of their information and files makes them worth a try. If a newsletter editor thinks that you will quote him or her and mention the newsletter in your article, you will get better cooperation.

▪ The *Directory of American Scholars* and *American Men and Women of Science* provide listings by academic and scientific specialty and brief educational and career data on each scholar or scientist. The latter work is available online from DIALOG.

▪ The *Research Centers Directory* and its supplement, *New Research Centers*, can help you track down many of the best university-affiliated research experts; at most centers, the public affairs office can help you find the most appropriate scholar or scientist to interview.

▪ Faculty directories and course guides from local universities will help you to find experts in every field in which courses are being offered. This will include some very practical fields, such as real estate finance and hotel administration, as well as the liberal arts. To find out what the spe-cialties of each department member are (if the course guide doesn't tell you), check the *Faculty Directory of Higher Education*, which will list the courses each professor teaches. Note that universities love to see their faculty members quoted in the media, and therefore most univer-sity news services maintain lists of quotable faculty experts on a variety of topics. Also, your local university publicist can use ProfNet, the na-tionwide computer network of university public information officers, to find academics or research center scientists in any locality to speak au-thoritatively on the most obscure or arcane topic (see the appendix).

Local professors will rarely be the ranking experts in their specialty, but they will be more likely to spare time for you than will a national academic celebrity. In addition, you can talk face to face with them, and perhaps get access to their personal research files, without having to in-vest in an airplane ticket. Be aware that local professors often toil away unappreciated in a narrow but important field. They are frequently de-lighted to be contacted by a journalist.

▪ The catalogs of local alternative education centers and college continu-ing education programs list teachers with very unusual specialties. Al-though you are unlikely to need an expert on Hot-Air Ballooning or How to Flirt in Art Museums, such centers and programs also offer courses in very hard-nosed practical subjects. The teachers are often freelance writers, consultants, or editors of specialty newsletters. As avid self-promoters, they will usually cooperate with a journalist.

- Textbooks and works of scholarship that relate to your field of interest will guide you to a wide range of experts. Look in the bibliography and also note the authorities cited in the text and in the footnotes or endnotes. If you find the right book, this is often the quickest way to track down the very best experts.

- Dissertation indexes and abstracts (see section 11.1) can help you narrow your search for an academic expert to the most minute subspecialties. Once you find a dissertation that deals directly with your topic, its author, if located through the *National Faculty Directory*, will probably be so flattered that someone other than his dissertation adviser actually read his turgid tome, that he will cooperate and even give you the names of experts whose knowledge is more up to date than his own. (Of course, you can also find subspecialists via searches of the scholarly and scientific journals; for tips on how to do this online and via CD-ROM, see section 11.3.)

- Investigative Reporters and Editors (IRE) can aid you in finding journalists who specialize in the topic you are researching. IRE maintains a file of the subject specialties of its 4,500 member–journalists (the 1995–96 membership directory will include this information). IRE also publishes *The Investigative Journalist's Morgue*, a subject index (with brief abstracts) to over 9,000 investigative articles and series over the past 20 years. You can obtain photocopies of any articles included in the index, and also the telephone numbers of the reporters who worked on them, from the IRE office.

- In many communities, at least one private citizen collects and files away all the dirt and scandal involving local politicians, businesspeople, etc. Some of these amateur muckrakers are like pack rats, collecting everything they can get on everybody around them. Others are "selective" muckrakers concerned with a particular subject. For instance, a corrupt trade union local may have at least one rank-and-filer who occupies his or her spare time with collecting evidence of the union leadership's misdeeds.

Unlike newspaper reporters, who must flit from assignment to assignment, amateur muckrakers have the leisure to concentrate on their pet target(s) year after year, gathering every scrap of documentation they can find. Frequently their files will overflow the basement or attic. Almost invariably, they are eager to cooperate with anyone who shares their interests.

Let's say you need an expert on Sun Myung Moon's Unification Church. National newspapers will have one or more reporters who cover religious cults, although not too closely. Get their names from IRE and then call them and ask for a referral to someone with special knowledge of the Moonies. They may give you the name of their favorite amateur muckraker as a favor to the muckraker rather than as a favor to you. After all, by providing the muckraker with a new potential collaborator (you), they are placing the muckraker in their debt.

Once you find an amateur muckraker, he or she may refer you to other muckrakers, including those who like to keep their identities secret.

▪ Federal government bureaucrats are often remarkably conscientious in helping journalists, corporate researchers, high school science project students, and any other member of the public in need of information. As an example: I was backgrounding a businessman who was involved in offshore banking schemes in several small Third World countries. Looking in various directories, I obtained the names and telephone numbers of the State Department and Commerce Department country officers for these nations as well as other relevant officials. None had ever heard of Businessman X, nor would it have been appropriate for them to discuss him if they had. They did, however, share with me their intimate knowledge of the countries in question, citing various government and private reports, and they sent me clippings from newspapers in these countries. In addition, they referred me to experts in other government agencies and the private sector. One official referred me to a white-collar criminal in a federal penitentiary whom he described as the best expert on certain aspects of offshore banking. A second official referred me to an investment promoter long active in one of the countries involved; he, in turn, was willing to make a few inquiries for me.

To find government experts, look first in *Lesko's Info-Power II* (see bibliography).

▪ Congressional committee and subcommittee research staffers are among the most valuable contacts in government for an investigative reporter. The committees for which they work frequently investigate areas such as white-collar crime, government waste and inefficiency, labor racketeering, offshore banking, and corporate pollution of the environment. Quite often, these investigations will shed light on the activities of an individual, corporation, or nonprofit organization in which you are interested.

To find the right committee for your purposes, look in the *Congressional Directory* and consult the Congressional Information Service's cumulative index and abstracts, which cover congressional hearings and reports since 1970. You may find that a committee investigated and held hearings on your topic of interest several years ago, but the committee staffers who did the research have moved to new jobs. Track them down!

▪ Your local congressman may not be an expert on much of anything, but he has a personal legislative staff at his disposal as well as the research staffs of the House committees to which he belongs. In addition, he has the entire resources of the Library of Congress to draw upon through the Congressional Research Service, and he can make the congressional liaison staffs of every department and agency of the federal government jump to his tune. You are his constituent; if you are also an investigative journalist he will have a very strong incentive to keep you happy. Put him to work for you!

- Look in your state and local government handbooks to figure out who's most likely to be useful, both in the various departments and agencies and in the legislative bodies. Remember that state legislative committees, like congressional committees, hold hearings, publish reports, and employ staff researchers.

- Tap the energies of retired experts. Throughout the United States there are millions of retired civil servants, college professors, scientists, and corporate executives with a vast wealth of knowledge and experience in every conceivable field. Many of these retirees are tired of playing golf and would be delighted to cooperate on a volunteer basis with a journalism project that impinges on their specialty. Note that retired experts will often talk more frankly about the Way Things Really Work than might an expert who still has to worry about his or her job. (Thus, if you are looking into industrial pollution, seek out retired chemical engineers who may have spent much of their working lives reluctantly doing the bidding of the polluters.)

- Get on the Internet and advertise for help via the thousands of online bulletin boards and e-mail groups (or "lists," as they're called) concerned with hobbies and popular fads as well as serious scholarly, scientific, or political topics. If you join an e-mail list, you will be able to receive the messages sent out by all members and send your own messages to the entire list or to selected members. Thus if you're investigating whether or not Elvis is still alive, you can send a message to members of your Elvis list soliciting any hard facts they may have (if it's a large list you might receive dozens of responses within the first hour).

  In addition to the e-mail lists, there are also thousands of "newsgroups" on Usenet, an international conferencing system closely linked to the Internet; what we said about advertising for help via e-mail lists applies equally to these groups.

  In general, computer networking has advantages over most other ways of searching for expert knowledge in that it ropes in not just the people we normally think of as "experts" (i.e., those with credentials in a recognized professional field) but also those people from all walks of life with knowledge of thousands of obscure "nonprofessional" topics, e.g., the guy who knows every group of bikers on the West Coast and where they usually hang out. Also, insofar as you join in electronic conferences on scholarly or scientific subjects, you can reach out not just to the recognized academics in the field but also to the independent scholars, self-styled generalists, and amateur enthusiasts whose names appear in no published directories but who sometimes have insights as valuable as those of the "official" experts.

There are a number of online directories of lists and newsgroups; for instance, SRI International's directory of e-mail lists, the BITNET directory of Listserv lists, and Kent State University's directory of scholarly electronic conferences. (For further information, see the appendix and also consult the Internet manuals listed in the bibliography.)

14.2 Finding the Books You Need

If there is a thorough, up-to-date book on the topic you are researching, you should spare no effort to find it—no matter how obscure the publisher. This lesson was brought home to me in 1979 while researching Lyndon La-Rouche's ties to the Teamsters Union. I had been making phone calls for weeks with only modest results. Then, I happened to mention to a Teamster dissident the name of an obscure (I thought) Midwest Teamster official who had been cooperating with LaRouche. "Oh, that s.o.b.," said the dissident, "you can read all about him in *The Hoffa Wars*." He then told me about a book that, if I had begun my research at the public library, I would have found long before. I rushed out and bought the book (Dan Moldea's classic account of Teamster strife) and looked in the index. There I found dozens of references to the thuggery of this "obscure" Teamster official and his underlings.

In searching for the right book, you can always just stroll down to your local public library and look in its catalog. But if you're dealing with a complicated or obscure topic, you might begin by searching the comprehensive online catalogs, i.e., Books in Print Online, LC MARC, and REMARC—all available via DIALOG. Then check with your public library (note that its catalog may also be available online) to see if it has any of the key titles you wish to consult.

If a certain book is unavailable at your local library but is in print, you can get your local bookstore to order it or you can purchase it through Book Stacks Unlimited, the online bookstore that claims to be the world's largest with over 250,000 titles. If the book is out of print, you can try UMI's Books on Demand service, which offers photocopies of over 100,000 out-of-print titles (costing about 25 cents per page). Or you can obtain the book through a dealer in out-of-print or used books. One of the largest out-of-print book dealers is Elliot's Books in Northford, Connecticut. Others can be found in *Book Dealers in North America* and *Directory of Specialized American Bookdealers*.

If the price of an out-of-print copy is too high, you can ask the research librarian at your public library to search the RLIN and OCLC databases (which describe in detail the holdings of member libraries nationwide) to find out which nearby public libraries, university libraries, or special libraries have what you need. If the book is available at, say, a local university library and you can't wait to borrow it through interlibrary loan, you can arrange through your public library to get a one-day pass to examine the book and photocopy the pages you need. If the book is not available locally, RLIN or OCLC will identify libraries elsewhere that have a copy and are part of the interlibrary loan system.

An alternative to RLIN and OCLC is to get on the Internet and search over 500 library catalogs worldwide from your own computer. Hopefully at least one of the catalogs will be that of a library in your locality. In many cases the catalog will not only give you bibliographic information but will also tell you if the book is currently checked out or if it's a noncirculating copy, and whether or not it can be borrowed through interlibrary loan. Note that as you search these catalogs you may find some titles that weren't included in any of the databases you searched earlier.

A search of catalogs by subject, by title key words, and by the names of authors whom you know specialize in the given field may guide you to the books you need. If not, you should check in the relevant specialized bibliographies (see H.W. Wilson's *Bibliographic Index*, a cumulative subject guide available in print back to 1937 and in online and diskette versions back to 1984). Also, a thorough search should always include a trip to the library stacks. I have often found relevant books—books I had not identified through my catalog search—by browsing on either side of where the catalog had informed me that a relevant book (usually missing!) was located.

It would be wonderful if library catalogs contained abstracts of each cataloged book to help you decide if a given book is worth obtaining for your purposes. Although no such catalog exists, you can quickly find detailed information online or on CD-ROM about tens of thousands of books. First, full-text book reviews can be accessed via the full-text databases covering both general-interest newspapers and periodicals and scholarly and scientific journals offering reviews. Second, some online and CD-ROM newspaper and periodical journal abstracts include abstracts of book reviews. Third, H.W. Wilson's Book Review Digest is available online and on CD-ROM dating back to 1983; it covers over 6,500 English-language books each year with brief critical evaluations culled from reviews in over 90 periodicals. Fourth, summaries of reviews and other descriptive material about an author's books are contained in the nearly 100,000 biographical/bibliographical entries in Gale Research Inc.'s Contemporary Authors on CD. Fifth, Dissertation Abstracts Online will give you abstracts of thousands of works of scholarship that, after acceptance as dissertations, were published as books. (For information on book reviews, abstracts, etc., on the Internet, see the appendix.)

14.3 Finding the Right Library

Don't judge a library only by the size of its total collection. Instead, look at the strength of its collection in the field in which you are interested. If I were researching the history of a left-wing party, for instance, I would not go to the giant New York Public Library (NYPL); I would go to the Tamiment Institute Library at New York University. Tamiment is tiny compared to the NYPL, but radical labor history happens to be one of its specialties.

To find the strongest collection for your purposes both locally and nationally, look in *Subject Collections*, the *Directory of Special Libraries and Information Centers*, and the *Directory of Archives and Manuscript Repositories in the United States*. If the collection you most need turns out to be in another part of the country, its catalog may be searchable online. And if the collection's librarians are not too overworked and you can interest them in your research task, they may be willing to look up names in book indexes for you, photocopy material for you, and speed up the interlibrary loan process.

The Library of Congress (LC), with its 100-million-item collection, is the largest library in the world (the second largest in the United States, the New York Public Library, has only about half as many items). As well as having scholarly books and the nation's most complete periodicals collection, the LC has all kinds of miscellany, such as pamphlets and brochures, current and back-issue telephone books, and city directories for localities throughout the country. The LC's National Reference Service will help you over the phone with relatively simple questions. If you need complicated research done at the LC, its Reading Room maintains a list of private researchers who will help you for a reasonable hourly fee. Washington journalists on tight deadlines sometimes call the LC's public affairs office for research on urgent specialized questions.

For your everyday needs, investigate the various libraries in your locality. As noted above, access to the stacks is extremely important. Another crucial factor is the photocopying machines: Are they maintained in good working condition? Are there enough machines so that you don't have to stand in line? A third factor for any investigator is whether a library has basic tools of his or her trade, including the local city or crisscross directories, *BGMI*, *Directories in Print*, and crucial CD-ROM products (especially PhoneDisc and The Complete Marquis Who's Who Plus). If your local public library can't meet these needs, try a local university library (these are easier to gain access to than one would think).

14.4 The World of Research Cabinets

Nonprofit organizations often maintain clippings files on subjects of interest to their members or sponsors. These files may range from a single filing cabinet to vast clippings libraries (such as the one maintained by the Anti-Defamation League of B'nai B'rith in New York), which rival those of the great daily newspapers. In some cases, these files turn out to be a researcher's dream. They can greatly shorten the time it would otherwise take you to collect articles on your subject from indexed periodicals. In addition, these files will include articles from obscure unindexed periodicals that you probably would never come across on your own.

Often these clippings files have been developed as an adjunct of the organization's library, which may be listed in the *Directory of Special Libraries and Information Centers*. Many of the file collections themselves are listed in *Prospect Researcher's Guide to Biographical Research Collections*. But many small organizational libraries are not listed in any directory, and even when they are, the directory may not specify the existence of clippings files.

The easiest way to find such files is to ask the experts in the field you are researching. Failing this, check the *Encyclopedia of Associations* and also *National Trade and Professional Associations of the U.S.* Many organizations listed in these directories regard the dissemination of information to the general public as one of their major functions. Often, they will search their files for you and send you photocopies. Or if you visit their headquarters, they will help you find what you need and provide photocopying on the spot.

If an organization has extensive files relating to your topic and is within convenient distance, you should visit it to search the files yourself. Once you meet the staff in person, and explain your purpose in greater detail, they may let you look through files not ordinarily available to the public.

As an example: When I was researching Lyndon LaRouche's ties to the former apartheid government of South Africa, I went to an anti-apartheid research organization in New York, which was glad to help me. Within minutes I was looking through thick folders of clippings from South African daily and weekly newspapers, South African government reports, and reports by various anti-apartheid groups. When the office closed that afternoon, I left with my briefcase stuffed full of photocopies of materials directly pertinent to my investigation, such as an article from a South African newspaper praising LaRouche's economic theories, an article from another South African newspaper quoting a government commission as charging that the first newspaper was funded by BOSS (the South African secret police), and reports suggesting that BOSS propagandists had worked directly with the LaRouchians. I don't think I could have done much better with help from the CIA—and this is only one of many such experiences I have had with the clippings files of nonprofit organizations.

Bibliography
and Resources ·

I Books, Pamphlets, and Reports

Business Research
Community Press Features. *Open the Books: How to Research a Corporation.* Cambridge, Mass.: Urban Planning Aid, Inc., 1974. Valuable tips on researching and estimating the profits of local businesses.

Daniells, Lorna. *Business Information Sources.* 3d ed. Berkeley: University of California Press, 1993. A thorough guide, highly recommended.

Fuld, Leonard, M. *Competitor Intelligence: How to Get It, How to Use It.* New York: John Wiley, 1985.

Kluge, Pamela H., ed. *Guide to Economics and Business Journalism: The Columbia Knight–Bagehot Handbook.* New York: Columbia University Press, 1993.

Tracy, John A. *How to Read a Financial Report: Wringing Cash Flow and Other Vital Signs out of the Numbers.* 4th ed. New York: John Wiley, 1994.

Courts and the Law
Denniston, Lyle W. *The Reporter and the Law: Techniques of Covering the Courts.* New York: Columbia University Press, 1992.

Wren, Christopher G., and Jill Robinson Wren. *The Legal Research Manual: A Game Plan for Legal Research and Analysis.* 2d ed. Madison, Wisc.: Adams & Ambrose Publishing, 1988.

Credentials and Identity Documents
Bear, John. *College Degrees by Mail.* Rev. ed. Berkeley, Calif.: Ten Speed Press, 1993. Successor to *Bear's Guide to Non-Traditional College Degrees.*

Newman, John Q. *Understanding U.S. Identity Documents.* Port Townsend, Wash.: Loompanics Unlimited, 1991.

Reid, Barry. *The Paper Trip I & II.* Rev. ed. Fountain Valley, Calif.: Eden Press, 1994.

Yeager, Wayne. *Status for Sale: The Complete Guide to Instant Prestige*. Los Angeles: Charter Publications, 1992.

Finding People
Askin, Jayne, with Molly Davis. *Search: A Handbook for Adoptees and Birthparents*. 2d ed. Phoenix: Oryx Press, 1992.
Gunderson, Ted. L., with Roger McGovern. *How to Locate Anyone Anywhere Without Leaving Home*. New York: E.P. Dutton, 1989.
Johnson, Richard S. *How to Locate Anyone Who Is or Has Been in the Military: Armed Forces Locator Directory*. 6th ed. Burlington, N.C.: MIE Publishing, 1995.
Thomas, Ralph D. *How to Find Anyone Anywhere*. 4th ed. Austin, Tex.: Thomas Publications, 1993.

Freedom of Information Laws
Adler, Allan R., ed. *Litigation Under the Federal Open Government Laws: The Freedom of Information Act, the Privacy Act, the Government in the Sunshine Act, the Federal Advisory Committee Act*. Washington, D.C.: The American Civil Liberties Union Foundation, annual editions.
Buitrago, Ann Mari, and Leon Andrew Immerman. *Are You Now or Have You Ever Been in the FBI Files: How to Secure and Interpret Your FBI Files*. New York: Grove Press, 1981. Explains the terminology, abbreviations, and acronyms used in FBI documents, plus the organizational structure and office procedures of the FBI in past years.
Daugherty, Rebecca, ed. *How to Use the Federal FOI Act*. 7th ed. Washington, D.C.: Reporters Committee for Freedom of the Press, 1994. Pamphlet.
House Committee on Government Operations. *A Citizen's Guide on Using the Freedom of Information Act and the Privacy Act of 1974 to Request Government Records*. Washington, D.C.: Government Printing Office, 1993. Pamphlet.
Marwick, Christine M. *Your Right to Government Information*. New York: Bantam Books, 1985.

Interviewing
Brady, John. *The Craft of Interviewing*. New York: Random House, 1977.
Metzler, Ken. *Creative Interviewing: The Writer's Guide to Gathering Information by Asking Questions*. 2d ed. Englewood Cliffs, N.J.: Prentice Hall, 1989.
Royal, Robert F., and Steven R. Schutt. *The Gentle Art of Interviewing and Interrogation: A Professional Manual and Guide*. Englewood Cliffs, N.J.: Prentice Hall, 1987.

Investigative Journalism and Public-Interest Research
Benjaminson, Peter, and David Anderson. *Investigative Reporting*. 2d ed. Ames: Iowa State University Press, 1990.
Harry, M. *The Muckraker's Manual: Handbook for Investigative Reporters*. 2d ed. Port Townsend, Wash.: Loompanics Unlimited, 1984.
Mollenhoff, Clark R. *Investigative Reporting: From Courthouse to White House*. New York: Macmillan, 1981.

Pawlick, Thomas. *Investigative Reporting: A Casebook*. New York: Richards Rosen Press, 1982.

Rose, Louis J. *How to Investigate Your Friends and Enemies*. Rev. ed. St. Louis: Albion Press, 1992. Especially valuable are Chapter IV ("Investigating Real Estate") and Chapter V ("Finding the Hidden Owners").

Weberman, A.J. *My Life in Garbology*. New York: Stonehill Publishing Company, 1980.

Weinberg, Steve. *Trade Secrets of Washington Journalists*. Washington, D.C.: Acropolis Press, 1981.

———. *Telling the Untold Story: How Investigative Reporters Are Changing the Craft of Biography*. Columbia: University of Missouri Press, 1992.

———. *The Reporter's Handbook: An Investigator's Guide to Documents and Techniques*. 3d ed. New York: St. Martin's Press, 1995. Indispensable for every journalist and investigator.

Williams, Paul N. *Investigative Reporting and Editing*. Englewood Cliffs, N.J.: Prentice Hall, 1978.

Zilliox, Larry, Jr. *The Opposition Research Handbook: A Guide to Political Investigations*. McLean, Va.: Investigative Research Specialists, 1993. Highly recommended for beginners.

Zilliox, Larry, Jr. and Larry Kahaner. *How to Investigate Destructive Cults and Underground Groups*. Alexandria, Va.: Kane Associates International, Inc., 1990.

Library and General Research

Barzun, Jacques, and Henry F. Graff. *The Modern Researcher*. 5th ed. New York: Harcourt Brace College Pubs., 1992. Although written for historians, there is something in almost every chapter for both investigative journalists and private investigators. See especially the chapters on "Verification" and "Truth and Causation."

Berkman, Robert I. *Find It Fast: How to Uncover Expert Information on Any Subject*. 3d ed. New York: HarperCollins, 1994.

Harris, Sherwood, ed. *The New York Public Library Book of How and Where to Look It Up*. New York: Prentice Hall, 1991.

Lawton, Henry. *The Psychohistorian's Handbook*. New York: The Psychohistory Press, 1988.

Lesko, Matthew. *Lesko's Info-Power II*. Kensington, Md.: Information USA, 1993.

Luebking, Sandra Hargreaves, and Loretto Dennis Szucs, eds. *The Source: A Guidebook of American Genealogy*. Rev. ed. Salt Lake City: Ancestry Incorporated, 1995.

Mann, Thomas. *A Guide to Library Research Methods*. New York: Oxford University Press, 1990.

Prucha, Francis Paul. *Handbook for Research in American History*. 2d ed. Lincoln: University of Nebraska Press, 1994.

Todd, Alden. *Finding Facts Fast*. Berkeley, Calif.: Ten Speed Press, 1992.

Online Databases and the Internet

Braun, Eric. *The Internet Directory*. New York: Fawcett Columbine, 1994.

Dern, Daniel P. *The Internet Guide for New Users*. New York: McGraw-Hill, 1994.

Gilster, Paul. *The Internet Navigator: The Essential Guide to Network Exploration for the Individual Dial-Up User.* 2d ed. New York: John Wiley, 1994.

Glossbrenner, Alfred, and John Rosenberg. *How to Look It Up Online: Get the Information Edge with Your Personal Computer.* 2d ed. New York: John Wiley, 1995.

Goldman, Nahum. *Online Information Hunting.* Blue Ridge Summit, Pa.: Windcrest, 1992.

Maxwell, Bruce. *How to Access the Federal Government on the Internet.* Washington, D.C.: Congressional Quarterly Books, 1995.

Orenstein, Glenn S., and Ruth M. Orenstein. *CompuServe Companion: Finding Newspapers and Magazines Online.* Needham Heights, Mass.: Bibliodata, 1994.

Privacy

Larson, Erik. *The Naked Consumer: How Our Private Lives Become Public Commodities.* New York: Henry Holt, 1992.

Rothfeder, Jeffrey. *Privacy for Sale: How Computerization Has Made Everyone's Private Life an Open Secret.* New York: Simon & Schuster, 1992.

Smith, Robert Ellis. *Collection and Use of Social Security Numbers.* Providence, R.I.: Privacy Journal, 1990.

———. *Compilation of State and Federal Privacy Laws.* Rev. ed. Providence, R.I.: Privacy Journal, 1992.

———. *The Law of Privacy Explained.* Providence, R.I.: Privacy Journal, 1993.

———. *Our Vanishing Privacy and What You Can Do to Protect Yours.* Port Townsend, Wash.: Loompanics Unlimited, 1993.

Smith, Robert Ellis, with Eric Siegel and James S. Sulanowski. *War Stories: Accounts of Persons Victimized by Invasions of Privacy.* Providence, R.I.: Privacy Journal, 1993.

Private Investigators' and Legal Investigators' Methods

ACM IV Security Services. *Secrets of Surveillance: A Professional's Guide to Tailing Subjects by Vehicle, Foot, Airplane, and Public Transportation.* Boulder, Colo.: Paladin Press, 1993.

Anacapa Sciences, Inc. *Sources of Information for Criminal Investigators.* Rev. ed. Santa Barbara, Calif.: Anacapa Sciences, 1990.

Binder, David A., and Paul Bergman. *Fact Investigation: From Hypothesis to Proof.* St. Paul, Minn.: West Publishing Co., 1984.

Blye, Irwin, and Ardy Friedberg. *Secrets of a Private Eye.* New York: Henry Holt, 1987.

Carroll, John M. *Confidential Information Sources: Public & Private.* 2d ed. Stoneham, Mass.: Butterworth-Heinemann, 1991.

Culligan, Joseph J. *When in Doubt Check Him Out: A Woman's Survival Guide for the 90's.* Miami: Hallmark Press, 1993.

Golec, Anthony M. *Techniques of Legal Investigation.* 2d ed. Springfield, Ill.: Charles C. Thomas, 1985.

Pileggi, Nicholas. *Blye, Private Eye.* Chicago: Playboy Press, 1976.

Probe, Inc. *Private Investigators Pretext Manual.* Beverly Hills, Calif.: Probe, 1989.

Rapp, Burt. *Shadowing and Surveillance: A Complete Guidebook.* Port Townsend, Wash.: Loompanics Unlimited, 1985.

Sample, John. *Methods of Disguise*. 2d ed. Port Townsend, Wash.: Loompanics Unlimited, 1993.

Slade, E. Roy, and James R. Gutzs. *The Pretext Book: "Sweet Talking"—The PI's Black Book*. Houston: Cloak & Data Press, 1991.

Thomas, Ralph D. *How to Investigate by Computer*. 4th ed. Austin, Tex.: Thomas Investigative Publications, 1994.

———. *Investigator's and Information Broker's Guide to CD ROM Technology*. 2d ed. Austin, Tex.: Thomas Investigative Publications, 1994.

Thompson, Josiah. *Gumshoe: Reflections in a Private Eye*. New York: Ballantine Books, 1989.

Public Records—General

Morehead, Joe, and Mary Fetzer. *Introduction to United States Government Information Sources*. 4th ed. Englewood, Colo.: Libraries Unlimited, 1992.

Murphy, Harry J. *Where's What: Sources of Information for Federal Investigators*. New York: Warner Books, 1976.

Murray, Thomson C. *The License Plate Book: How to Read and Decode U.S. and Canadian Plates*. Rev. ed. Jericho, N.Y.: Interstate Directory Publishing Co., 1994.

National Employment Screening Services. *The Guide to Background Investigations*. 6th ed. Tulsa, Okla.: National Employment Screening Services, 1994. Convenient one-stop directory.

———. *Social Security Number Guide*. Rev. ed. Tulsa, Okla.: National Employment Screening Services, 1994.

Sankey, Michael, and Carl Ernst. *The County Locator—LOCUS: The Ultimate Place Name and Zip Code Locator*. The Public Record Research Library, Tempe, Ariz.: BRB Publications, 1993.

———. *The Sourcebook of County Asset/Lien Records*. The Public Record Research Library, Tempe, Ariz.: BRB Publications, 1994.

———. *The Sourcebook of County Court Records*. 2d ed. The Public Record Research Library, Tempe, Ariz.: BRB Publications, 1994.

———. *The Sourcebook of Federal Courts—U.S. District and Bankruptcy*. 2d ed. The Public Record Research Library, Tempe, Ariz.: BRB Publications, 1995.

———. *The Sourcebook of Local Court and County Record Retrievers*. 2d ed. The Public Record Research Library, Tempe, Ariz.: BRB Publications, 1995.

———. *The Sourcebook of Public Record Providers: The National Guide to Companies That Furnish Automated Public Record Information, Search Services and Investigative Services*. 3d ed. The Public Record Research Library, Tempe, Ariz.: BRB Publications, 1995.

———. *The Sourcebook of State Public Records*. 2d ed. The Public Record Research Library, Tempe, Ariz.: BRB Publications, 1995.

———. *The MVR Book*. The Public Record Research Library, Tempe, Ariz.: BRB Publications, annual.

———. *The MVR Decoder Digest*. The Public Record Research Library, Tempe, Ariz.: BRB Publications, annual.

U.S. Dept. of Health and Human Services. *Where to Write for Vital Records: Births, Deaths, Marriages, and Divorces*. Washington, D.C.: U.S. Government Printing Office, 1993.

Public Records—Local and State Guidebooks

Davis, Aurora E., ed. *Access to Public Information: A Resource Guide to Government in Columbia and Boone County, Missouri.* Rev. ed. Columbia, Mo.: Freedom of Information Center, 1990.

Dolan, John P., Jr., and Lisa Lacher. *Guide to Public Records of Iowa Counties.* Des Moines: Iowa Title Company, 1987.

Guzik, Estelle M., ed. *Genealogical Resources in the New York Metropolitan Area.* New York: Jewish Genealogical Society, 1989.

Jeffres, Leo W., et al. *Cleveland State University Journalists' Handbook Series.* Vol. I: *News Strategies.* Volume II: *Public Records Guide* (includes Cuyahoga County, City of Cleveland, and regional, state, and other offices). Cleveland: Communication Research Center of Cleveland State University, 1988.

Kronman, Barbara. *Guide to NYC Public Records.* 4th ed. New York: Public Interest Clearinghouse, 1993.

Levine, Stephen. *Paper Trails: A Guide to Public Records in California.* 2d ed. San Francisco: Center for Investigative Reporting, 1994.

White-Collar Crime

Bologna, Jack. *Handbook on Corporate Fraud: Prevention, Detection and Investigation.* Stoneham, Mass.: Butterworth-Heinemann, 1993.

Clinard, Marshall B., ed. *Illegal Corporate Behavior.* Washington, D.C.: U.S. Government Printing Office, 1979.

Dickinson, Peter S. *Civil RICO: A Research Guide to Civil Liability for Business Crimes.* Buffalo, N.Y.: William S. Hein, 1989.

Edelhertz, Herbert. *The Investigation of White-Collar Crime.* Washington, D.C.: U.S. Government Printing Office, 1977.

Hoy, Michael. *Directory of U.S. Mail Drops.* Rev. ed. Port Townsend, Wash.: Loompanics Unlimited, 1991.

Luger, Jack. *How to Use Mail Drops for Privacy and Profit.* Port Townsend, Wash.: Loompanics Unlimited, 1988.

Nossen, Richard A., and Joan W. Norvelle. *The Detection, Investigation, and Prosecution of Financial Crimes.* 2d ed. Tucson, Ariz.: Thoth Books, 1993.

Schilit, Howard M. *Financial Shenanigans: How to Detect Accounting Gimmicks and Fraud in Financial Reports.* New York: McGraw-Hill, 1993.

II CD-ROM and Floppy Disk Products

CIABASE. Ralph McGehee, P.O. Box 5022, Herndon, VA 22070.

The County Locator—CD. BRB Publications, Inc., 4653 South Lakeshore, Suite 3, Tempe, AZ 85282.

Death Master File. CSRA, 23 Rocky Knoll, Irvine, CA 92715.

NameBase. Public Information Research, P.O. Box 680635, San Antonio, TX 78268.

The National Geographic Names Data Base. U.S. Geological Survey, 523 National Center, Reston, VA 22092.

PhoneDisc. Digital Directory Assistance, Inc., 6931 Arlington Road, Suite 405, Bethesda, MD 20814.

The Public Record Research System. BRB Publications, Inc., 4653 South Lakeshore, Suite 3, Tempe, AZ 85282.

SelectPhone. ProCD, Inc., 8 Doaks Lane, Marblehead, MA 01945.
Social Security Death Benefits Index. J&D Distributing, 1160 South State Street, Suite 220, Orem, UT 84058.
Street Atlas USA. DeLorme Mapping Systems, Lower Main Street, P.O. Box 298, Freeport, ME 04032.

III Journals, Magazines, and Newspapers

Everton's Genealogical Helper, 3223 South Main Street, Nibley, UT 84321. Bimonthly.
The IRE Journal, 100 Neff Hall, University of Missouri, Columbia, MO 65211. Bimonthly. Contains state-of-the-art trade tips found nowhere else. Cumulative index (1978–94) and complete backfiles available.
The Legal Investigator, 3304 Crescent Drive, Des Moines, IA 50312. Quarterly.
Link-Up, 143 Old Marlton Pike, Medford, NJ 08055–8750. Bimonthly.
P.I. Magazine, 755 Bronx, Toledo, OH 43609. Quarterly.
Searcher: The Magazine for Database Professionals, 143 Old Marlton Pike, Medford, NJ 08055. Nine issues per year.
Special Libraries, 1700 18th Street N.W., Washington, DC 20009. Quarterly.

IV Newsletters

The Database Files, 5622 Wood Lane, St. Louis Park, MN 55436.
Lesko's Info-Power Newsletter (formerly *Data Informer*), Information USA, P.O. Box E, Kensington, MD 20895.
Privacy Journal, P.O. Box 28577, Providence, RI 02908. Indexes available covering 1974–93.
Private Investigator's Connection, National Association of Investigative Specialists, Inc., P.O. Box 33244, Austin, TX 78764.
Uplink, National Institute for Computer-Assisted Reporting, 120 Neff Hall, University of Missouri, Columbia, MO 65211.

V Reference Book, Microform, and Electronic Publishers (*includes producers of online databases*)

BRB Publications, 4653 South Lakeshore, Suite 3, Tempe, AZ 85282.
Burrelle's Information Services, 75 East Northfield Road, Livingston, NJ 07039.
Cole Publications, Inc., 901 West Bond Street, Lincoln, NE 68521–3694.
Commerce Clearing House (CCH), 4025 West Peterson Avenue, Chicago, IL 60646.
DeLorme Mapping Systems, Main Street, P.O. Box 298, Freeport, ME 04032.
Dow Jones News/Retrieval Service, P.O. Box 300, Princeton, NJ 08543–0300.
Dun & Bradstreet Information Services, Three Sylvan Way, Parsippany, NJ 07054.

Gale Research Inc., P.O. Box 33477, Detroit, MI   48232–5477.

The H.W. Wilson Company, 950 University Avenue, Bronx, NY   10452.

Information Access Company (IAC), 362 Lakeside Drive, Foster City, CA   94404.

Journal Graphics, 1535 Grant Street, Denver, CO   80203.

Learned Information, Inc., 143 Old Marlton Pike, Medford, NJ   08055.

Meckler Corporation, 11 Ferry Lane West, Westport, CT   06880–5808.

Metromail, 360 East 22nd Street, Lombard, IL   60148.

Moody's Investors Service, Inc., 99 Church Street, New York, NY   10007.

NewsBank, Inc., 58 Pine Street, New Canaan, CT   06840–5426.

PR Newswire, 1515 Broadway, New York, NY   10036.

Reed Reference Publishing, 121 Chanlon Road, New Providence, NJ   07974.
    Includes: R.R. Bowker, Marquis Who's Who, National Register Publishing,
    and Martindale-Hubbell.

R.L. Polk & Co., 1155 Brewery Park Boulevard, Detroit, MI   48207.

Standard & Poor's Corporation, 25 Broadway, New York, NY   10004.

Thomas Publishing Company, Five Penn Plaza, New York, NY   10001.

TRW Information Services, 505 City Parkway West, Orange, CA   92668.

TRW REDI Property Data, 3610 Central Avenue, Suite 500, Riverside, CA
    92506–9858.

UMI/Data Courier, 620 South Third Street, Louisville, KY   40202–2475.

University Microfilms International (UMI), 300 North Zeeb Road, P.O. Box 1346,
    Ann Arbor, MI   48106–1346.

West Publishing Company, P.O. Box 64779, St. Paul, MN   55164–0779.

VI Online Database Vendors

DataTimes, 14000 Quail Springs Parkway, Suite 450, Oklahoma City, OK   73134.

Dialog Information Services, Inc., 3460 Hillview Avenue, P.O. Box 10010, Palo
    Alto, CA   94303–0993.

Mead Data Central (LEXIS/NEXIS), 9443 Springboro Pike, P.O. Box 933, Dayton,
    OH   45401.

NewsNet, 945 Haverford Road, Bryn Mawr, PA   19010.

ORBIT Search Service, 8000 Westpark Drive, McLean, VA   22102.

VII Online Gateways

America Online, 8619 Westwood Center Drive, Vienna, VA   22182.

CompuServe, 5000 Arlington Centre Boulevard, P.O. Box 20212, Columbus, OH
    43220.

Delphi Internet Services, 1030 Massachusetts Avenue, Cambridge, MA   02138.

EasyNet, c/o Telebase Systems, Inc., 435 Devon Park Drive, Suite 600, Wayne, PA
    19087.

GEnie, 401 North Washington Street, Rockville, MD   20850.

Prodigy, 445 Hamilton Avenue, White Plains, NY   10601.

VIII Online Information Brokers Used by Investigators

CDB INFOTEK, 6 Hutton Centre Drive, Santa Ana, CA   92707.

Datafax Information Services, P.O. Box 33244, Austin, TX   78764.

Information America, 600 West Peachtree Street, N.W., Suite 1200, Atlanta, GA   30308.

Prentice Hall OnLine, 18200 Von Karman Avenue, Suite 100, Irvine, CA   92715.

IX Mail Order Publishers/Distributors of Investigative Books

Eden Press, P.O. Box 8410, Fountain Valley, CA   92728.

Loompanics Unlimited, P.O. Box 1197, Port Townsend, WA   98368.

Paladin Press, P.O. Box 1307, Boulder, CO   80306.

Thomas Investigative Publications, Inc., P.O. Box 33244, Austin, TX   78764.

Appendix ·

Investigative Resources on the Internet

The Internet offers a unique way to reach out to individuals and organizations having the special knowledge you need. Properly worded, a single query to the appropriate BBS (bulletin board system), e-mail list, or newsgroup can do the work of hundreds of phone calls.

Less clear is the usefulness of the hodgepodge of free government, academic, and scientific databases that one can access via the Internet. As things stand now, these databases are no substitute for the systematically compiled business, news, and legal databases available from commercial vendors such as DIALOG or LEXIS/NEXIS. It would be a mistake for any investigator or researcher to think that he or she could cut corners and obtain from noncommercial databases anything remotely like a systematic search of the available online information in most fields. Even in the case of SEC filings (see I.1 below), you are advised to go through commercial vendors if you need a thorough search of a given company's filings.

Yet the free databases on the Internet can sometimes be a valuable adjunct to the commercial databases—it all depends on who or what your target is. For instance, if you are backgrounding a businessperson who uses his or her computer for pleasure as well as work—or a scientist who communicates with his or her colleagues via the Internet—you may be able (if you know subject's username) to download some of his or her e-mail ramblings as preserved in the archives of various newsgroups, lists, or conferences. If you are backgrounding someone who has not yet joined the online revolution, however, you may not find very much hard information about him or her via the Internet.

The following is an outline of mostly noncommercial Internet services and related electronic resources that journalists and investigators may find useful. Note that the Internet is a volatile and rapidly changing social dimension: Several of the resources listed below may be defunct or have changed their Internet addresses by the time this book is published.

A. Basic Aids to Investigating (supplements section 2.1)

1. **Investigative Reporters and Editors listserv and National Institute for Computer-Assisted Reporting listserv.** To join either or both: **mailto:jourire@muccmail .missouri.edu.** Services include: IRE and NICAR discussion groups where you can post messages for help from other members, an international directory of over 300 journalists in 70 countries (with areas of expertise), abstracts from the IRE Resource Center (over 10,000 investigative articles), abstracts from the IRE tip sheets (conference panel handouts) database, the *IRE Journal Index* (covers 1978 to 1994), and the full text of the *IRE Journal* and *Uplink* beginning in 1994.

2. **Archive of the Index to Journalism Periodicals.** Over 20,000 citations to articles from 40 journalism-related trade, professional, and academic periodicals. **gopher .uwo.ca** (choose UWO News and Publications).

3. **Privacy Forum.** Moderated discussion of privacy issues; full archives available. **ftp.vortex.com** (path:/privacy/*) or **gopher://cv.vortex.com** (choose Privacy Forum).

4. **NBONLINE, the online version of NameBase** (annotated diskette index and photocopy/fax retrieval system for articles and books of investigative journalism; see section 6.5). You can access it via PeaceNet: **mailto:apc-info@igc.apc.org.** Note: NBONLINE offers only two of the eight NameBase search options, but you do get the annotated descriptions of each listed title. The indexing is selective in both the online and diskette versions, so if you fail to find a citation for the given individual, company, or organization in a book or article that seems promising, you should consult the book's own index (if it has one) at the public library or do a full-text search of the article (if it's available online). Public Information Research, which produces Namebase/NBONLINE, will send you a copy of any cited article or the cited pages of any book in its collection. In addition, you should consult CIABASE (see bibliography), a diskette subject index with 30,000 citations of books, articles, congressional reports, and special publications regarding the intelligence community (this covers from a different angle many of the same books and periodicals indexed by NameBase/NBONLINE).

5. **Library science electronic journals:** gopher://vienna.hh.lib.umich.edu.

B. Finding "Missing" People (supplements chapter 4)

1. **Finding people via their Internet addresses.** A wide range of resources are at **gopher: //marvel.loc.gov** (choose Internet Resources/Directories: Finding People and Organizations) and at **gopher://yaleinfo.yale.edu** (choose About the Internet/People on the Internet). How to use the many online finding aids is described in detail in the various Internet manuals (see bibliography). (Of course you can also check for subject's name in the hard-copy *Internet White Pages*.) Note: Even if you don't think subject has ever used a computer, you should send messages to every e-mail address that includes (as the username or as part of the username) subject's surname or the surname of subject's wife prior to her marriage to subject. This might turn up a relative. It also might turn up subject's computer-crazed teenage son or daughter, listed here under his or her real surname even though the family is using another name in the telephone white pages to

hide from bill collectors. Also note: Usernames on the Internet may vary widely from the names given in a phone book. Typical variations include the user's first and last names run together as one word; the first syllable only of the user's last name; the user's first name, middle name, or nickname (often followed by the first letter of his or her last name); a pseudonym; or a designation by subject's occupation or special interest. Fortunately, gateway services such as DELPHI and many Internet newsgroups and conferences have user directories and/or entry logs by which you can sometimes match the username to the real name; such a directory will often include subject's address, job title, and other identifying information.

2. **Finding people via those who share their interests.** To obtain a comprehensive list of Usenet newsgroups, go to **news.lists** and **news.groups** and **news.announce .newusers.** (Example: If you are searching for your lost biker brother, you might try **rec.motorcycles** or **alt.motorcycles.harley.**) For the directory of BITNET lists: **mailto:listserv@bitnic.bitnet.** For SRI International's directory of Internet lists: **ftp .nisc.sri.com** (path:/netinfo/interest-groups).

3. **Finding people on college campuses.** For finding campus e-mail addresses, see B.1 above. For finding work and/or home addresses and phone numbers of students, faculty members, administrators, and support staff, check the relevant directories on the given college's Campus-Wide Information System (CWIS). What's available will vary from campus to campus, but the directory at a particular campus very well may include home telephone numbers and addresses that are unavailable from the local telephone company's white pages. For an up-to-date list of CWIS servers: **ftp.oit.unc .edu** (path:/pub/docs/about-the-net/CWIS). Also see the menu of campus and research center directories at **gopher.nd.edu** (choose Non-Notre Dame Information Sources/Phone Books—Other Institutions/North America).

4. **Finding people via Freenets.** You can post messages for a person you need to contact—or anyone who might know him or her—via hobby-oriented, local government, and local nonprofit BBSs on the Freenet serving any locality in which you believe subject might be residing (for instance, if you are searching for a homeless relative, you would post to the BBSs of social service agencies and charities). For a list of Freenets: **mailto:exr@nptn.org.** To access Freenets: **gopher.tamu.edu** (choose Hot Topics/Freenets).

5. **Finding ham radio operators.** The online call-sign directory provides addresses, dates of birth, and license information on amateur radio operators throughout the country. It can be searched by name, call sign, city, or zip code. **telnet://callsign.cs .buffalo.edu 2000** (login: hamradio).

6. **Advice on posting your messages anonymously.** This can be important if you're searching for someone who would be hostile to your search, or if you're searching for a lost birthparent and feel too embarrassed to let the electronic public know your name. **mailto:help@anon.penet.fi.**

7. **National Geographic Names Data Base (NGNDB).** Over 2 million names of places, features, and sites throughout the United States with exact location, alternate or former name(s), and variant spellings of the official name. Includes towns, villages, rivers, creeks, mountains, TV towers, shopping centers, cemeteries, campus dormitories, churches—almost everything except streets, roads, and railroads. Useful in finding and/or backgrounding someone if you have only a fragmentary address, or if the village where subject was born is now 20 feet under the waters of a reservoir, or if the rural church where he or she was christened has been destroyed to make way for a shopping mall or interstate highway. The NGNDB can be found at **gopher://info.er.usgs.gov** (choose National Mapping Division) or at **gopher**

.peabody.yale.edu. Note that this resource is best used in tandem with Street Atlas USA (see bibliography).

8. **Genealogical records.** First check the National Archives and Records Administration's online database at **gopher.nara.gov**. For state and local genealogical records, check state government or university gophers for the relevant region, e.g., for New York genealogies check the New York State Archives database at **gopher://nysernet.org**.

C. Biographical Background Information (supplements chapter 5)

Biographical sketches on candidates for federal office (and, for some localities, candidates for state and local office) can be found at **telnet://ora.rsch.oclc.org 6020** or **http://www.oclc.org/VoteSmart/lwv/lwvhomex.htm**. For biographies of state officials, see the various state government gophers, e.g., **gopher.revisor.leg.state.mn.us** for Minnesota state legislators and **gopher.election.ca.gov** for California judges.

Biographical and career data is also available from CWISs, e.g., the biographical sketches of California State University administrators and trustees at **gopher.calstate.edu** (choose CSU Public Affairs) and the biographical data on Texas A&M faculty members at **gopher.tamu.edu**. Especially detailed biographical information can be obtained from résumé databases, e.g., the résumés of consultants at **news:misc.jobs.contract** and the résumés of thousands of job seekers (mostly in technical fields) at **gopher://garnet.msen.com 9062** (choose Search Resumes) and at **news:misc.jobs.resumes**.

D. Newspapers, Periodicals, and Television News Programs (supplements chapter 6)

1. **Online collections of campus newspapers.** About 35 U.S. and Canadian campus publications (mostly student newspapers) are available at **gopher://blick.journ.latech.edu**. Also, 13 student dailies and 16 weeklies can be found at **http://www.utk.edu** (choose Daily Beacon/Campus Newspapers on the Internet). Note that full-text searches of student newspapers will turn up information not just on students and faculty but also on politicians and others in the surrounding community.

2. **UnCover.** A service of Colorado Alliance of Research Libraries (CARL). Each member library sends its latest periodical issues to CARL, which creates the UnCover records from the table of contents of each issue (title, author, and any article summary on the table of contents page). UnCover contains records of over 5 million articles from scholarly journals and popular magazines. You can search by author's name, by key word, or by the periodical issue's full table of contents, and then order a fax of the article you need. **telnet://pac.carl.org**.

3. **Alternative press.** PeaceNet provides access to the electronic archives of left-liberal-activist magazines, newsletters, and news services, e.g., *Mother Jones*, *Z Magazine*, *The Nation*, and the Pacific News Service; while the EDIN gopher provides a fascinating mixture of left-wing and right-wing periodicals. For more on PeaceNet and EDIN, see J.5 below.

4. **Electronic journals, newsletters, and "zines."** To obtain the Directory of Electronic Journals and Newsletters: **listserv@acadvm1.uottawa.ca** (commands SEND EJOURNL1 DIRECTRY and SEND EJOURNL2 DIRECTRY). For a list of zines: **ftp://netcom.com** (path:/pub/john1/zines/e-zine-list). For archives of electronic periodicals, see H.4 below.

5. **Television news programs.** The online version of *Television News Index and Abstracts* (see section 6.26) can be found at **gopher://tvnews.vanderbilt.edu** or **http://tvnews.vanderbilt.edu/hh/**. This database covers evening news programs and news specials (e.g., conventions and presidential speeches) from all three major networks back to 1968 as well as "Nightline" back to 1988. Similar abstracts of CNN programs are at **gopher://info.umd.edu**. Transcripts of offbeat political programs on public-access cable TV can be found at **gopher://garnet.berkeley.edu**.

6. **Research library periodical indexes.** Many libraries have compiled indexes and/or abstracts of local or specialized periodicals not covered by standard reference works or commercial databases; some are available online. Example: the North Carolina Periodicals Index at **gopher://fringe.lib.ecu.edu**.

E. Federal Election Commission Records (supplements section 10.10)

The FEC's Direct Access Program offers online information on candidate, PAC, and party committee finances. It includes the Individual Search System (which corresponds to the FEC inhouse database's Contributor Search System), the 5I report (which corresponds to the inhouse G Index), FEC advisory opinions, and FEC court abstract texts. Costs $20/hour. To sign up, call (800) 424-9530 or (202) 219-3730. Note that this database covers only the most recent three election cycles. To access earlier cycles, you must either purchase the mag-tapes or else order computer printouts from the inhouse database and/or photocopies from the microform files (floppy disks not available); call the public disclosure office at (202) 219-4140.

F. Subject's Campus Career (supplements section 11.1)

1. **Newsletters, minutes of meetings, etc., of the student government and of fraternities, religious societies, and other campus organizations.** These records will often be available on the college's CWIS for the current academic year, but the organization in question may not have bothered to create an electronic archive for the records of past years. At the least, the current records will give you an indication of whether or not it will be worth your time to search through the manual files (at the college library) of a particular organization for the years in which subject was an active member.

2. **Faculty records** (departmental newsletters and announcements, indexes of grants and fellowships, minutes of faculty senate meetings, etc.). These can be important in gathering background information on faculty members and graduate students. Again, the records from previous years may not have been electronically archived.

3. **Catalog/index of the campus archives** (the official repository for the records of campus activities dating back to the college's earliest years). Look in the university li-

brary's electronic catalog, which can easily be accessed via HYTELNET at **gopher: //liberty.uc.wlu.edu** or LIBTEL at **telnet://bbs.oit.unc.edu.**

4. Campus newspapers. See D.1.

G. Library Archives (supplements section 11.2). See B.8 and F.3 above.

H. Subject's Writings (supplements section 11.3)

1. **Library catalogs.** See F.3 and K.2.

2. **U.S. Copyright Office.** All copyrights since 1978. **telnet://locis.loc.gov** (password: copyright information).

3. **Electronic indexes and archives of scholarly, scientific, and professional journals** (apart from the versions offered by DIALOG and other commercial database vendors). Examples include the Iowa State University SCHOLAR System (agriculture-related science and technology articles) at **telnet://isn.iastate.edu** (login: scholar); the National Archaeological Database at **telnet://cast.uark.edu** (login: nadb); and ERIC, the U.S. Department of Education's giant bibliographic database, at **telnet://acsnet .syr.edu** or **gopher://cwis.syr.edu** (choose Non-S.U. Internet Resources/Discipline Specific Internet Resources).

4. **Electronic journals, newsletters, "zines."** For directories of these publications, see D.4 above. For archives of electronic journals and zines: **ftp.cic.net** or **gopher.cic .net** (choose Electronic Serials) and **gopher.virginia.edu** (choose Library Services/ Electronic Journals). For zines on various topics: **gopher://wiretap.spies.com** (choose Wiretap Online Library/Zines) and **ftp://nigel.msen.com** (path:/pub/newsletters/*) and **gopher.well.sf.ca.us.** For science-fiction zines: **news:rec.mag.fsf.**

5. **Preprints.** Scientists or scholars who don't want to wait years for a refereed journal to finally print their work may prepublish it electronically. The criticisms elicited via prepublication as well as the journal editing process may result in heavy revisions, so check both versions if available. For examples of preprints, see the theoretical physics archive at **ftp://xxx.lanl.gov** (paths:/gr-qc/* and /hep-th/*), the mathematics archive at **gopher://archives.math.utk.edu** and the management science archive at **gopher://chimera.sph.umn.edu.**

6. **Archives of working papers.** Scientists or scholars who wish to elicit suggestions and criticism regarding their work in progress may put it on the Internet. See, e.g., the archive of working papers in economics at **ftp://econwpa.wustl.edu** (path: /econ-wp/*).

7. **Archives of technical reports.** A good example is at **gopher://arthur.cs.purdue. edu** (choose Non-Purdue Information/FTP Servers outside Purdue/FTP Archives of Technical Reports).

8. **Speeches and interviews.** A collection of speeches and papers by prominent conservatives can be found at **ftp://cathouse.org** (path:/pub/cathouse/conservative/*). A list of C-SPAN transcripts of National Press Club speeches and Booknotes interviews can be found at **gopher://c-span.org.**

9. **Poetry.** An index of all poems and reviews in the prestigious Chicago-based *Poetry* magazine since 1987 is accessible via the WAIS at **sunsite.unc.edu** (resource

name: **POETRY-index.src**; database name: /home3/wais/POETRY-index). Recent plagiarism in the poetry field may result in additional electronic indexing and archiving of poetry magazines in the near future. Meanwhile, you can find the work of amateur Internet poets at **news:rec.arts.poems** and an archive of original works in both poetry and fiction at **gopher://quartz.rutgers.edu** (choose Quartz BBS Original Works Archive) or **ftp://quartz.rutgers.edu** (path:/pub/origworks/*).

10. **Unpublished scholarly discussion.** See the Directory of Scholarly Electronic Conferences at **ftp://ksuvxa.kent.edu** (path:/library/acad/*) or **gopher://nysernet.org** (choose Special Collections: Higher Education/Electronic Conferences of Interest to Scholars).

11. **Unpublished newsgroup or e-mail list discussion.** See B.2. Note that many participants in sexually oriented lists or certain of the "alt" newsgroups use anonymous remailers (secure network sites that delete from e-mail messages any information that could reveal the sender's identity).

12. **Catalog of "uncataloged" titles.** You can find brochures, pamphlets, self-published books, audiocassettes, research reports, and other hard-to-locate items in the UNCAT database at **http://www.sapphire.com**.

I. Businesses and Nonprofits (supplements chapter 13)

1. **Internet EDGAR Dissemination Project.** This experimental free service offers all Securities and Exchange Commission public filings since 1994 that were filed electronically (some corporations still file nonelectronically). For access to EDGAR: **ftp.town.hall.org** (login: anonymous; password: your e-mail address) or **gopher://town.hall.org** or **http://www.town.hall.org.jour**. For SEC records prior to 1994, see LEXIS/NEXIS (subscription information is at **telnet://nex.meaddata.com**).

2. **Federal and state business databases.** One of the best places to search for evidence of corporate misdeeds is the Food and Drug Administration's BBS at **telnet://fdabbs.fda.gov** (login: bbs). A wide range of government online services relating to the corporate world can be accessed at **telnet://fedworld.gov** and at **gopher.micro.umn.edu** (choose Libraries/Information from the U.S. Federal Government). To search for federal government contracts awarded to a particular company or within a particular industry, see the online version of the Commerce Business Daily at **gopher.counterpoint.com**. State government contract information has also been put on the Internet by a few states, e.g., the New York State Office of General Services' database of current and expired contracts at **gopher://ogs.nysernet.org**.

3. **The labor movement.** This is a much-neglected but vital source of business intelligence data. You can contact trade union leaders and activists throughout the United States via LaborNet. See J.5.

J. Finding Experts (supplements section 14.1)

1. **Profnet.** This is an online network of 1,440 public information officers at 770 universities and research centers in 17 countries. Profnet can put you in touch with experts on even the most obscure scholarly, scientific, or technical subject. E-mail queries: **mailto:profnet@sunysb.edu**. Fax queries: (516) 632-6313. Telephone queries: (800) 776-3638.

2. **National Referral Center Master File.** Maintained by the Library of Congress; describes thousands of organizations willing to provide expert advice. **telnet://locis .loc.gov** (password: Organizations).

3. **Directory of Scholarly Electronic Conferences.** See H.10.

4. **Usenet newsgroups and Listserv lists.** See B.2.

5. **Liberal activists.** These folks (environmentalists, feminists, labor organizers, etc.) regard investigative journalists as natural allies and often provide excellent research help. To communicate online with activist organizations such as Greenpeace, Community Farm Alliance, and the American Indian Movement, as well as individual activists, join one of the Institute for Global Communications (IGC) networks—PeaceNet, EcoNet, ConflictNet, or LaborNet (by subscribing to any single network you have full access to the resources of the others). For further information: **mailto: apc-info@igc.apc.org.** An equally useful activist-oriented service is the Economic Democracy Information Network (EDIN) at **gopher://garnet.berkeley.edu.**

K. Finding the Books You Need (supplements section 14.2)

1. **Book Stacks Unlimited.** The online bookstore; over 250,000 titles in catalog. **telnet://books.com.**

2. **Online Public Access Catalogs (OPACs).** The Library of Congress catalog is at **gopher://marvel.loc.gov** or **telnet://locis.loc.gov.** Hundreds of other research library catalogs worldwide are also searchable online; see F.3 above. For obscure works that are not easy to find in library catalogs, see UNCAT (H.12 above).

3. **Descriptive information online about books.** For miscellaneous book reviews, see **news:alt.books.reviews** and the archive at **ftp://csn.org** (path:/pub/alt.books .reviews/*). Newsgroups and lists devoted to a particular topic will often produce multiple reviews of an important book in the given field. In addition, electronic journals often include multiple reviews along with a summary or precis by the book's author; see, for instance, the archives of the journal Psycoloquy at **ftp://una.hh.lib .umich.edu** (path:/journals/psyc/*). Promotional descriptions of books can be found in the collection of publishers' catalogs at **gopher.virginia.edu** (choose Library Services/University Library Collections/Alphabetic Organization). Excerpts and tables of contents of recently published mathematics books are at **gopher.siam.org.** Tables of contents (but not excerpts) of books that have multiple contributors but a single editor are often included in research library catalogs, as are the tables of contents of some short-story collections and business texts.

L. Organizational Files (supplements section 14.4). See J.2 and J.5 above.